Soldiers of Uncommon Valor

The History of Salvationists of African descent in the United States

by

Warren L. Maye

THE SALVATION ARMY
USA Eastern Territory
West Nyack, New York
2008

Published by Others Press
The Salvation Army Eastern Territory Headquarters,
440 West Nyack Road, West Nyack, New York 10994
Commissioner Lawrence R. Moretz, Territorial Commander
Lt. Colonel Larry Bosh, Chief Secretary
Major Richard Munn, Secretary for Program
Linda D. Johnson, Literary Secretary

Printed in the United States of America

Cover illustration by Warren L. Maye, design by Lily Chen, Keri Johnson
(Rendering of Thomas Ferguson, prolific composer and lyricist)

Book design and layout by USA Eastern Territory Literary Department

Library of Congress Control Number: 2007042695
Soldiers of Uncommon Valor, the history of Salvationists of African descent in the United States, by Warren L. Maye

1. The Salvation Army
2. Christian history
3. Interracial issues and leadership in the Church
4. Interracial issues within an ordained ministry
5. Black church leaders
6. Social services
7. Civil rights movement

ISBN (9780892161126) Soft Cover
ISBN (9780892161119) Hard Cover

Also by Warren L. Maye

Orita: Rites of Passage for youth of African descent in America (2000)
http://members.aol.com/orita1

Warren Maye is editor and contributing writer of *Good News!*, the Salvation Army's USA Eastern Territory monthly news magazine, as well as contributing editor and writer to *Priority!*, a quarterly magazine about people who have been touched by the Army's ministry nationwide.

www.GoodNews.use-salvationarmy.org
www.PriorityPeople.org

International Mission Statement

The Salvation Army, an international movement, is an evangelical part of the universal Christian Church.
Its message is based on the Bible.
Its ministry is motivated by the love of God.
Its mission is to preach the gospel of Jesus Christ and to meet human needs in His name without discrimination.

This book is dedicated to:

Major Norma T. Roberts,

who wrote the first booklet about Salvationists of African descent entitled *The Black Salvationist: people of African descent in The Salvation Army, USA*. Having served as the first and only African–American territorial social service secretary, Roberts retired in 1985.

Major (Dr.) George Evans,

who relentlessly challenged Salvation Army leadership in the United States to care for officers of African descent with respect, justice, and equity.

The soldiers of uncommon valor

whose faith and commitment to the work of the Kingdom will remain indelibly imprinted on our minds.

Lillie Hinnant Maye

whose example as a writer, photographer, and family historian gave her son Warren an appreciation for the contributions of people of African descent to the world and encouraged him to preserve their history for future generations.

Endorsements

"The quality of research and of writing makes for fascinating reading. Crafted is a well–informed text, integrating vital events in significant areas in the American experience and the related impact on being black and a Salvationist. I consider that to be crucial as one does not merely abandon, nor should they, their cultural history as they embrace the culture of a movement such as The Salvation Army."

—Commissioner Israel L. Gaither
National Commander

"Warren L. Maye, a distinguished author and highly respected Salvation Army employee, editor of *Good News!*, the monthly publication of the USA Eastern Territory, has captured the legacy of our fellow missioners in their struggles and victories as soldiers and officers of The Salvation Army.

As I read this exciting work I realized that many of the great leaders Maye writes about I have had the personal privilege to serve along side in my own 45 years of officership. I have grown in my own spirit and character by their example of determination and tenacity for justice, equality and respect, and have been blessed to call them brothers and sisters.

One learns best of friends and fellow soldiers as you serve with them on the battlefield and I commend this book to all who want to discover and appreciate more the soldiers of uncommon valor.

Maye honors us by allowing us to journey with these soldiers in the heritage of loving yet demanding service to God and The Salvation Army. It is a book worth your reading and I'm sure you will, with me, offer a prayer of thanksgiving for the soldiers of uncommon valor past, present, and yet to come."

—Commissioner Lawrence R. Moretz
Territorial Commander
USA Eastern Territory

"*Soldiers of Uncommon Valor* is a wonderful, well–researched manuscript, excellently written. As I read it, I was drawn into the reality of what many of my well–known sisters and brothers faced during these last decades and have had many thoughts evoked as well as feelings of admiration for those who have crossed my path and been such a blessing to me."

—Commissioner Nancy A. Moretz
Territorial President for Women's Ministries
USA Eastern Territory

"It was with great anticipation that I waited for *Soldiers of Uncommon Valor*; I was not disappointed. In fact, I was simply riveted once I began reading. The history of these soldiers has finally been unearthed. The struggles were chilling, but the victories were compelling and exhilarating. From James Jermy to Commissioner Israel L. Gaither, the book clearly shows how God's hand has guided these soldiers. I strongly urge anyone with interest in The Salvation Army to read this book. Thank you, Major Norma T. Roberts, Major Allan Wiltshire, Daniel N. Diakanwa for the vision; and thank you, Warren L. Maye, for completing the vision."

—Kenneth Burton, O.F.
Harlem Temple Corps Bandmaster

"I believe [*Soldiers of Uncommon Valor*] will take its place among the significant works of [Salvation Army] history in America, and its author will take a place in the pantheon of Army editors and writers. You make us proud."

—Colonel Henry Gariepy, O.F.
author of 26 books

"Excellent; a job well done. We can be proud of it. Thank you, Warren."

—Lt. Colonel Abraham Johnson
Officers' Counselor

"I wish to congratulate you on a job well done. I felt quite privileged to have had the opportunity to review it.... I personally know it is not easy to write a book—unless one is a 'writer' by occupation."

—Major Norma T. Roberts
author of The Black Salvationist: people of African descent in The Salvation Army, USA

"I now understand why it took long to produce this excellent and attractive book. Most history books are boring, but this one is definitely exciting to read because of the pictures and the interesting style in which it is written."

—Daniel N. Diakanwa
author of three books on cross–cultural ministries

"Wow, what a great expression of African descent history for people serving within The Salvation Army movement. Brother Warren and his [researchers] have compiled a blessed blueprint that all of us would be glad to add to our spiritual arsenal. This [history book on black people in The Salvation Army] will indeed play a vital role in communicating the mission of ministry of people of color who plowed new ground within our movement yesterday, today, and tomorrow. All Salvationists will find *Soldiers of Uncommon Valor* an outstanding tool that will bring about a real awareness of the contribution people of color have offered to God, through the 'soup, soap, and salvation' movement of The Salvation Army."

—Major K. Kendall Mathews
Divisional Secretary and
Detroit Metro Area Coordinator

Contents

Preface

On July 28, 1896, Booker T. Washington wrote these words in a letter to Major T.C. Marshall: "I am very glad to hear that The Salvation Army is going to undertake work among my people in the Southern States. I have had the greatest respect for the work of The Salvation Army, especially because I have noted that it draws no color line in religion."

The history of "Salvationists of African Descent" (a term used to include black American, Caribbean, and African Salvationists) is a captivating story that needs to be told to future generations. It started when the Army first set foot in America, and it continues to evolve. Blacks were members of the very first "Christian Mission" congregation established in the United States of America by James Jermy and James Fackler in 1872.

My fascination with the history of Salvationists of African descent grew out of *The Black Salvationist,* a booklet written by Major Norma T. Roberts. Reading her work aroused my interest in doing further research on Salvationists of African descent as well as in publishing articles on black Salvationists in *Good News!,* the USA Eastern Territory's monthly newspaper. Some of the published articles were "From Ethnic Committee to Cross–Cultural Ministries Department" (a history of Black Ethnic Committees), October 1994; "McIntyre's 'Blood and Fire' challenge," February 1995; "Legacy of Envoy Thomas D. Ferguson," February 1997.

In 1995, I expanded Major Roberts's booklet into a book by adding some information and pictures. *The Black Salvationists: People of African Descent in The Salvation Army USA* drew much interest among Salvationists of African descent in the United States and the Caribbean. One thousand copies were sold within six months, and more requests flooded the Cross–Cultural Ministries Department.

In response to this demand, Major Allan Wiltshire and I decided to do further research in order to write an expanded version of the book. Warren

L. Maye, who had also been compiling Black Salvationist history material since the early 1980s, shared his research with us in order to help in this project. The project was proposed during a meeting of the Territorial Committee for Salvationists of African Descent, which Commissioner Ronald G. Irwin, the then–territorial commander, and Colonel Israel L. Gaither, the then–chief secretary, attended. Commissioner Irwin heartily endorsed the publication of the new book. "I want this book to be worth reading," he said. "And that it conveys the struggle and triumphs of the Black Salvationists." The project was also endorsed by the then–Colonel Gaither and the Territorial Committee for Salvationists of African Descent.

Upon Territorial Administration clearance, the Cross–Cultural Ministries Department appointed me to coordinate the research and Warren Maye to write the book. We received much material and information from soldiers and officers throughout the United States, Canada, England, and the Caribbean. We received further information from Dr. Edward H. McKinley, author of *Marching to Glory: The History of The Salvation Army in the United States, 1880–1992*, Second Edition. After exhaustive work in compiling information and material for the book, we were able to gather enough material to tell the story of people of African descent and their involvement in The Salvation Army in the United States.

I hope that this book will not only encourage Salvationists of African descent but also give them a sense of ownership, belonging, and commitment to an Army of God that they helped pioneer in the United States of America. I also hope that all American Salvationists will welcome the book as part of their proud heritage.

DANIEL N. DIAKANWA

Foreword

It is my privilege to welcome you to this tribute to Salvationists of African descent. Whether we choose to be identified as "people of color," "black," or by our country of origin; whether we trace our more recent family history to the Caribbean, the West Indies, or Africa, we share a common ancestry. Our roots are in the great continent of Africa, and our forefathers were kings and warriors and builders of nations.

Thousands of years before England existed or before America was even a dream, our forefathers founded great civilizations and influenced the destinies of other nations.

It is written of King Solomon that he took as his wife the Queen of Sheba, a ruler in a highly civilized nation of great wealth. She was an African.

Yes, we have royal blood flowing in our veins. We are representatives of some of the greatest cultures and civilizations this world has known.

There is an erroneous belief that persons of African heritage came to this nation only as slaves.

Prior to the War for Independence from England, many men and women of African heritage lived in the colonies as free people. They made a contribution as artisans, craftsmen, tradesmen, and farmers.

In fact, the blood of many of our freeborn ancestors watered the seeds of America's independence.

Did you know that Crispus Attucks, a former slave and free man, was among the first Americans to die on March 5, 1770, in what was to become know as the "Boston Massacre," the opening volley of the Revolutionary War?

On April 19, 1775, seven men of African descent fought in the little band of colonials at Concord Bridge in Massachusetts. They turned back the British soldiers in a hail of musketry.

Salem Poor, an African, was cited for bravery in action at the Battle of Bunker Hill.

African Americans crossed the ice–choked Delaware River with General George Washington on Christmas Eve to defeat the British forces at Trenton.

On August 11, 1778, 125 African–American soldiers were among the rear guard who, for four hours, held greatly superior British forces at bay in the Battle of Long Island so that Washington and the remnant of the Continental Army might escape. By 1779, one in seven soldiers in Washington's Army was of African descent.

Our forefathers served this country with honor and distinction during the War of 1812.

During the Civil War, 186,000 free African Americans served in the Union Army, and 29,511 served in the United States Navy—all with honor and distinction.

In the dark hours of the night of June 18, 1863, the 54th Massachusetts Regiment, an all African–American regiment, charged heavily entrenched Confederate troops at Fort Wagner, South Carolina. Returning to their lines after hours of hand–to–hand combat, they were cheered by white troops standing in reserve. Sergeant William H. Carney, an African American, was awarded the Medal of Honor for gallantry in the battle.

Following the War Between the States, African–American soldiers were posted to the Western frontier, where Native Americans highly praised the "buffalo soldiers"—so–called because of their black, curly hair—for their courage and bravery.

During World War I, the African–American "Fighting 369th" Division received France's highest military honors for heroism under fire after 191 days in the trenches. It was recorded that the 369th never gave a yard of ground and never retreated during any battle.

On December 7, 1941, Dorie Miller, a mess attendant on the USS Arizona, saved his wounded captain and destroyed four attacking Japanese aircraft. He was awarded the Navy Cross for gallantry in action.

And who has not heard of the 99th Pursuit Squadron, the much-decorated Tuskegee Airmen? During 1943–45, in more than 15,500 bomber escort missions, these African Americans, under the command of Colonel Benjamin O. Davis Jr., never lost a single escorted bomber to German aircraft—a record that has never been equaled by any other air unit.

I have recited this great roll call of heroes because I want you to understand that we are a warrior people. We are not intimidated by overwhelming odds; we are not given to retreat or surrender; we have done and will do all that is necessary to take the victory over that which is evil and unjust.

The courage, bravery, and valor that our people have shown in battles for freedom, liberty, and honor constitute our heritage.

It is this inheritance that enables us to be soldiers of uncommon valor in another army—The Salvation Army.

With warrior blood coursing through our veins, it is not unexpected that our forefathers would have been attracted to and captivated by William Booth's fledgling Army, which was attacking poverty and evil in the slums of London.

Beginning in 1869, newspaper articles and reports noted attendance and conversions of "Negroes," "blacks," and "people of color" in Army meetings.

In 1872, James Jermy, a former Christian Missioner (the Christian Mission founded by William Booth later became The Salvation Army), and his family opened a Mission Station in Cleveland, Ohio. Jermy was known as "the Nigger preacher" because of his work among blacks.

In the 1880s, corps with black congregations opened in Baltimore, Maryland; Richmond and Alexandria, Virginia; and Washington, D.C. The Army opened corps in Cleveland, Ohio, in 1891 and 8th Street in New York in 1892.

The Army, with its focus on the internal and eternal condition of man, apparently gave little thought to external appearance and ethnic origins.

In 1894, six black Salvationists were prominent in the 23–member American delegation to the Army's Jubilee International Congress in London, England.

Racial harmony and commitment to the Army's ministry and mission, especially to the poor, were paramount in the beginning of the century until racism, fueled by national attitudes and events, surfaced in The Salvation Army in the United States. Racial segregation emerged as a dark and foreboding shadow.

The evangelical ministry of the Army, coupled with social service to aid the desperately poor, flourished among the black populations in major cities.

In 1924, the Harlem Corps relocated to West 135th Street to serve what was an increasing number of black families moving into the area.

The corps' early history was characterized by rapid growth and outstanding service to the poor in the community. The corps also birthed a large number of multi-generational Salvation Army families. From their ranks came outstanding Christian women and men destined to succeed in professional careers and in Army ministry.

In the late 1940s, the specter of racism in America was evident in the Army. Norma T. Roberts, daughter of Brigadier James N. Roberts, was denied admission to the Training College for Officers in Atlanta.

The denial of admission is perceived to have been based on the fact that the Army simply could not accept more black candidates for officership than could be assigned to black corps.

For more than a half century, given the national climate of segregation, the assignment of black officers to command corps with primarily white congregations was not viable.

Thank God, the specter of racism that caused so much personal sorrow and distress to our beloved Army is a vanishing nightmare. Today, candidates for officership who are of African heritage are welcome and urgently needed.

In our veins flows the blood of kings and priests; of saints and martyrs; of great people and humble people. Like the saints in the vision of St. John, they have washed their robes in the "blood of the Lamb" and have made them white.

They have responded to the voice of the Holy Spirit. They have confessed sin and have been born again in Christ. They have answered His call to become soldiers in the Great War against evil. They have been counted faithful.

And now they look to you and to me to lay hold of our heritage of the sword and the shield that we might engage the enemies: ignorance, poverty, racism, and evil.

They call us also to the ministry of the proclamation of the Gospel. We are called to serve the hungry, the homeless, the hopeless, and the lost.

We are of the lineage and family of all Soldiers of Uncommon Valor. Let us commit to be like them, that all may say of us, "he was counted faithful; she was counted faithful; faithful unto the end!"

COMMISSIONER ISRAEL L. GAITHER

Introduction

In this world's economy, life is a precious commodity. I hold the task of telling the stories of these soldiers of uncommon valor as an honor and sacred trust.

It is my hope that *Soldiers of Uncommon Valor* will heighten your appreciation for life as well as expand your worldview. I also hope you will enjoy reading stories about Salvationists who have a made a difference in their communities and have moved the Salvation Army's mission forward.

What roles did people of African descent play in building The Salvation Army of the United States into the organization it is today? The answer to that question is important to people of every race and culture influenced by the Army's ministry in this country.

Black Salvationists have been vital in the spiritual development of the Army from its inception in the United States. Black Salvation Army soldiers lived the Army's "Blood & Fire" motto as they struggled at times to hold fragile communities together, sometimes amid the spilling of actual blood and in the heat of real fire.

Documentation dating back to 1872 shows that people of color added something special to Army ministry. In fact, they were often called to "special"—a term coined by Salvationists in the late 1800s to describe guest worship leaders who were particularly gifted at preaching, singing, praying, or evangelizing potential converts. Today, people of color continue this legacy of service in the Army. In 1999, for instance, Commissioner Israel L. Gaither, an African-American officer, received the distinction of being called "the spiritual leader of the [USA] Eastern Territory" by a USA Eastern Territorial Headquarters department chairperson. On that occasion, the Army in the East was saying farewell to Gaither, who had been appointed the first black leader of the Southern Africa Territory. In 2006, he became the first black to command The Salvation Army in the United States.

Salvationists such as Gaither have gone to battle on three fronts: the first, spiritual, against Satan; the second, organizational, against Salvationists who failed to accept them as equal partners in ministry; and the third, internal, against members of the African–American community who did not understand the important role black Salvationists were playing in urban communities.

Despite these obstacles, black Salvationists established a beachhead of spiritual influence. And from that place, they have marched forward into the lives of people in need. From Washington, D.C., to Washington State, Salvationists of color have brought healing, comfort, and hope to the physically and spiritually wounded.

In African nations, black people make up the fastest–growing segment of new Salvationists in the world. In the United States, ministries to black people make up much of the Army's work in urban areas. Such ministries—in addition to churches—comprise ongoing Adult Rehabilitation Center, social service, shelter, and recreation programs that benefit men, women, and children.

The material in this book is drawn from published works, newspaper and magazine articles, unpublished writings, internal communications, photos, letters, and many personal interviews. I have gone to great lengths to affirm the credibility, authenticity, and accuracy of each account, and I have attempted to tell the story of black Salvationists from their own perspectives.

Soldiers of Uncommon Valor begins with the founding of the "Salvation Mission," in London, England, by William and Catherine Booth. It then chronicles the ministry of James Jermy and James Fackler, two men—one white, the other black—who successfully launched Booth's first outreach in the United States. Jermy and Fackler, like the many who would later minister to African–American communities, learned through their experience that the basic need of every human being is to be respected and valued.

This book is designed to take you on a fascinating journey through distinct eras in Salvation Army and African–American history. As you meet the many people woven throughout this text, perhaps you will recognize yourself among them. It is my earnest prayer that the victories of these soldiers of uncommon valor will inspire, inform, and enlighten you as you seek to overcome the challenges you face.

WARREN L. MAYE

Chapter 1

The first Salvationists in the United States

'That which your first little band is, succeeding societies will be.'

—General William Booth

"THAT WILL BE 50 CENTS,"[1] THE BUTCHER SAID TO THE WOMAN as he wrapped a fresh lamb leg in crisp white paper. She reached into her purse and handed him the money. He smiled, handed her the package, and put the coins in the wooden drawer below the counter.

It was the last sale of the day; closing time. After clearing the counter and bagging his earnings, James Jermy took off his apron, put on a heavy overcoat, locked the door behind him with an iron key, and started his walk down Garden Street.[2]

James Jermy

For some reason, Cleveland seemed even colder than Canada had been. Jermy had lived there until just one year ago when he brought his family to the United States. People living in Cleveland said the penetrating cold came from the city's location on the shore of Lake Erie, one of the five Great Lakes. Although the lake measured only 64 meters at its deepest point, it spanned a distance of more than 55 miles, stretching all the way back to Canada. Standing on its shore, as with a vast ocean, one could see nothing but water and sky meeting at the horizon.

As Jermy headed for home at 239 Erie Street,[3] he could almost feel the lake preparing to deliver another bitter winter. Frost formed on the bushy mustache[4] just below his nose. Perhaps Clevelanders would remember 1872 as one of the coldest winters on record, he thought. As he walked, he found comfort in the fact that, as a meat market owner, he could at least work inside. His other skill, carpentry, was something he practiced during the warmer months from his shop at 96 Muirson Street.[5]

William and Catherine Booth

Jermy's thoughts turned to the ministry he had left behind in Canada. He may have been a carpenter and butcher by trade, but spreading the Gospel message of Christ was his passion. Even before he immigrated to Canada, he had made a name for himself as an evangelist in his home country of England.

As a protégé of William and Catherine Booth, Jermy had learned the true meaning of evangelistic outreach to the poor. He had seen the Booths in action in London's streets. They had preached to the homeless under bridges and in the city's notorious East End. Booth, a Methodist minister, took Jermy, his cousin Joseph, and Joseph's sister, Mrs. Payne, under his wing. They had seen Booth challenge the invisible barriers of class, caste, race, and culture that divided the people of London.[6]

Jermy saw William and Catherine touch the helpless and pray for downtrodden men, women, and children. Their congregation, sometimes as large as 800–900 people, would gather for a Sunday morning free breakfast. The crowd from the slums included black residents and many people from distant countries. Collectively, the upper crust referred to the Booths' people as "denizens."[7]

Color was an issue, even within Jermy's own family, who were members of the Christian Community, a group of believers in town. Everyone called him "fair" and his cousin Joseph "dark."[8] "Are our names not good enough?" James probably wondered at times.

Issues of race and color notwithstanding, Jermy chose to

focus his attention on the Booths' compassion for the poor, which led to a unique ministry. Before long, the couple had amassed a sizable following. However, the Methodist church refused to take in the new converts, and the Booths asked themselves, "What do we do with them now?"

William and Catherine had taken their case to denominational leadership, only to be rebuffed. "No, we have no place for these people in our churches!" the leaders had said. Jermy then saw the Booths make a decision that changed their lives, his life, and the lives of many converts forever. They broke free of the Methodist church and started a new ministry.

Although critics mockingly called the new Christians "Booth's Army," the Booths continued to meet with the lost souls of London and share the Gospel of Christ with them. They eventually gave their movement a name, the "Christian Mission." Jermy attended the mission meetings and became a member of the Bethnal Green Station in 1868.[9]

He recorded his ministry milestones in an informative journal,[10] which he brought with him when he immigrated to Canada in 1871. Anne, his wife, and six children were also in tow. He worked as a carpenter by day, but he felt God had called him to Canada to teach the poor about Christ.

Ministering to poor blacks accounted for the most rewarding days of Jermy's life to that point. He wrote to William Booth saying, "My happiest times in Canada were with colored people. Bless God, when I was preaching, power came down; they shouted, jumped, and danced."[11]

Jermy remembers being called "the nigger preacher" in those days.[12] He didn't take the name as an insult but as a badge of honor. "A lot of little black children in the streets would call after me, 'Mr. Jermy, Amen!'" The blacks Jermy encountered in Canada were the children of ex–slaves, freed by Harriet Tubman and other heroic Americans of the Underground Railroad.

But as Jermy walked home that cold September evening in Cleveland, he realized that he couldn't continue living on the memories of yesterday's meetings. He wanted to be in the soul–saving business. He needed to be back in ministry—now.

He soon found an opportunity. On his third Sunday in Cleveland, Jermy came upon a little hall in one of the poorer sections of the city. He looked up at the sign, which read, "Christian chapel, the poor have the gospel preached unto them." He almost shouted! He went inside and found a few blacks who seemed to be waiting for someone.

They looked hard at Jermy and someone asked, "Don't you preach?" Jermy said, "A little that way." They wanted him to speak the next Sunday. "If the [minister] don't come [next Sunday], will you oblige?" someone asked. Jermy responded with an enthusiastic "Yes!" The next Sunday, Jermy found, no doubt to his disappointment that a young man was in the pulpit.[13] Afterward, Jermy discovered he had been listening to James Fackler, a Methodist Episcopal Church minister who had written to William Booth to ask that Booth come to Cleveland and help with the ministry.[14]

Jermy told Fackler all about the Christian Mission work in England. Fackler said in response, "Brother, that is what I have been waiting for!" Jermy gave him his hand and said, "Let us come out for God and souls!" "Yes!" Fackler said. "I will pray about it." Jermy said, "I *have* prayed." Jermy and Fackler met with another church brother and prayed some more.[15]

As they did, Jermy remembered feeling the Lord come down in power. The three men said, "It is of God!" When Jermy wrote to Booth to say he had met Fackler and that together they had "unfurled the flag of the Christian Mission in America," Booth was so excited that he rose up from a bed of affliction to read the letter to the workers at a Friday morning meeting in London. They responded with tokens of deep appreciation and thanksgiving. Then they all knelt down and spread the letter before the Lord and prayed that God would bless and guide the two men in their endeavor.[16]

When Booth wrote back, he said, "He [God] will give you this. I feel He will, even while I write. All glory to His name!" The ailing Founder continued, "So you have raised the banner of the Christian Mission in Ohio. Amen! May it never be dishonored, but may it float over an Army of men and women whose sole aim shall be the glory of God in the salvation and happiness of men."[17]

Booth gave them more words of advice, saying, "Remember, our motto is, 'Holiness to the Lord, and the world for Jesus!'" Booth then wrote to his friend William Crow on December 16, saying, "Our flag has been unfurled, and a branch started in Cleveland, Ohio."[18]

Booth's response marked a significant change in his attitude toward the idea of a global Christian Mission ministry. Fackler and Jermy had not been the only people who had written requesting Booth's endorsement and support. By 1872, William and Catherine Booth found themselves forced into an unsought and almost undesired advance. William Booth was utterly exhausted from overwork. He was on the edge of a nervous breakdown when Fackler's letter reached him. Close associates had wondered if Booth would ever return to his previous level of health and productivity.[19]

But the letters from Cleveland encouraged William and Catherine. Jermy and Fackler forged ahead on the strength of the Booths' counsel and coaching. "Start fair," William Booth wrote to Fackler.

> Remember quality is of far more importance than quantity. Like produces like. That which your first little band is, succeeding societies will be. There-

fore, aim at thoroughness and whole–heartedness in the company you allow to associate with you. You ask me for advice. I hardly know enough of your position to give you counsel. One or two things I think I may say, and when I hear from you again, I will write further.

1. Ours is an extraordinary work, and therefore, we try to accomplish it by extraordinary means. We gave up all concern for our reputation at the commencement, and were resolved we would succeed and have souls at all costs. The great curse of the church is RESPECTABILITY. Throw reputation and so–called respectability overboard. Let others have the finery and oratory. Go in with all your might for souls and God. 2. Be a man of prayer, and teach your colleagues the power and virtue of knee–work [prayer]. 3. I rejoice that you have grasped Jesus as a Savior from all sin. Push this blessing wherever and whenever you labor. 4. Aim at souls at every service. 5. Do plenty of open–air work. I believe there is also much to be done in house–to–house visitation. Try all or any means. May He guide you and give great sincerity, and, I was going to say, above all other blessings, humility.

"Oh, the mightiness of meekness! There are thousands whom God is yearning to use in the soul–winning work, but dare not. Success would turn their heads and be their ruin. Be very careful of the kind of spirits you associate with you. One contentious, masterful spirit can make you and the work endless sorrow. Such spirits have almost broken my heart. Beware of men who will want to come in because they can be great among you, and indulge the natural love of talking that exists in many. One humble though illiterate worker,

> full of simplicity and the Holy Ghost, is worth a regiment of such," Booth wrote.[20]

Jermy and Fackler's efforts paid off. Within a year, the ministry had grown to the point where their hands were full. They had opened two "stations," and, as Jermy put it, "the converting work was going on gloriously." They went on to open a large shop on "the Broadway," the main market street in the city. Meetings took place continuously, which required that volunteers work unending shifts.

Souls came to Christ every night. In 1873, at the Christian Mission Chapel, located at 75 Broadway, Jermy and Fackler held Sunday meetings at 11 a.m. and at 7:30 p.m.[21] Fackler and an associate, Thomas K. Doty, launched a monthly periodical that year called the *Mission Harvester*. The eight–page magazine had an estimated circulation of 1,250 during its first year. Doty, a printer by trade and an employee of the Evangelical Association Publishing House, was the editor.[22]

Open–air ministry was vital to the ministry, but poor weather in the Haymarket District sometimes brought the

Haymarket Street

meetings to a premature end. One day, the wife of a tavern owner who had became interested in the meetings going on outside her door said to Jermy, "Next time it rains, move your meeting inside the saloon." The next rainy day, he and Fackler took the woman up on her offer. They saturated the secular atmosphere with sacred songs and sermons! Later, when a child of the saloonkeeper and his wife died, they asked Jermy to conduct the funeral.[23]

However, the nonstop ministry and cold Cleveland winters proved more than Fackler could handle. In 1874, he returned to his home in the South because of failing health,[24] stopping to conduct an open–air meeting in Solon, Ohio, on his way.

Jermy, then 36, struggled on without Fackler. Ann, Jermy's wife, five years older than her husband, raised the couple's six children and supported James in his ministry. The two would often walk through the snow and frost to get to one of their five mission stations.

In 1874, the *Mission Harvester* announced that the ministry was still in operation although its success had been sporadic during the winter. Nonetheless, people were still becoming Christians during outdoor meetings held every month under Jermy's oversight.

Eventually, however, Jermy's trek between his home on Erie Street, the carpenter shop on Muirson, the meat market on Garden, and his ministry on the Broadway began to take its toll. "I have much more to do in the work than I am able," he said in a letter to William Booth.[25]

But Booth, feeling that the growing number of outposts in England alone already overextended the Army, wasn't ready to launch a full–fledged assault on the United States by sending reinforcements. Had he done so, the fledgling Cleveland ministry might have received a much–needed boost. But the Founder, struggling with his own problems—which included Catherine's angina—did not send the help for which Jermy pleaded.[26]

Booth's failure to respond probably sent a chill through Jermy worse than he had felt even on Cleveland's coldest day. By 1875, Ann could no longer endure the extremes in temperature; it was too cold in Cleveland in the winter, too hot and humid in summer. So, after much thought and resistance, and following three nonstop years on the spiritual battlefield, Jermy left Cleveland to return to England in October 1875. "The way opened, in the providence of God, for us to return to the land of our birth," he said.[27]

Booth met Jermy upon his return but could not offer him the financial support his family needed so that he could become a full–time minister in the Christian Mission in London.[28] The Cleveland Mission in Ohio continued for about a year without Jermy. Although it eventually folded, the *Mission Harvester* did not. Under Doty's leadership, the publication continued as the *Christian Harvester,* a nonsectarian holiness monthly that, until 1904, printed items of evangelical interest to a growing readership.[29]

Jermy lived the rest of his life as a faithful Salvationist and local preacher based at the Congress Hall, Clapton Corps. He often witnessed to the time in Cleveland when God's "power came down," at worship meetings and people of color, filled with the Holy Spirit, shouted, jumped, danced, and praised the Most High God.

Chapter 2

"My Lord, what a morning!"

Spirituals and hymns are used to inaugurate the Army in America

By 1878, The Christian Mission had become The Salvation Army, and William Booth was in a better mindset to offer support to protégés interested in expanding the ministry beyond the British Isles to the United States. Lieutenant Eliza Shirley and Commissioner George Scott Railton, two such persons, both effectively used African–American music in the forms of spirituals and hymns to dramatically communicate to Americans the Salvation Army's commitment to equality and racial and gender diversity.

When Eliza Shirley arrived in Philadelphia in 1879, she used such African–American songs as, "We are going to wear a crown, a starry crown," to attract attention and draw people out of local saloons. When people in the bars heard the music, they listened. Although she was only 17 years old, Shirley had courage and vision to match those of her elders; it may have been fueled by the stories Jermy shared upon his return home.

Shirley had committed herself to similar adventures in ministry in the United States. Her father, Amos Shirley, had secured a job as a weaver at the Adams & Company silk mill in Kensington, near Philadelphia. He and his wife, Annie, had been members of the Army's Coventry Corps in England.[30]

The cold Cleveland winters that Jermy and Fackler endured were nothing compared to the spiritual freeze Shirley experienced from residents of the "city of brotherly love." But her ministry eventually ignited one night and souls came to the Lord.[31]

The Shirleys—father, mother, and daughter—soon opened two stations. Eliza sent William Booth conversion reports that rivaled the ones he had received from Jermy and Fackler five years earlier. Booth read the newspaper clippings and letters with enthusiasm. But he was still hesitant about taking bold steps to secure the Salvation Army's future in America.

Booth's eventual decision to take over the work in Philadelphia was due in no small part to George Scott Railton, another protégé who longed to leave England and join the battle for souls in the United States. A strong advocate for women's rights to equality in ministry, he arrived in New York a year after the Shirleys with "Seven Hallelujah Lassies" to accompany him in the mission.[32] He brought them to "show what women, inspired by the power of the Holy Ghost, could do," as he had said. He also expected each woman to marry an American, thus insuring, through intermarriage, "that the Army in America would be American."[33]

So, on March 10, 1880, "Commissioner" Railton, Captain Emma Westbrook, a ten–year Christian Mission veteran, and six women Salvationists arrived at Castle Garden in New York City. The women wore blue uniforms with ankle–length skirts and long–sleeved, high–collared tunics with the name "The Salvation Army" inscribed in large letters. When the "invasion party" marched onto the docks of the greatest port city in the world, they boldly proclaimed the name of Jesus Christ in Battery Park and sang distinctively African–American songs, such as "Way down on the Suwannee River" and "Old Kentucky Home."[34]

African–American women (seated right) listen as George Scott Railton preaches.

Why did they come all the way from England to sing such songs, particularly when just 10 years before, New York City had endured the worst race riots in its history? Those events had been so devastating that the mayor had banned all open–air meetings for fear they would lead to even more riots.[35]

Railton held his meeting anyway. And if the music and the diverse crowd who gathered weren't enough to signal Railton's intention to reach people of color, he stated it plainly when he said he wanted to get "Africans…fairly started."[36] Railton recognized that African Americans had the potential to bring a special something—an ability to engage, to combine passionate worship with soul–stirring music—to The Salvation Army. On the docks that day, he offered a promise.

A black woman inspires a "holy dance" during an open–air meeting.

> We are honored today to be the only white people in whose company, whose platforms, whose operations, colored people have had the same wel-

> come as others ... if they will not join themselves with other races, we will go farther still, and there will be found officers ready to leave off association with their own race in order to rescue those of another.[37]

Time would reveal Railton's prophetic vision to be true. Some brave and daring white officers would be willing to make that commitment, despite the social consequences that came with it.

After the landing, news reporters from *The New York Times* and other local papers interviewed Railton, who commenced the Army's first official public relations campaign by telling them about the organization's origin, purpose, and projects. He also gave them comprehensive statistics printed on flyers, listing numbers of officers; services, both indoors and outdoors; people in attendance; and souls saved.[38]

In their articles, the reporters pointed out that African Americans were present at the meeting. Artists included them in renderings of the scene. Unfortunately, the reporters also used derogatory adjectives to describe the crowd. Their choice of words reflected the classism and racism of the day. One reporter wrote: "A more motley, vice smitten, pestilence breeding congregation could seldom be found in a house of worship. There were Negroes, dancing girls, prostitutes, and station house tramps sandwiched in between well–dressed visitors."[39]

Although Railton had planned to locate the Army's national headquarters in New York City, local ordinances on street preaching and public assembly restricted such privileges to clergy of already established denominations. To his dismay, Railton was prohibited from holding mass open–air meetings.

So he headed for Philadelphia, where the Shirleys had conducted their breakthrough open–air meeting just six

Eliza Shirley prays with converts in Philadelphia (re–enactment).

months before. It was a historic moment for The Salvation Army in the United States when Railton's contingent met Eliza Shirley's followers in Philadelphia on March 24, 1880. They held a special public meeting so that Railton could formally present the Army flag—sent by Catherine Booth—to Amos, Annie, and Eliza Shirley.

Railton was amazed by the crowd's size. "This was the biggest meeting of my life," he later wrote. More than 200 soldiers, wearing Army hatbands, cheered on the platform. Approximately 1,500 people—both black and white—had made their way into the Athletic Hall, rented for the occasion.

Railton would remember for the rest of his life the way the three Shirleys led the singing of the African–American spiritual, "My Lord, What a Morning, When the Stars Begin to Fall!"[40]

Chapter 3

'A new influence'

Black worship style draws converts to the Army

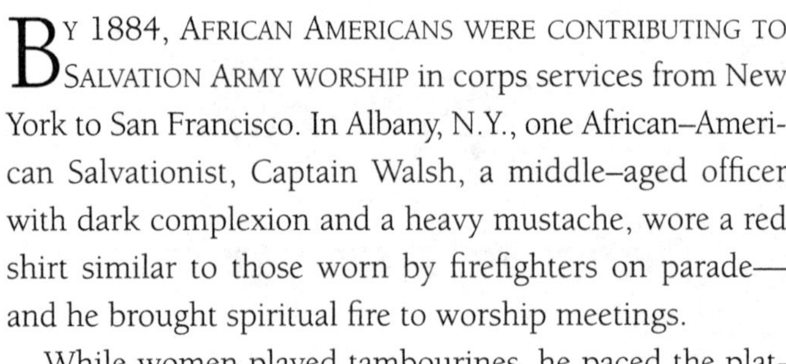

By 1884, African Americans were contributing to Salvation Army worship in corps services from New York to San Francisco. In Albany, N.Y., one African–American Salvationist, Captain Walsh, a middle–aged officer with dark complexion and a heavy mustache, wore a red shirt similar to those worn by firefighters on parade—and he brought spiritual fire to worship meetings.

A banjo

While women played tambourines, he paced the platform, singing and playing his banjo with great dexterity.[41] He clapped his hands, rolled his eyes forward, and, at times shouted at the top of his voice.

Walsh, who once had belonged to a minstrel group, felt at home on the platform. When he initially accepted Christ as his Savior, Walsh wrestled with whether he should part with his instrument. Fortunately, at this time, The Salvation Army placed no restrictions on musical expression or instruments used during corps meetings. So he felt free to "make a joyful noise unto the Lord" with his banjo.

Walsh consecrated his instrument to the Lord's service, and it became his constant companion. The freedom he brought to worship inspired many conversions at the Mercy Seat (altar). He held meetings in the old Hudson Avenue Methodist Church, where three women soldiers helped manage the large crowds. Among them were long-standing members of the church who assisted the women and later testified that "a new influence" had spiritually awakened them.[42]

That influence was also apparent once again on the streets of Cleveland, and it was fomenting trouble. The *Cleveland Gazette*, a black newspaper, reported that residents in the vicinity of Brownnell and Ohio streets were complaining about the great disturbance caused by Salvation Army parades. Others complained about the Army's "noisy manner of worship" indoors. And as in New York City, authorities labeled the Army a "public nuisance" and arrested its leaders. The Salvationists hired lawyers to challenge the fines and demanded that a jury hear their case.

A reporter wrote, "Now that the street disturbance has been so summarily dealt with, whatever steps are possible in the suppression of the continual and usual rackets raised at the Army's meeting should be immediately taken by the authorities for the speedy relief of the citizens in that vicinity."[43]

In Washington, D.C., Salvation Army Commissioner Frank Smith's assessment of a meeting held at a black corps one cold winter evening was positive and enthusiastic. "The snowstorm will spoil the meeting," he heard someone say. "The hall is snowed–up, no one can find the entrance!" But the meeting took place. Smith later wrote:

> But at last, above the roar of the wind, we heard a sort of chanting noise. It was the roll of a good old salvation song, which made our hearts and feet jump together, and answered the purpose of a star leading us to the salvation table. We were into the thick of it with a rush and a 'Hallelujah!' and found, in a moment, our highest expectations, as to the zeal and enthusiasm of our colored corps, more than realized.
>
> A big crowd was packed together, and a lot more who had been breasting the snowstorm outside in order to be the first to see us arrive, came tumbling in after us. The sensation of facing a crowd is always fresh. But here was the very essence of novelty.
>
> To face a very large crowd of enthusiastic colored faces is the acme of new sensations. From the mulatto to the jet–black African, every face there bade us welcome, and as the entire audience rose to give us one, it was only to voice what we felt was already ours, the good will of every colored brother and sister present. Never did we

> feel more convinced than then that salvation is the only missing link between the races; the golden link, which if we will only let it, will bind all men together in love and unity, irrespective of class, caste, or color.
>
> Socially, it was a very representative crowd. Old and young; some well off, some ill off; but all, for the time being, under the dominion of the gospel spirit—'peace on earth and good will towards men.'

Smith heard testimonies that he described as "intense" and "earnest."

> We turned and looked at the speaker and oh!, her whole body seemed to tremble with suppressed emotion as, walking up and down the platform, she cried: 'Salvation! Salvation! Salvation! I am ready to carry the news anywhere!'
>
> Suddenly, a fine young fellow springs to his feet and cries out in a sing–song strain, 'I'se a long, long ways from home, many miles are 'atween me and my Father's house. I was a big sinner all the way; but in Africa The Salvation Army met me, picked me up, and led me to Jesus. Then he sang a native African song, ending something like, 'Tut a nu, Tut a nu, Tut a nu.'"

Smith also recalled "Old Auntie" who stood up and shared a stirring testimony. "I remember years ago," she said, "in the dark days on the plantation, when things were hard, how I prayed for something like this." Smith had been praying for something like this too. He called it "… one of the most remarkable public services I have ever attended." Smith and his entourage left the meeting to catch a midnight train, but he had also caught a spirit that would motivate him to take the gospel to black people in the aftermath of the Civil War.[44]

Smith's testimony revealed his compassion and an unusual sense of justice for black people. He wrote:

> There was one calamity, which penetrated furtively into the world, and, which was at first scarcely distinguishable amidst the ordinary abuses of power. It was wafted like some accursed germ upon a portion of the soil, afterwards, matured itself, and grew without effort, and spread naturally with the society it belonged to. That calamity was slavery. As a community, until within the last few years, our colored brethren have been very much wronged, the victims of a cruel avarice, their bodies turned into merchandise and treated as cattle. All this has passed away in theory, and most of it has, we grant, passed away in fact; our colored brother is supposed to occupy the same platform with the white, but we see by daily experience that the assertion is a benevolent fallacy. But we desire to make that a living, practical reality, which the last generation have only succeeded so far, in making the written right.[45]

Towering over New York Harbor, a copper–skinned statue that had evolved from images of North African women, symbolized an even broader vision of the "new influence" Smith felt that night. The sculpture had been a special gift offered from one anti–slavery society to another. French Anti–Slavery Society chairperson Edouard de Laboulaye, a historian, and Frederic Auguste Bartholdi, a sculptor, had proposed the work of art to their government. They had suggested that the American Abolitionist Society present the statue to the United States government in recognition of those who had given their lives for the

American democratic ideal.

An earlier concept of the statue portrayed the woman with broken chains at her feet and in her left hand. However, after Laboulaye and Bartholdi presented their 151–foot work to the U.S. Minister to France in 1884, they, at Laboulaye's request, decided to change the image showing a broken shackle and chain in the statue's left hand to tablets inscribed with the date "July IV, MDC-CLXXVI" (July 4, 1776), the day the United States won its independence from Britain. Thus the design changed and the world eventually embraced the icon, not just as a memorial for American heroes, but also as a Statue of Liberty for people of all nations.[46]

Black converts spread the new influence—their particular worship style—throughout the Army as they appeared in meetings and shared their testimonies. Some soldiers became popular "specials," and many congregations received them enthusiastically. George Washington Stroud Peck Bradford, better known as "Special George," a black soldier who played cornet, harmonica, and guitar, was popular in the Eastern cities.[47]

Isaac Smith, converted in 1885, became the corps sergeant–major at New York's Number 3 Corps and did not miss a single open–air meeting for the next 15 years. A corps sergeant–major is comparable to a head deacon in most other Protestant denominations; he or she has oversight of the corps boards and committees and manages its business and religious meetings.

In 1888, George Washington, a black man living in Danbury, Conn., marched alongside Samuel Logan Brengle, a young Salvation Army captain who would later become a legendary writer and teacher on holiness. Tough times had hit the corps, which had only 13 members. Brengle, who was new to the Army, had little credibility and reputation in a community that pelted his motley band of Salvationists with firecrackers one Fourth of July holiday when they marched through the streets. Brengle's complaints to the authorities fell on deaf ears; the police offered little protection from the "roughs," as Brengle called them.

Nonetheless, the soldiers marched, singing, "We are marching on to war, we are, we are, we are!" Washington, who stood 6', 3," towered above everyone else, so he made an easy target. When a firecracker exploded near his head, he continued undaunted. The diverse crew also included a young but hunchbacked woman and a lame lieutenant who dragged his leg behind him. When such difficult days caused Brengle to endure "fierce soul battles," or bouts of self–doubt, he would turn to Washington and the others. They reminded him that, despite their shortcomings, "God's Word would see them through," Brengle wrote.

He later testified that he had experienced one of the greatest spiritual victories of his life in those days. "[God] liberated my spirit and made me free as a bird in the midst of the cramping circumstances in which we were living and working," he said. "The Army may have put me into the darkest little corners it has, but by the grace of God, I will preach the Word until it reaches around the world, for the Word of God is not bound!"[48]

Alexander Beck and family, territorial evangelists.

In 1889, groups called "Colored Jubilee Singers" sang and testified at the Number 1 Corps in Chicago, and in 1896, ministered in all three Los Angeles corps. Among the Army's Jubilee Singers was the Beck family of Los Angeles. As the Army's first territorial evangelists on record, they helped spread Christ's Gospel. Exposure in *The War Cry* magazine gave their ministry national attention.

Alexander Beck, originally from Jackson County, Tenn., was the son of ex–slaves. He made music on a cane whistle and could readily sing in plantation "hoe–down" style. He met his wife, also from Tennesee, while he was battling an addiction to alcohol in Kansas. A Christian woman, she gave him a reason to win the struggle. They eventually married and headed west. After they arrived in Los Angeles, his wife discovered The Salvation Army and became a Salvationist. Four years after Alexander gave his life to the Lord, he too joined the Army. The Becks taught Pearl, their only child, to serve God and pray. Pearl became a "*War Cry* Boomer," or a seller of that Salvation Army publication.

A drawing of Alexander Beck and wife.

Members of the Los Angeles Number 1 Corps, the Becks ministered to many people as "specials" to corps throughout California and saw hundreds of souls saved at the Army's Mercy Seat, also called a "penitent form" or "altar."[49]

In Nevada County's Grass Valley, a mining town settled by ex–slaves in the 1850s, a "dear, old colored sister" proved to be another strong spiritual influence in the Army. "Auntie Mae" Norton had been born into slavery. She didn't know her exact age, which was between 82 and 100 years at the time the Army's *Conquerors* magazine published an article about her.

Despite enduring great pain from sickness, Auntie Mae was always at her post at the Grass Valley Corps and set an example for other corps members. One Sunday, she came across a Salvation Army version of a popular song, which mixed in some dialect from her plantation days. She stood before everyone and triumphantly declared, with the glory of God shining on her wrinkled face, "I don't want to serve old Satan, I don't like him any more; He'll be sorry when he sees me, sliding down the cellar door."

The petite woman's eyes showed strength and resolve as she sang out the words. The crowd cheered. Captain R. A. Ironside, her corps officer, was astonished. He had never heard the song sung that way.

This was the young man's second appointment to Grass Valley. He called it spiritually "the hardest place he had ever gotten into." But after hearing Norton sing, Ironside began to have hope for the corps' future.

Auntie Mae Norton

That hope translated into as many as 17 converts who enrolled as soldiers during Ironside's appointment. He sent one cadet to training to become an officer. Members paid off a $90 debt the corps owed, and the circulation of the Salvation Army magazines *The War Cry* and *Conquerors* rose.

Faithful old "Father Mills," as he was affectionately called because of the paternal role he played at the church, and his wife, both black, served as spiritual kindling wood for the corps. Mills had lived a wild, reckless life before coming to the Lord. When he stood on the platform to sing, he closed his eyes tight as if to hold back tears of joy. His songs comforted the congregation, many of whom needed that after a hard week working in the mines. "Jesus, lover of my soul, let me to Thy bosom fly!" Mills sang. "Methinks it would have done Charles Wesley's heart good to have seen [Mills]," Ironside said.[50]

Evangelism on a different stage

A booming social and cultural revolution took place in the 1890s that spotlighted theatrical productions like never before. In the age of vaudeville—which included singing, comedy sketches, acting, and dancing in a variety-show format—The Salvation Army emerged as an innovative, creative organization that took full advantage of the secular trend for evangelistic purposes. Salvationist Emma Booth

Tucker's traveling lantern (slide) show, for example, was one of the first multimedia productions used for fund–raising purposes by a charitable organization. Army parades became elaborate—complete with floats and costumed battalions. Street evangelists attracted spectators with loud bands, circulated flyers advertising staged "trials" of the devil, preached from open coffins, held marathon hymn–singing contests, and appeared as specialty acts with names such as the "Golden Minstrel," "The Saved Cowboy," and "The Converted Pugilist."[51]

Using secular theater technique moved the Army into the mainstream of American life and consciousness. Later, legendary actors such as Clark Gable and Joan Crawford played uniformed Salvationists in major motion pictures. In the 1890s, the Army—including black Salvationists—became grist for creative writers' mills. A song written in 1897 for mainstream consumption is one case in point. It tells the story of a bold, black, outspoken Salvation Army woman captain. "Ise Gwine to Save Yo Soul" debuted 52 years before the premiere of Damon Runyon's Broadway hit, "Guys and Dolls," a satire whose central character was a Salvation Army woman captain.

Music score cover

The lyrics of "Ise Gwine," written in "darkie dialect" by Edward Abelles and Nathaniel D. Mann, were a stark reminder that the vaudeville era was also the minstrel era of American entertainment. To be able to work in theater, African Americans had to cover their faces with black paste made from burnt cork and speak in a plantation dialect. People called it performing in "blackface." The cover art for the music score of "Ise Gwine" showed black uniformed Salvationists singing and dancing. They were the stereotypical, big–lipped, bug–eyed caricatures common in that day. Perhaps because the background was dark, the artist did not blacken their faces.

The lyrics of the song began, "The Army is a comin' down the street just like a cloud. And there's goin' to be a heap o'great commotion. For the captain is a colored lady, large and very proud. Who can save the soldiers when she takes a notion. They're going to have a meeting and the crowds will flock aroun'. 'Mong the colored folks there'll be great devastation. For she'd rather save the sinner than to eat a possum dinner. She's the greatest Army captain in the nation."

M. Witmark and Sons, Inc., distributed the song in New York, Chicago, London, and Toronto.[52] It was one of many ways in which the Army became an icon in popular American culture and the nation's most beloved charity in years to come.

The Great Colored Campaign

While black Salvationists made their way from east to west, another movement headed south. Commissioner Frank Smith, the Salvation Army's newly appointed national leader, launched a "Great Colored Campaign and Combined Attack on the South," an attempt to make good on the promise of racial and ethnic pluralism that Commissioner Railton had articulated some years before. But unlike Railton, who, in his zeal for change, failed to solidify his organization, Smith proposed and implemented a long–range plan.[53]

Smith, from Great Britain, wanted to change the Salvation Army's image as an organization principally for white, British men. He began the campaign by appointing Captain S. W. Braithwaite, a black man who was a former Methodist pastor from British Guyana, to lead the effort. Braithwaite had the theological and cultural background needed to establish rapport with Smith and other Brits.

As an immigrant, Braithwaite also offered a much–needed freshness to the cause that most war–weary African–American Salvationists lacked. After 400 years of slavery and oppression, many of these Salvationists just wanted to leave the South, not stay and try to reform what many blacks perceived to be a white organization.[54]

As a student of medicine in London, an attorney, and a graduate of Harvard College, Braithwaite was arguably the most educated leader in the Salvation Army world at that time. However, his peers saw him first and foremost as a humble man. He knew that education hadn't saved him from sin—Christ, working through The Salvation Army, had done that.

At a meeting in Asbury Park, N.J., Braithwaite emerged from a "backslidden" life and said, "Here am I Lord, send me!" Smith sent Braithwaite to conduct fund–raising meetings in New York, parts of New England, and Michigan. Braithwaite secured funds, recruited volunteers, and solicited prayers for the "expedition." He emphasized taking action to save the "immortal souls" of "the colored race settled in our midst."[55]

The strategy worked. Because of Braithwaite's efforts, the Army opened a corps in Alexandria, Va., in August 1885; the Fredericksburg, Va., Corps opened four months later. Two of the four pioneering officers were African Americans: Captain Johnson, a smart young man of mixed parentage from Maine, and Lieutenant Minor, an attractive woman who was an ex–slave from Virginia. Their congregations were multiracial, with the majority being black.

Even after Braithwaite left the work some time later over a mysterious charge leveled against him by someone in leadership, the fruit of his labor continued to ripen. The Army opened black corps in Washington, Frederick, Richmond, and Norfolk. Speculators contend that Thomas E. Moore, the former national commander who took over after Railton returned to England, had lured Braithwaite to his side during a schism that took place within The Salvation Army.[56]

Despite these challenges, the spiritual breakthrough Commissioner Frank Smith had experienced while worshipping at the Washington, D.C., corps drove him to take bolder action in the South. He launched another campaign called the "Colored Skins and White Hearts Crusade," to win more volunteers.[57] The Army had every good intention, but many African Americans, eager to rid themselves of racist stereotypes, reacted negatively to the idea that being "colored" meant they were bad and that to be changed, their hearts needed to become "white."

Upon Smith's recommendation, William Booth gave Joseph Pugmire, his aide–de–camp (A.D.C., or personal assistant), the job of making this new but awkward initiative work.[58] To accomplish this, Pugmire took advantage of the momentum his predecessor, Braithwaite, had generated.[59]

Smith had great expectations of A.D.C. Pugmire, whom he had personally summoned from England; he believed that Pugmire would make a significant contribution to Reconstruction in the South. Smith wanted to see the full realization of the Emancipation Proclamation, the statement issued by President Abraham Lincoln in 1863 declaring freedom for all enslaved people in states still in rebellion against the federal government. Smith hoped that in some significant way, the "Great Colored Campaign and Combined Attack on the South" would complete the work started by the Thirteenth, Fourteenth, and Fifteenth amendments to the U.S. Constitution.

Smith said, "A whole race remained to be, not only liberated, but civilized, and saved.... We are determined, by the help of God, to be among the first white Christian communities of America, who would faithfully and wholly break down this wall of partition, separating the white from the colored, whom the Lord has brought from a common captivity and bondage."[60]

In response to this mandate, young Pugmire immersed himself in ministry. He moved into the neighborhood to live among the African–American people. However, by eating, drinking, and living with blacks,[61] Pugmire also essentially cut himself off from the white community. His actions fulfilled Railton's promise made the day he landed in New York City. "If they will not join themselves with other races," he proclaimed, "we will go farther still, and there will be found officers ready to leave off association with their own race in order to rescue those of another."[62]

At first, the black people Pugmire was trying to reach did not understand or trust him and his group. Eventually, however, through song, prayer, and preaching, the blacks began to hear Pugmire's message. In 1885, Pugmire wrote a hymn, in minstrel–show dialect, entitled "Southern Colored Work," to the tune of "When de Stars ob de Elements Are Falling." The song served as an effective tool designed to promote the Salvation Army's evangelical outreach to blacks. "It does not matter," said the lyrics, "wedder we are black or white; blessed be de name ob de Lord! For God says, 'Whoever,' can come and be put right."[63]

In Fredericksburg, Va., the scene of bloody Civil War battles, white and black congregants sat in the same pews praising and worshipping God. Smith and Pugmire wept with them as they knelt at the altar and confessed together their need for the Lord.

But the road to reconciliation would not be an easy one. Pugmire wrote,

> We have been through many a battle, many a heavy conflict, face to face with the old enemy. Men have attempted to take our lives, and we have had to bear black eyes for Jesus, but God has brought us through with a shout of victory, and we will never give up, but stick to our guns,

> and sweep through the South, and win it for God and The Salvation Army.... We have heavy odds to contend with here, which nobody knows of but those engaged in the deadly warfare, but our Captain is Jesus Christ.[64]

Racism accounted for the "deadly warfare" Pugmire alluded to. Only black and white Christians who had the courage to defy prevailing social norms dared pray together at the same Mercy Seat. For blacks, violating such taboos could easily result in an early "promotion to Glory" (death, in Salvation Army parlance). Often, ministries fell victim to sabotage and acts of terrorism perpetrated by a post–Civil War insurgency. The Ku Klux Klan alone murdered hundreds of innocent black men. Klansmen would hide their faces under white sheets, break into homes of unsuspecting targets, and hang them from trees in the middle of the night or in broad daylight.

Daytime lynchings could often attract several hundred people, who would witness the hangings and then sit on the lawn and have lunch. The commercialization of these events included sideshows and sales of various products by entrepreneurs looking to take advantage of an opportunity.[65]

The Salvation Army spoke out frequently against "the lynching craze" in *War Cry* articles. At one time, two Salvation Army officers begged and pleaded with a mob for a black man's release, but the crowd refused to let him go. Under these horrific circumstances, there was not much the officers could do except pray for the man. Their last hope was that they could shame the crowd into releasing him. But after everyone respectfully prayed with the officers, the hanging proceeded.[66]

Despite setbacks such as these, the Army pressed forward, determined to bring to fruition the longterm strategies it had written on paper and articulated in public meetings. Smith's management style and flair for public relations during his two and a half years at the helm helped increase the number of Salvation Army corps worldwide—which included a number of corps with black membership in the United States—from 17 to 143.[67]

These efforts did not go unnoticed. On July 28, 1896, Booker T. Washington, a black man and principal of the Tuskegee Normal and Industrial Institute in Alabama, wrote a letter to Major T. C. Marshall, editor of the Salvation Army's *Conqueror* magazine. Washington was responding to a letter he had received from Marshall to thank Washington for "his remarkable speech," in which he made some favorable remarks about the Army, and to let Washington know about the plans of the Army to reach African Americans in the South for God.

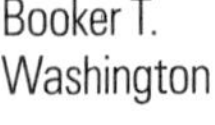

Booker T. Washington

My Dear Sir:

I am very glad to hear that The Salvation Army is going to undertake work among my people in the southern states. I have always had the greatest respect for the work of The Salvation Army, especially because I have noted that it draws no color line in religion. I feel that there is a large class of colored people in the South, especially in the cities, who are not reached by the churches, but who will be reached by your work. In reaching the neglected and, I might say, outcasts of our people, I feel that your methods and work have peculiar value. Certainly, there is plenty of room in the South for your work, and I feel that the colored ministry and others will give you a hearty welcome. There are thousands of my people in the cities who do not go to church. These as well as others I feel you will reach and help in a permanent form. God bless you in all your unselfish Christian work for our country! If I can serve you at any time, please let me know.

Yours for the Master,
Booker T. Washington,
Tuskegee Normal and Industrial Institute,
Tuskegee, Ala."[68]

William and Catherine Booth no doubt took courage as they read those words from a Christian who was one of America's strongest advocates for poor and disenfranchised Americans. Washington recognized, as did the Booths, that their destinies were inextricably intertwined with the poor. The 20th century would test the bond forged between the black community and Army pioneers. Soon Reconstruction would end. The glory days would fade, creating a need for new ways to keep the spiritual flame alive.

Chapter 4

'Fading Glory'

Blacks struggle to move forward

"I WAS DELIGHTED TO SERVE IN THE UNION ARMY DURING THE CIVIL WAR... " said a tall black man standing before a crowd attending the International Congress in 1894. It was testimony time, and the ex–slave was about to make a startling confession: "... because I enjoyed seeing white men kill each other," he said. He told his audience how he had carried hatred toward white men in his heart as a child slave and had taken that hatred with him to the battlefield.

Then one day, long after the war had ended, his testimony continued, he happened upon a Salvation Army meeting. When a young woman officer in charge of the meeting called out, saying, "If you want to be saved from your sins, stand up now!" the former Union soldier stood. A black woman sitting behind him pulled at his coat and hissed, "She don't mean you!" But the repentant sinner stayed on his feet. He had resolved that this day he would trade in his sword for a plowshare and give his heart to the Lord. He no longer wanted pleasure from memories of screaming, dying men.[69]

After he shared his testimony at the Congress in London, the man joined four other African Americans in song as part of Commander Ballington Booth and Colonel Richard Holz's American delegation. On their tunics they wore stars and stripes in red, white, and blue. Their hats had Salvation Army bands around them, and their delegation carried the U.S. flag. Their very presence at this international event demonstrated the Army's commitment to evangelizing blacks in the United States. The group sang before audiences numbering in the thousands in London and in other English towns and cities, delighting everyone who heard them.

Despite the flattering attention the black Salvationists received, their actual names were never mentioned in articles covering the Congress. And after taking center stage overseas, they returned to a marginal life in the United

States. By the end of the 19th century, African Americans had lost many of the gains they had enjoyed during Reconstruction. Sometimes, the loss came suddenly and tragically. From lynchings in the middle of the night to the destruction of entire towns populated by blacks, they watched as their oppressors stripped them of a briefly held prosperity. Other changes happened gradually; a solidly Democratic South moved toward barring blacks from holding further public office for the next 70 years.

In the midst of these horrific setbacks, many African Americans sought their fortune in the West. Some became cowboys: One of every six cowboys who rode the Plains was black. They wore wide–brimmed hats and high boots. Their tight woolly hair reminded Native Americans of their beloved buffalo.[70]

The only cowboy of that era—black or white—to write an autobiography was Nate Love, better known as "Deadwood Dick." Although he was black, his book became a classic and, in years to come, the model for Hollywood's legendary but fictional cowboy movies and television shows.[71]

From the Eastern United States, a group of African Americans wearing broad–brimmed hats of a different kind set out for a frontier across the ocean. Wearing the flaming red, "wide–awake" hats of The Salvation Army, they made their way to the Army's international congresses held in London in 1904 and 1914. These massive meetings of Salvationists from around the world provided an outlet for these black Army pioneers to let the world know of the oppression they were suffering in the United States in the wake of Reconstruction.

Thomas Ferguson

At the Congresses, they participated in ministry through music and testimony. In 1914, Thomas Ferguson's music emerged

> **"When I left Old Egypt's land, Oh, my! Oh, my! Pharaoh fairly cried, While he was promise making, My heart was aching, aching, Good–bye, Pharaoh, good–bye. Good–bye, Pharaoh, good–bye."**
>
> *—Tom Ferguson, "Goodbye, Pharaoh"*

as the kindling that lit the spiritual flame among delegates. Commissioner John McMillan said to Ferguson, "When your song [Goodbye Pharaoh, Goodbye] was sung before an audience of over a thousand people in Congress Hall, the impression was so great, it touched us in spots which words of eloquence rarely reach."[72]

That evening, the sun glowed red over the Hall. One delegate later wrote,

> "In spite of the disguises of the skin, [the delegates] are obviously one people. It is the common citizenship that ignores the boundaries of kings and states, of color and of speech. They have some secret of fellowship that unites them—a secret too, which makes them conspicuously happy!" Another writer echoed those sentiments; "There is nothing that shows more clearly the unity that exists between Salvationists, black, white, bronze, or yellow than the readiness with which they

Gifford, Malpass and the Brigade to ICC, 1914

speak of God in their own hearts among their own people."[73]

They came from the Caribbean

In 1912, the *HMS Titanic*, the ill–fated ocean liner, set sail for America on its first voyage. Joseph Laroche, a black man from Haiti, and his wife, Juliette, who was white, had boarded the ship at Cherbourg, outside Paris. They were awestruck by the ship's size and accoutrements in the second–class section. The Laroches didn't know that Salvationists had been among the shipbuilding crews who constructed the vessel and were also among its passengers.

When the *RMS Carpathia* carried 705 *Titanic* survivors to Manhattan, Salvationists were also among the first to meet them. When the ship pulled in to Pier 54 at the end of 13th Street on April 18, Evangeline Booth, The Salvation Army's national commander, and her troops were waiting. They had been summoned to provide comfort to the survivors, their families, and the families whose loved ones had died. "Mothers, children, husbands, and wives called aloud the names of their loved ones lost," she said, "and strong men were overcome by their emotions."

Juliette Laroche, 22, and her two small daughters were among the survivors. "[Joseph] gave me this coat," she cried. It was stuffed with money and family valuables. "He told me I would need it. He said he would see me in New York. Where is he? Where is Joseph?" Unfortunately, her husband and 1,660 other second–class passengers lost their lives when the *Titanic* sank.[74]

During this era, many Caribbean–born men like Joseph Laroche left their island homes on ships to start a new life in Europe, Canada, or the United States. Fortunately, most did not experience failures of *Titanic* proportions.

In fact, many succeeded. Captain Lambert Bailey, born in British Guiana, was one of those success stories. He set eyes on America in 1913. On July 25 of that year, he wrote a letter to Evangeline Booth seeking permission to come to the United States.

In his letter, Bailey offered to volunteer in the "Salvation War" waged for colored people's souls in America. "I am not doing this today with any selfish motive," he wrote. "I am doing it with this motive; that whether the reply be favorable or unfavorable to my conviction, to take it as from God and would not murmur, as He does all things well!"

Lambert Bailey

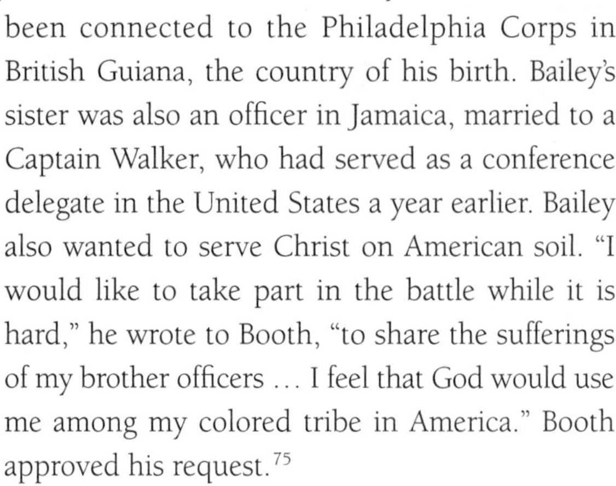

Bailey was the son of Salvation Army officers who had been connected to the Philadelphia Corps in British Guiana, the country of his birth. Bailey's sister was also an officer in Jamaica, married to a Captain Walker, who had served as a conference delegate in the United States a year earlier. Bailey also wanted to serve Christ on American soil. "I would like to take part in the battle while it is hard," he wrote to Booth, "to share the sufferings of my brother officers … I feel that God would use me among my colored tribe in America." Booth approved his request.[75]

Another Caribbean islander, Pearl Hurdle, emigrated to the United States in 1916 from Antigua, British West Indies, at age 19. A Christian from age 8, she attended the New York #8 Corps in Harlem. In June 1921, Hurdle entered the School for Officer Training. Less than a year later, she was commissioned and appointed as assistant officer to the New York #8 (Harlem) Corps. She also assisted at the Brooklyn #12 Corps. Hurdle took command of the Cleveland, Ohio (Central), Corps in 1925. She rebuilt that congregation and gained a reputation for being an outstanding open–air meeting campaigner.[76]

But Hurdle and other islanders who immigrated to the U.S.A. discovered that they had much to learn about American culture in general and African–American history and culture in particular. Similarly, African Americans knew little about the West Indies and the culture of its people.

Pearl Hurdle

In those days, the concept of an "African diaspora" had not yet been born. Blacks from the United States, the Caribbean islands, South and Central America, and the African continent lived in isolation from one another. All they knew about one another were stories told by traveling merchants or tales written in print or shared via word–of–mouth. The prevailing parlance of that era caused even the most well–intentioned authors to inadvertently paint derogatory images of people of color and the poor. For example, when Samuel Logan Brengle, a legendary figure in Salvation Army history and a prolific writer on holiness, wrote his "Impressions of the O.C.C.," (a meeting held at the International Congress of 1904), he said, "...the Congress was a vast object–lesson. Here were officers who for years had devoted themselves without stint to the outcast and criminal tribes of India, the lepers of Java, the ignorant natives of Africa, the unspeakably vile slums of London and Glasgow, New York, and Chicago, and the godless, sneering libertines of Paris and Antwerp."

With no malice intended, Brengle further denigrated delegates of color by using language common in his day. "Officers connected with the proudest aristocracy were one with the humblest and most illiterate while those from the most favored countries and the highest civilization were glad to serve those from the most backward and depraved races."[77] Although Brengle was clearly praising God for the spirit of unity at the Congress, his language unfortunately reinforced prevailing race and class stereotypes. When the people of India, at that time resisting British colonial rule, were described as "criminal"[78] in *The War Cry* and Africans were described as "ignorant," "depraved," or "backward" for not being versed in European languages and culture, racial stereotypes were set in type. When people from such backgrounds began to live together in the United States, they began with those stereotypes in mind and had difficulty appreciating one another's positive attributes.[79]

On the one hand, African Americans generally saw West Indian immigrants as an ambitious but self–serving people who refused to participate in the Civil Rights struggle yet felt free to take advantage of its benefits in pursuit of the "American dream." On the other hand, West Indian immigrants saw African Americans as they were depicted in books such as *Gone with the Wind*—as an indolent bunch, who, after 400 years of slavery and exploitation, could no longer believe in a work ethic, much less pursue the American dream.[80] And thanks to writers such as Edgar Rice Burroughs, creator of the "Tarzan" stories, Africans who had immigrated to the United States were pegged as uncivilized savages.[81] Native Americans, who played a large role in the formation of African–American communities—particularly in the southern United States following the Civil War—were viewed by the larger society in much the same way.[82]

Estava Maughn

Against this backdrop of disinformation and the resulting climate of distrust between people groups of color, Salvationists of African descent struggled to establish pluralism by attempting to overcome cultural imperialism, replacing the lies with truth; substituting positive messages for negative ones. They sought to eradicate misconceptions and cultural biases and to nurture tolerance throughout the black diaspora.

On April 29, 1915, Captain Lambert Bailey, originally from British Guiana, and Captain Estava Maughn, a woman from Trinidad who was the daughter of Episcopalian parents, joined forces in the war for souls by getting married. She had been in the United States for three years and had graduated from the Salvation Army's School for Officer Training in New York City. Her first appointment as a single officer had been as corps officer in Charleston, S.C., where she had a female lieutenant to assist her. The poor black community readily accepted Maughn. She distributed Salvation Army Christmas baskets full of vegetables, canned fruits, toys, and candies for the children and later persuaded one family with 10 children to send them to the first Sunday school at the corps. In less than a month, as many as 25 children and their parents were attending Sunday school and morning services.[83]

During this period, Bailey had been a cadet in training in Jamaica, W.I. Then he was commissioned and assigned to serve as assistant to one of the colonels at the college; his duties included teaching a course to incoming cadets. One day, he saw a photo of Captain Maughn and read about her accomplishments in Charleston. He immediately found her attractive and sought a way to contact her through his superior officer.

The couple corresponded for six months before Lambert sent a marriage proposal to her that Estava accepted. As was the custom, the territorial commander granted permission for the union. In time, their love for each other proved to be as true and lasting as their love for The Salvation Army.[84]

"While crossing on life's ocean, they're devils like submarines; they'll attack your boat in the dark. Don't you think 'tis mean? But when to open fighting, you'll find all devils shy to approach a Christian soldier, who's not afraid to die."

—Tom Ferguson, "Honey in the Rock"

After their marriage, Lambert and Estava both served together in Charleston; Richmond, Va.; Elizabeth, N.C.; and Norfolk, Va. They saw many souls saved and encouraged young Salvationists to become officers. And the Baileys' careers were not over yet. In 1927, they assumed command of the Harlem Temple Corps after having pioneered the work in Brooklyn, N.Y.[85]

Changing racial attitudes

Correcting misconceptions within the black diaspora was a trivial matter compared to coping with physical attacks perpetrated against all people of color, primarily in the South. Establishing racial pluralism was no small task in a land where, in 1919 alone, domestic terrorists such as The Ku Klux Klan killed as many as 70 black men, some of them war veterans.[86]

Blacks who did not die by the rope suffered character assassinations at the hands of hostile journalists and authors who inflicted insult and injury with their pens. Leading sociologist William Dunning's book, *Reconstruction, Political and Economic*, had labeled Reconstruction "a corrupt outrage perpetrated on the prostrate South by a vicious and vindictive government controlled by Northern Republican radicals." Writers quoted "The Dunning School" view in scholarly papers and magazine articles across the nation. His view—that blacks, who had just emerged from slavery, were utterly ignorant and in every way unfit for self–government—became widely accepted.[87]

Many white Southerners viewed themselves as "the purest Anglo–Saxon strain in America" and a dominant race, and they were not willing to agree to being governed by "Negroes." Believing that it was possible to deny them political and social equality and "befriend" them at the same time, these whites exhibited an ambivalent, almost schizophrenic attitude toward blacks.[88]

However, in the 1940s, C. Vann Woodward, David Herbert Donald, Thomas B. Alexander, and other historians re–examined the record of the Reconstruction governments of the South. They concluded that the record of African Americans in politics, business, and education showed they had contributed significantly to rebuilding the South.[89] Even during the so–called "Dunning era," blacks were making strides in the post–Civil War South as early as 1914. For example, Colonel William Holz, a leader in The Salvation Army, wrote an article in *The Officer* magazine in which he cited a large number of "educated, prosperous, and clean–living Negro people throughout the Southland." Holz said their schools and colleges were "excellent. And [they had] thousands of churches, all managed and controlled by themselves." He said they had acquired hundreds of millions of dollars' worth of property and had shown themselves to be "hardworking, honest, and thrifty" and would "sooner or later … own their own farms." He also acknowledged their significant spiritual presence at Salvation Army open–air meetings in white areas, where frequently as much as 50 percent of the congregation was black.[90] In addition, blacks—who had been elected to public office as members of the new abolitionist–inspired Republican Party—passed legislation that dramatically improved the standard of living for both blacks and whites in the South. Perhaps the most important of those accomplishments was the establishment of the first public education system in the South.[91]

The Great Depression and Prohibition

The November 12, 1932, *War Cry* featured on its cover an artist's rendering of a black WWI soldier in uniform kneeling with his face against his mother's breast. The cotton–field worker looks toward heaven with her right hand across her breast and sings the words seen in a music score printed above her head, "Ain't goin' to study war no mo'…" In the background, black workers are picking cotton in a vast field.[92]

Perhaps readers found comfort in the calm, peaceful image. But it belied the reality of the day. The world had just experienced a bloody, devastating war. Jobs were scarce. And for African Americans, a domestic war with white society was intensifying. The city of Chicago, where the *War Cry* cover originated, had experienced its worst race riots on record just 12 years before. As many as 15 blacks and 23 whites died during clashes. Nearly 1,000 people had lost their homes.[93]

For ten years, the "Blackshirts," a nationwide organization of white men who insisted that every white man have a job before any black man could have one, had campaigned in the streets, causing riots that resulted in many deaths in major cities across the country.[94] Despite President Herbert Hoover's "prosperity propaganda," as journalists called it, the nation's economic health spiraled downward. Unemployment rose dramatically when the Bank of the United States closed; it was the biggest bank failure in history and left 400,000 depositors stranded. And the worst was yet to come.

Ironically, the depressing financial news hastened the sale of home radios. People depended on them for information, entertainment, and the opportunity to live their dreams vicariously through real and fictional heroes. Joe Louis, a black man, became such a hero when he won the heavyweight boxing crown in 1939. Amid painful poverty, Americans, both black and white, rooted for the "Brown Bomber."

For every Joe Louis, there were millions of other black "Joes" struggling to survive. "Chappy" was one of them. Addicted to alcohol and homeless, he had a dream that was impossible, to become a prizefighter like his hero, Joe Louis.

But one day, Chappy came across The Salvation Army in New Brunswick, N.J., and his life changed forever. He accepted Christ as his Savior and became a giver as well as receiver of God's blessings. Jake Hohn, who was white and would retire as a Salvation Army lieutenant colonel, watched Chappy bond with his newfound church family.

Hohn loved Chappy's outgoing personality, and his consistent, encouraging testimony.[95] Chappy remains a symbol of salvation, transformation, and rehabilitation of the body, mind, and spirit.

The Great Depression taught many lessons. For Doris Bailey, the teenage daughter of Captain Lambert "Pop" Bailey at the Harlem Temple Corps, it was to always help those less fortunate. She also became aware of the Salvation Army's social and religious strength. In those days, her father arranged for the children of the Harlem community to attend the Army's Fresh Air Camps where they had a chance to enjoy lovely lakes, hills, and countryside. And at Christmas, Pop Bailey gave them toys and candy.

The Baileys planned Christmas programs and plays that required the participation of the Sunday school children. Their parents not only felt proud to see their children perform, but the activity also took their minds off the nation's dismal economic plight and focused them instead on the goodness of God and the thoughtfulness of The Salvation Army. As the Harlem corps grew, services became more

James N. Roberts (center) and party

structured. The combination of social and religious activities created in young Doris a lasting desire to serve others that would carry her through difficult times ahead in her own life.[96]

Ministry milestones (1913–1944)

Ensign James N. Roberts, a Bermuda national, leads a brigade of black officers to open a work among blacks in the segregated South, after having served 20 years in New England in interracial corps. During the next 28 years, he and his wife establish ministries to soldiers returning from the war, as well as community outreach and camps. Twice a delegate to the International Congress in London, Roberts serves faithfully in Washington, D.C.[97]

Mabel Vivian Broome

An African-American officer, Mabel Vivian Broome, enters training in 1915 after being a soldier for four years. Broome does not train in the South or the North, but becomes the first African-American cadet in the Army's Central Territory, graduating from its school in Chicago. (At the time the Chicago headquarters was considered part of the West, but by 1920, the Army officially named the region the Central Territory.)

Broome completes the course in nine months, receives her ordination and commissioning as a lieutenant, and takes her first appointment at the Chicago #22 Corps. Subsequent appointments take her to Chicago #1, Des Moines Rescue Home, Glen Ellyn (pro tem), and Chicago #2 Slums. As a "Slum Sister," Broome joins other Salvation Army women in house-to-house visitation, scrubbing floors for disabled people, caring for new mothers and their children, ministering to the sick and shut-ins, mending clothes and seeking donations of food and clothing. The Slum Sisters also conduct religious services in chapels and in the open air for the Army, visit brothels and saloons, and sell *The War Cry.*[98] The sisters encounter a variety of responses, from acceptance to outright hostility. For a woman of African descent living in a segregated America, the duty is particularly hard.[99] On March 15, 1918, Broome, suffering from ill health, resigns.

In 1920, Broome, still in delicate health, reapplies for officership in the Eastern Territory and is appointed to the Boston Rescue Home in February. In 1921, Broome is appointed

Pearl Hurdle

captain, then ensign, while serving at the Boston Rescue Home. In 1930, she is promoted to Glory after an appendicitis attack leads to infection. Her mother and her sister Edith, both living in Chicago at the time, bury her in the Salvation Army section of Glen Oak Cemetery in Hillside, Ill., on October 11.[100]

After serving many years on the other side of the ocean, another pioneer passes on. James Jermy, "the nigger preacher" and co–founder of the first Christian Mission outpost in the United States, is promoted to Glory in 1929. His surviving family members bury him near the grave of William Booth in Abney Park Cemetery, Stoke Newington, England.[101]

Another pioneer Salvationist, Pearl Hurdle, is becoming known as a musician as well as an officer. In 1937, she moves to Brooklyn and takes command of the Bedford Temple Corps, where she also displays her talent as a cornet and triangle player.[102]

As pioneer Salvationists go on to Glory in the Central Territory and in England, others continue to hold up the Army's flag in the USA Eastern Territory. B. Barton McIntyre receives his commission from the School for Officer Training in New York as a member of the Climbers session (each class of Salvation Army cadets worldwide has such a name) in 1921. For nine months of training, McIntyre made a daily trek through the Bronx, past Loring Place, over to Andrews Avenue, and up the steep training school steps to get to class.

B. Barton and Mildred McIntyre

McIntyre, a Canadian, is appointed to command the Harlem Temple Corps, then, in 1933, to the Brooklyn (Bedford) Corps in 1933. In February 1937, the last year of that appointment, he meets Lieutenant Mildred Ernestine Bowen. She had come to the United States as a child, serving as a Corps Cadet, Girl Guard, and Sunbeam leader (the Salvation Army's equivalent to the Girl Scout organization). After her graduation from the School for Officer Training in 1938, the Army appoints Lieutenant Bowen to serve at the Catherine Booth Hospital in Cincinnati, Ohio. The following year, she and Captain McIntyre marry.

The Army reassigns them to serve together as Cleveland (Central) Corps officers. Captain Mildred receives acclaim for her work with young people and later attends the Central Nursing School. For the next 30 years, the McIntyres will put their education and passion for ministry to work against social ills.[103]

In 1941, Brigadiers Adrian and Eualee DaCosta, who had served in Lagos, Nigeria, since 1920, transfer to the United States Eastern Territory to command the Harlem Temple Corps. The Jamaican-born officers had also commanded corps in Barbados, Antigua, and Trinidad prior to serving in Africa. As missionary officers, the DaCostas had adapted to the rigors of African life. They mastered the Yoruba language, preached the Gospel, and led people to Christianity. Adrian had also started a brass band there. But at the end of his second term of missionary service in Africa, Adrian was weakened by malaria, which necessitated the transfer to the U.S. Now they begin the last chapter in their careers, which will take them from Harlem to their final post in Philadelphia.[104]

Adrian and Eualee DaCosta

In Washington, D.C., that same year, an early Army pioneer, Brigadier James Roberts, retires from active service. He had given 57 years of his life to The Salvation Army—50 as an officer. He was the highest-ranking black officer in The Salvation Army at that time.[105]

Roberts' retirement did not mark the end of that family name in the Army's ranks. His daughter, Norma, then in government work, would soon declare her intention to become the next member of the family to wear an officer's uniform.

Senior Majors Lambert and Estava Bailey assume command of the Washington, D.C., Corps, their final appointment before retiring. They had spent many years in the South, having served in Richmond and Norfolk, Va.; Charleston, S.C.; and Elizabeth, N.C.[106]

In 1944 in Cleveland, Ohio, The Salvation Army conducts a ceremony on Haymarket Street to remember its official founders in that city. Veterans with more than 55 years of service unveil a plaque that commemorates the Army's start in 1889—17 years after James Jermy and James Fackler had, with William Booth's blessing, marched, preached, taught, ministered, and prayed for souls seeking Christ.

By this time, these early pioneers, who had never flown the Salvation Army flag, had become the forgotten heroes of the old Christian Mission. The marble tablet embedded in the sidewalk at Central Avenue and Nickel Plate Way, S.E., does not commemorate the founders of Booth's first outpost in the United States but instead states: "Here on Nov. 5, 1889, the work of The Salvation Army began in Cleveland. God is our refuge and strength."[107]

On July 10, 1944, Senior Major Maurice A. Smith marries Adjutant Grace Bean in Washington, D.C.[108] Born in Bermuda, Bean had graduated from the Army's training college in Kingston, Jamaica, in 1930 and had served in the Canada and Bermuda Territory. Prior to coming to the U.S., Bean had served in numerous Central American and Caribbean appointments. Smith had trained in the USA Eastern Territory in 1925 following the ministry of then–Captain B. Barton McIntyre in the New England Division. Maurice was an excellent euphonium player who had been taught by his father, Edward Smith, once a vaudeville entertainer. Out of eight children, Edward Smith had fathered five boys and he taught all of them to play instruments in the Salvation Army band in Bangor, Maine. (At that time, girls were not allowed to play in Army bands). Maurice taught himself to play the piano as an assistant at the New York #8 Corps before he transferred to the Southern Territory in 1927 to serve as assistant officer at the Washington (Seventh Street), D.C., Corps. He had become one of two black bandsmen to play in the National Capital Band from 1937–1945. Victor Smith, his brother and a soldier at the Washington (Seventh Street) Corps, was the other.[109]

Maurice A. and Grace Bean Smith with son Maurice E.

Major and Mrs. Smith with Bible School students at Fort Pickering Corps, Memphis, Tenn., 1952

The Smiths' 1944 distinctively Salvation Army–style wedding takes place in the beautifully decorated Vermont Avenue Baptist Church. Major James A. Longino, divisional commander, leads the service. He had been a sessionmate of Smith and had introduced the couple to one another via letters. The audience falls silent as Adjutant B. Barton McIntyre, who had traveled from Cleveland, reads Scripture. From a hush, strains of grand music burst forth.

The flag and color bearers enter the sanctuary dressed in Salvation Army uniforms. As Brigadier Charles Walker performs the ceremony, he reflects on how he had recommended Adjutant Smith for officership some 20 years earlier. Maurice and Grace repeat their vows clearly during the double–ring ceremony. Brigadier James Roberts and Major and Mrs. Lambert Bailey offer their felicitations. Then, Norma T. Roberts sings, and the benediction follows. The event is a virtual "who's who" among black Salvation Army officers.

As the wedding party retires to the lower auditorium, they discover that it is adorned with beautiful flowers, which add an elegant touch to the social hour prepared by the soldiers, comrades, and friends of the Washington, D.C., No. 2 Corps.[110]

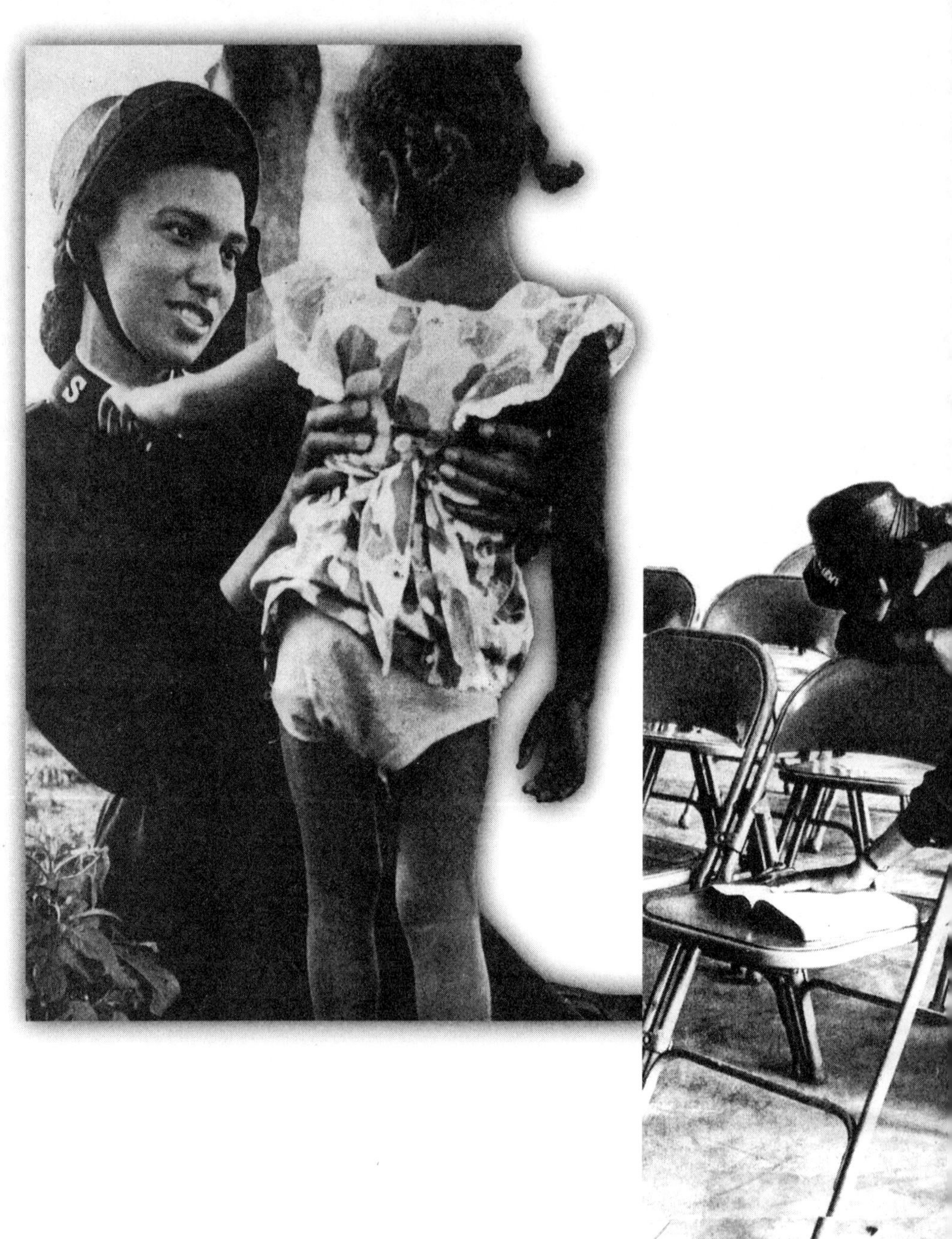

Chapter 5

'An opportunity to be of service to humanity'

Norma Roberts launches a ministry

SEVERAL YEARS BEFORE THE MARRIAGE OF SENIOR MAJOR MAURICE A. AND ADJUTANT GRACE BEAN (see Milestones, Chapter 4, July 1944), young Norma Roberts felt the call to become a Salvation Army officer. She left government service after just five years and applied for officership at the Southern Territory's School for Officer Training (SFOT). But she was denied a place there because of racial restrictions. Undaunted, Roberts applied to SFOT in New York City and was accepted. "I decided to give lifetime service to The Salvation Army because, through the Army, I can be of greater service to humanity," she said.[111]

The Bronx campus green reminded Roberts of the South, where she envisioned having a thriving ministry one day. But a plan to have her run a new home and hospital in Tulsa, Okla., was scrapped when the fund–raising project failed to reach its goal. The Army decided to have her serve instead at the Booth Memorial Hospital in New York City until another plan could be formulated to move her back to her home territory.

In 1949, Robert's prayers were answered. Lt. Colonel

SFOT campus in Bronx, New York, c. 1955

Florence Turkington, Women's Social Service secretary for the Eastern Territory, wrote, "The Lieutenant [Roberts] has been very happy in her appointment in the Eastern Territory and for many reasons would like to remain in the North." Lt. Colonel Turkington continued, "However, she had definite convictions that her work should be in the South with those of her own race."

Norma T. Roberts

Indeed, Roberts had established herself as a dedicated officer with "a beautiful spirit" during her short stay in New York, but she always wanted to serve in the South even though she knew she would face discrimination there. "She thought this through and recognizes the sacrifice which she must make in returning to the South, where opportunities for herself and those of her race are so limited," Turkington wrote.

Roberts spoke freely about taking an appointment in a racially segregated South. More than anything, she wanted to be an evangelist. Turkington wrote, "While I shall be very loath to let this officer go, I also appreciate her feelings and convictions, and would raise no barrier to her returning to the Southern Territory if this is the plan finally decided for her."[112]

By 1949, Roberts was working at a small, dilapidated Salvation Army center on East 6th Street in the East End of Little Rock, Ark. Although not one church or government agency had offered the area's 6,000 blacks a consistent social–service program in 12 years, the Army had nonetheless determined that "a liberal element" existed in this city more than in others. Activities at the center included social services every Monday, Wednesday, and Friday for young people, preceded by visits to homes in the community.

Roberts, dressed in her new uniform and bonnet, was hard–pressed to ignore the stench and squalor she found when she walked through the shabby dwellings. When she looked around, Roberts realized why God had called her back to the South—the need was so great. Poverty–stricken residents had stuffed the walls of their homes with cardboard and rags to keep out the cold; they used old trunks and garbage cans as end tables; and they covered some walls with old newspapers to hide the decaying, splintered boards.

Sunday meetings began at 10 a.m. in the form of an adult Sunday school class. Roberts let it be known that she needed young women assistants willing to be trained to give "lifetime service to the cause of humanity." The 27–year–old Roberts and her assistants conducted open–air meetings under the Cassinelli's Liquor store sign. A small group would gather to hear Roberts sing and preach. Only about 18 percent of the people in town actually attended religious services; 60 percent didn't belong to any church at all. Roberts found standing outdoors under the liquor store sign more comfortable than sitting at the East 6th Street center, where there was a lack of adequate furniture, paint was peeling from the walls and ceiling, and weeds were growing on the ill–kept property.[113]

Roberts was determined. She continued her community visits, supervised children's play programs, and envisioned a better tomorrow. Having watched her parents under challenging circumstances, Roberts knew the virtue of patience and was equipped for the tasks at hand.

One day, a reporter knocked on the door. He was from the *Arkansas Gazette*, a local newspaper. He asked Roberts if she would agree to let him write a story and photograph her ministry. She agreed. Reader response to the article and its dramatic photos was sensational. The piece exposed a community in desperate need. In the spotlight was Lieutenant Norma Roberts, a young, dedicated Salvation Army officer working valiantly against great odds.

The public's outcry pressured the Army's advisory board, a group of business leaders charged with oversight of the corps, to take action. A subsequent newspaper report announced that the board would "meet Friday night to hear plans for the construction of a new center." At that meeting, Roberts eloquently pointed out that the Army planned to build similar centers across the South, not just in Arkansas. "The Salvation Army strives to promote the spiritual and material welfare of people all over the world—regardless of race or color," she said. "In that spirit, it seeks to bring its service to my people in the Southland."[114]

Roberts, now well on her way to truly making a difference, continued to minister to families by helping them overcome marital problems, domestic violence, and the

Norma Roberts helping a client

humiliation associated with abject poverty. Her vision of a new tomorrow was now on the drawing board.

In 1951 in Washington, D.C., Brigadier James N. Roberts was promoted to Glory. He would have been proud to see that just a year later, his daughter Norma's tireless efforts began to finally pay off in Little Rock, Ark. The new center opened in the midst of East End's poorest community. The Army spent $18,179 from its trust funds to plan, build, and furnish the new center. A community chest contributed to its expansion. The center sat across the street from the new 200–family Hollinsworth Grove housing project for blacks, which flanked the Arkansas River, Adams Field Airport, and industrial plants along the Missouri–Pacific Railroad tracks. The new 45×60 foot center, which offered programs to 5,000 people annually, had a large auditorium for recreational and group activities; meeting rooms that could be opened into another large room; as well as a kitchen, restrooms, storage rooms—and an office for Lieutenant Roberts.

The center was a dream come true for Roberts, who had come a long way from the dilapidated shack in which she had started. Although she now made only $21 a week (an officer's transportation, and other needs are provided), she was happy. "An opportunity to be of service to humanity," she said, "is more important than other worldly gains."[115]

Chapter 6

'Colored' corps no more!

Black Salvationists attack racial stigma

AMERICANS WILL LONG REMEMBER THE 1950S as a time when political paranoia and mistrust permeated the nation. It was the beginning of the Cold War and the rise to power of Senator Joseph McCarthy (R) of Wisconsin, the nation's outspoken leader and crusader against "domestic subversion." He accused many prominent citizens of being communists. And in doing so, he made their lives a living hell.

For African Americans, being called "liberal" or even "communist" would have been a step up from the usual names assigned to them by a racially intolerant society. Their worst nightmares remained being called "nigger," "boy," "girl," or "coon." African Americans faced the same old color line and kept fighting discrimination and rejection based solely on race. The Salvation Army, although well–intentioned, was no haven from such labeling. The Army had named corps predominantly populated by blacks "colored corps," while corps in white neighborhoods had names based on geographic distinctions. A group of African–American Salvationists in Cleveland eventually took a second look at the Army's Disposition of Forces (the organization's official internal directory, also known as "the Dispo") and determined that their corps was the only one in the territory whose name was based on race.

After 58 years as the Cleveland 33rd Street (Colored) Corps, also known as the Glory Shop, soldiers there requested that the name be changed to the "Central Area Corps." Brigadier Edward Carey, divisional commander for Northeastern Ohio, wrote in a letter to Colonel Samuel Hepburn of Territorial Headquarters, "There has been objection to some of these titles and the discriminatory designation 'colored' which was removed from the last Dispo. We recommend, as does the commanding officer and his census board, that the corps be officially designated as 'Central Area,' which is a descriptive name for the area and neighborhood served.... We recommend that this take effect immediately...." To the Army's credit, when blacks brought this problem to the attention of leadership, it responded.

The Army approved the name change with great fanfare. At a most auspicious ceremony, the Army declared the new name, "Central Area Corps," in the presence of top territorial and local leaders.[116] Then–Major B. Barton McIntyre, corps officer, was among the celebrants, a group that included a host of visiting pastors, officers, and members of the Cleveland Advisory Board. McIntyre, although pleased with this development, knew that paying attention to semantics was only the first step for African Americans along the long road to freedom from segregation and bias in America. To get the job done, he began a campaign that would last the rest of his career as a Salvation Army officer.

Cleveland Central Area Corps, c. 1971

Separate but not equal

For example, McIntyre knew that the Salvation Army's Men's Social Service Department had an unofficial segregation policy that discriminated against men of color. Even in centers located in predominantly black or racially mixed neighborhoods, the Army allowed few if any black "beneficiaries," as residents were called, to live there. The Army never had an official policy excluding black men, but managers of the centers had the freedom to admit whom they wanted—and admission records show that they didn't want blacks, except to serve as cooks or in various other low–level positions.

As early as 1944, Lester Granger of the National Urban League wrote to the Army's National Headquarters and condemned the "bad interracial relationships" in many Men's Social Service institutions. McIntyre read a paper at the National Conference of Social Work in which he denounced racial segregation at Salvation Army institutions, which he said raised "the Jim Crow" standard rather than the "Blood and Fire" flag. Many managers of those institutions blamed the need for segregated facilities on the attitudes of the Army's white clientele, who would simply not accept black men into the program with them. The white protesters were mostly men over 40 who were poorly educated and frustrated with their own station in life. Their effort to keep blacks down was born out of a desperate need to feel some sense of power in their seemingly powerless existence, wrote author Edward H. McKinley in his book *Somebody's Brother: A History of the Salvation Army's Men's Services Department, 1891–1985.*[117]

However, by 1945, many black men had returned from WW2 as heroes. These men believed, as did their predecessors from WW1, that they deserved fair and equal treatment for risking their lives for the United States and its democratic way of life.

In March 1946, the Salvation Army's Eastern Regional

© David E. Scherman/Getty Images

African–American soldiers, circa 1942

directors called for a "definite policy" on admitting blacks. Army leadership asked each center director to take a single black client as an "experiment" and to report the results to headquarters.

In December 1950, the Southern Territory also entertained the idea of inviting black men into its social service centers on an experimental basis. These preliminary tests proved so successful that more trial runs were conducted. The Men's Social Services Department slowly became one of many avenues opening to blacks interested in receiving services from—and participating in—The Salvation Army.[118]

On May 7, 1954, the Brown vs. Board of Education decision rendered by the United States Supreme Court declared that "separate but equal" schools were unconstitutional. The decision read, in part, "Segregation of white and Negro children in the public schools of a state solely on the basis of race, pursuant of state laws permitting or requiring such segregation, denies to Negro children the equal protection of the laws guaranteed by the Fourteenth

Amendment—even though the physical facilities and other 'tangible' factors of white and Negro schools may be equal. The 'separate but equal' doctrine adopted in Plessy vs. Ferguson, 163 U.S. 537, has no place in the field of public education."[119]

The Commissioners' Conference, the annual meeting of the Salvation Army's top national and territorial leaders, embraced the Supreme Court's famous decision with sincere conviction. The Army quickly issued an official Salvation Army position statement endorsing the decision in language that was almost uniquely enthusiastic for such documents: "The Supreme Court's historic decision outlawing segregation in the nation's public facilities is heartily endorsed by The Salvation Army. A ruling so soundly based on Christian principles cannot but receive understanding and cooperation from all Salvationists dedicated to the ideal that in Christ all are one. We accept our full Christian responsibility to work earnestly and sympathetically to the end that a practical implementation of the decision may be successfully effected."[120]

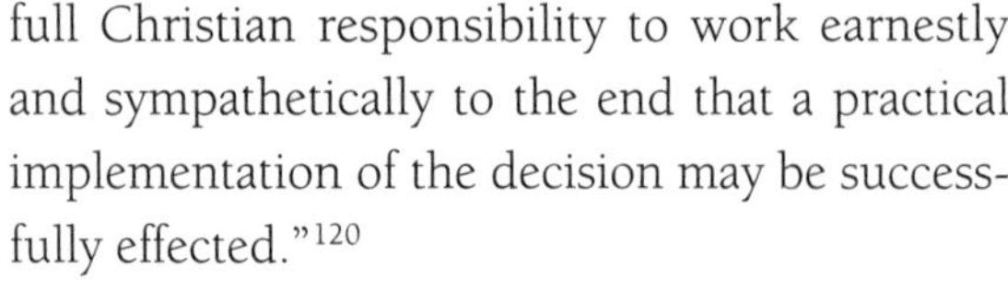

However, the Supreme Court soon learned that inscribing such a declaration in black ink on white paper was far easier than uniting people of those same colors. That year, Marian Anderson, the famous black contralto opera singer, sang on the steps of the Lincoln Memorial in Washington, D.C., because a prominent women's society, the Daughters of the American Revolution, would not allow her to sing at their affair at Constitution Hall. Former First Lady Eleanor Roosevelt resigned from the organization over the incident.[121]

© Gaston Paris/Getty Images

Marian Anderson

Ministry milestones (1949–1950)

In 1949, in the Southern Territory, Brigadiers Victor and Latrude Wilson arrive in the United States from Panama City's Central Corps to serve in Washington, D.C. The Jamaican-born Wilsons are appointed to the Washington #2 Corps (Washington Central). Because Brigadier Victor Wilson is fluent in Spanish, the Army asks him to speak to Hispanic residents. Wilson proves to be a kind, generous, humble lover of children and young people. He conducts an annual Gospel program for high school youth in the D.C. area. His motto becomes, "It is better to wear out than to rust out!" Wilson would contribute much more than a slogan to Army ministry before "wearing out."[122]

Victor Wilson

In Memphis, Tenn., 7-year-old Maurice E. Smith receives Christ as his personal Savior, as his parents, Senior Majors Maurice A. and Grace Smith, open a work among blacks in that city and name it the Fort Pickering Corps.[123]

In the East, another young man, Harmon Tate, an accomplished academician and Salvation Army musician, sets his sights on becoming an officer, but he later changes his mind when he see the limited opportunities for blacks. "A colored corps in New York, up in Harlem; seemed to me that was the only place you had to go ... as a black officer," he had said. "To myself, I said, 'I would [become an officer] but I don't want to be an officer in one place.'"

Harmon opts to stay close to the Army, however, through music and corps work, where he completes a six-year corps cadet course. He had recently graduated with a bachelor of Sacred Theology (STB) and a master of sacred theology (STM) degrees. Harmon had attended Salvation Army meetings since 1926 when he was a child in Boston, Massachusetts. His father, Carroll, was a Baptist and his mother, Hannah, a Christian Scientist, but Harmon enjoyed attending the Saturday night Army meetings at a corps on Erving Street in Malden. The Tate family lived in a small black community, but the children attended mixed schools. Harmon and his brother Myron become excellent band musicians. They audition and earn seats in the Kavalovski Orchestra.

Harmon Tate

Harmon Tate (second from left) with THQ team (l–r): Colonel John D. Waldron, chief secretary; CSM Gordon Cranford; Commissioner Norman S. Marshall, territorial commander; and Major Robert Watson.

During WW2, the Harmon brothers play stateside in U.S. Army bands. After the war, Harmon enrolls in Tufts University, where he completes a double major in sociology and theology in four years. He graduates in 1950 with an AB degree in sociology.[124]

In 1950, Commissioner Ernest Pugmire, national commander, delivers a national report at a White House Conference on Children and Youth and points out the particular difficulties in placing black foster children in homes and schools. In 1940, the Army had started The Salvation Army Nursery and Foster Home Service in Brooklyn, N.Y., where a program of foster care under professionally trained personnel cared for unwanted children, a good number of them black. The home frequently experienced problems in carrying out its interracial program, particularly in finding black foster and adoption homes for black children. Those kids tended to remain in the study homes longer than necessary, and transfers between foster homes were often delayed past the desirable point because of a lack of black foster homes. Yet the number of black children needing care away from their own homes continued to increase, and their problems were intensified because of inadequate care before placement. These problems tended to carry over into new foster home placements.

In his report before the White House conference, Pugmire says that life is difficult enough for most black children, and being a foster child often only exacerbates the problems caused by racial discrimination. He also points out that across the nation, the public school situation is becoming increasingly difficult for foster children of any race. Some schools openly state that they don't want them or demand tuition for them. Other schools are more subtle; they constantly report minor incidents at school to the caseworker, ask that children be removed from school, and evidence little or no sympathy for or understanding of the child and his (or her) problems.[125]

Chapter 7
'A soldier's story'

How three officers overcame adversity

In 1950, 13–year–old Abraham Johnson, along with his parents, and seven siblings moved from the suburbs to the city of Poughkeepsie, N.Y., where they found a Salvation Army corps. The Johnson children attended the soldiers' prep meetings, where they learned all about The Salvation Army, and later enrolled as soldiers. They became involved in every corps activity. Their white, foreign–born corps officers accepted the family.

Abraham Johnson

But as the only black family in the corps, the Johnsons encountered racism from some families who didn't want them there. In response, the corps officers spent many nights on their knees, praying for reconciliation between those corps families and the Johnsons.

The Johnsons were thankful to the corps officers for their heartfelt support and for the encouragement they received from other families that disagreed with their critics.

The following year, young Abe attended the Salvation Army's Star Lake Camp in New Jersey. One day, he entered the camp's rustic tabernacle and humbly knelt at the altar. There, he heard God call him to become a Salvation Army officer. With tears in his eyes, he accepted the call and at that moment, his destiny was sealed.[126]

In 1956, Abraham Johnson faced a major setback along the road to becoming an officer. He applied for training at the Eastern Territory's School for Officer Training, but he was not accepted. Territorial leaders, concerned about the civil rights unrest in the country, suggested that he go to England for training instead. But Johnson refused. "I want to be trained in my own territory so I can remain in this territory and serve with my people," he said.

The following year, Johnson entered SFOT in the USA East, becoming the first black man to do so in 12 years. The training school offered Johnson every opportunity to develop as a cadet. But the civil rights conflict continued to worsen, and school staff feared for Johnson's safety during field training exercises at white corps.

One day, while traveling through the state of Delaware, a group of male cadets stopped to eat at a restaurant. When the owner saw Johnson's black face among the sea of white ones, he refused to serve him. Humiliation and rage filled Johnson's heart. As for the white cadets, who had grown to love Johnson as one of their own, they suddenly lost their appetites. Despite the enticing aromas from the kitchen, they stubbornly refused to be served.

Both the restaurant owner and Johnson were amazed. His eyes filled with tears as he watched the cadets rise from their seats, one by one, and walk back to the bus. "I wasn't that hungry anyway," one cadet said as he adjusted his tunic and casually brushed away a piece of lint.

The following year, as Johnson stood on the steep steps of the training school and looked across the campus on Andrews Avenue in the Bronx, he reflected on that special moment when he felt so incredibly proud to be a Christian and Salvationist. He eventually graduated as a member of the Courageous session and was commissioned as assistant officer at Harlem Temple.[127]

Against this backdrop, a black woman entered the United States, this time from London. Salvation Army Captain Dorothy Purser had worked as a nurse in Army hospitals in London and Manchester, England, and in Scotland. Having heard numerous horror stories about racism in America, the Jamaican–born officer was reluctant to make the move. But the Army promised her a groundbreaking appointment at a new Booth Memorial Hospital in Cleveland. When she arrived in Ohio, however, she discovered that the hospital hadn't yet been built. So she took a position as director of nursing at the Catherine Booth Hospital in Cincinnati.

Purser had graduated from the Army's International

Dorothy Purser

Training School in London in 1941, during WW2. She had seen her parents, Ezekiel and Ethel Purser, senior majors, serve in appointments throughout the Caribbean. When she was only 6, Dorothy had also seen them in action in Nigeria, where the Army appointed her parents to help pioneer its work there. Now Dorothy was becoming a pioneer of a different sort.

On the way to the hospital in Cincinnati, she and a white woman officer decided to stop for some ice cream at Baskin & Robbins®. Little did Dorothy realize that she was about to receive her first taste of American racism. She sat in the car and watched as her friend's face grew red and her movements animated as she spoke to the clerk.

"Come on, Dorothy, we're leaving!" she said as she marched back to the car.

"Why? We haven't had our ice cream," Dorothy said.

"We don't need to eat here. Let's go!" her friend repeated.

Dorothy looked back through the window at the clerk, whose facial expression suddenly provided the answer to Dorothy's question. The clerk had refused to serve ice cream to Dorothy because she was black. In protest, Dorothy's friend had also refused to be served. The two women finished the journey to Cincinnati feeling angry, humiliated, and sad all at once.

This incident introduced Dorothy to life as a black person in the United States. At the hospital in Cincinnati, co–workers challenged her competence but were soon surprised by her confidence and resolve. Speaking on the phone sometimes proved comical. Her many years as a citizen of London gave Purser a British accent that most Americans assumed belonged to a white person. By the time callers met her face–to–face, it was frequently too late to say "no" or take back the information they had shared with her. Purser learned to deal with the racially intolerant culture with the same intrepid spirit that she had had to muster when she faced colonialism in the Caribbean, religious conflict in Africa, and German air raids in London during the war.

When the Booth hospital finally opened in Cleveland, the Army made Purser director of parent and nurses' aide education and assistant director of nursing. This marked the beginning of a ministry that would later become her most cherished accomplishment.[128]

In Quincy, Ill., a 6–year–old child, Vivian Taylor, heard a knock on her door. When her mother opened it, she saw a man wearing a blue uniform standing before her. "Hello, I'm Captain Herb Fuqua from The Salvation Army," he said. Vivian and her mother were transfixed. Fuqua continued, "For the next two weeks, we are having Bible school, and I would like to invite your children to attend."

Vivian's mom quickly asked him, "How many can go?" "How many do you have?" he asked. "Six in all, from age 3 to 13." "They all can come," he said. And so it was settled. However, all did not go well at first. Captain Fuqua's congregation was all white and unaccustomed to having blacks among them. But he was persistent. "It has taken me several years to get my foot in the colored neighborhood," he said, "and I'm not about to take it out!"

Vivian Taylor

To his critics, he said, "If you don't like it, you can leave." They didn't. And over time, many of the congregants fell in love with the Taylor children, and vice versa. Thus began their Salvation Army adventure. They attended Bible school, summer camp, and Sunday school. But a crisis would later challenge young Vivian and force her to make a difficult decision that would change the course of her life.[129]

Her turning point happened when a group of children called her "nigger" repeatedly at a Salvation Army summer camp. In tears, she went to her divisional youth secretary and complained. As he wiped her tears away, he said, "Vivian, there are some kids who don't know any better, and those who should be ashamed of themselves. What you need to remember is that God loves you, no matter what color you are or what names others might call you—and so do I. So, if they call you that nasty name again, just laugh at them and walk away, because as long as you cry, they are going to keep it up." He finished by saying, "And Vivian, last but not least, you need to pray for them."

From that moment on, God gave Vivian the gift of a loving heart—the ability to love people, no matter who they were or what walk of life they came from. She learned to look beyond their faults to see their souls and to love them as God does: unconditionally. Soon, Vivian's love for people would truly be put to the test. Not with strangers, but among her own family.[130]

By 1969, many things had changed for Vivian. She had just entered training in Chicago. She had heard God's call to officership at her first Young People's Council meeting in 1965. When her family had first arrived at The Salvation Army corps, some members of the all–white congregation had not accepted them. But, thanks to Captain Fuqua, the members eventually embraced the Taylor family. However, when a new corps officer assumed that appointment, Vivian's mom suddenly pulled the family out of the corps and returned to the local Baptist church. Vivian, who had heard God's call to Salvation Army ministry, chose to stay at the corps.

Those were difficult days for Vivian. She loved her family, but she also loved The Salvation Army. Had it not been for her corps family, her road to officership would have been a lonely one. They became her base of support and gave her full backing when she announced her decision to enroll as a cadet at the School for Officer Training. Ironically, the people who had once rejected her as a child now embraced her with their financial, material, and spiritual support.[131]

Ministry milestones (1955–1959)

In 1955, Brigadiers Adrian and Eualee DaCosta move from the Harlem Temple Corps to Philadelphia's Brown Street Community Center. To fill the Harlem post, the McIntyres leave the Cleveland (Central) Corps and return to New York City. Now the highest-ranking black officer in the Army, Barton McIntyre takes the lead in addressing racial issues on behalf of black Salvationists. He writes several scholarly papers on racial issues: "Experience in Lessening Racial Tension," "The Salvation Army Looks at the Negro," and "What Can We Do?" are among the titles. He also serves as executive director of the Army's largest Red Shield center for the aged. Under McIntyre's theme, "Watch Us Grow," Harlem Temple does grow substantially.[132]

Brigadiers Adrian and Eualee DaCosta

Black corps attract many children and teens. Some, such as Hester Burgess, would grow up to become officers. At just 6 years old, Hester notices a group of children having a wonderful time playing in the front yard of a local Salvation Army center. When she asks if she could play with them, an adult tells her, "You'll have to pay a quarter to become a member, and then you can play with them." The next day, Hester pays her quarter and joins the children. As she continues to go to the center, rain or shine, all the way through high school, she learns much about the Salvation Army's history and purpose.[133]

~

In the Southern Territory, the Smith family takes a severe blow. Sr. Major Grace Smith had been promoted to Glory in 1957 and now, two years later, the Army closes the Fort Pickering Corps that the Smiths had opened in Memphis, Tenn., among the black people there.

Sr. Major Maurice A. Smith moves to a new appointment in Washington, D.C. His son, young "Eddie" Smith, graduates from high school and enters the District of Columbia Teacher's College. He serves as a soldier and local officer at at the Washington, D.C., Central Corps. He takes on roles as Sunday school teacher, divisional bandsman, scoutmaster, and songster. Then one day, he picks up the book *The General Next to God* by Collier and captures a vision for his future as a Salvation Army officer.[134]

Louise Hagler

In the Eastern Territory, Louise Hagler enters SFOT as a member of the Greatheart session. Her introduction to The Salvation Army had come when she attended a Billy Graham Crusade in New York City's Madison Square Garden. There a Salvationist invited her to a worship service, where she began to learn more about the Army.[135]

In Cleveland, Ohio, William M. Haynes, a black, 56–year–old building supervisor at the Army's Men's Social Services Center on Euclid Avenue, pledges $500 of his hard–earned pay to the Army's building fund and he and his wife, Minnie, are prepared to give more if the Army's fund drive falls short of its $1,830 goal. William trusts and believes in the Army's willingness to help the poor. Wearing a wide–brimmed hat, blue collar, and a breast pocket full of writing pens, Haynes says to a *Cleveland Plain Dealer* newspaper reporter, "I've seen so much good that they have done for my people. I've seen people I wouldn't let in my backyard, and they take them right into the dining room. Some are dirty and ragged. Some are barefooted; and they get shoes. The Salvation Army people are God sent."[136]

William M. Haynes

The Men's Social Service ministry finally admits black men as beneficiaries, thanks to landmark legislation and outspoken leaders within the Army, such as Colonel B. Barton McIntyre.[137]

Chapter 8

Real blood and fire

"We must understand that this is not a game. [Racism] is demonic. We as a church must be on our knees praying for protection for ourselves and others because it's a spiritual battleground."

—Neil Rendall, Intervarsity Christian Fellowship

AMERICA HAD NOT SEEN ANYTHING LIKE IT SINCE THE CIVIL WAR. Once again, the focus of the entire nation, indeed the world, rested on the plight of African Americans in the United States. News agencies broadcast images of riot–torn urban communities from Newark, N.J., to Watts, Calif. "Freedom" became the battle cry of many blacks seeking to end a national policy of racial segregation and discrimination at water fountains, lunch counters, and college gates.

Demanding a hearing, African Americans boycotted, picketed, and marched through the streets of the nation's largest cities. Political upheaval on every front plagued the nation. The United States lost four of its most beloved leaders to assassins' bullets: President John F. Kennedy, Senator Robert Kennedy, Reverend Dr. Martin Luther King, Jr., and black Muslim leader Malcolm X.

Many more individuals, sung and unsung, also died in racially or politically motivated murders. Then there was the heated controversy over the war in Vietnam, from which an increasing number of American troops were returning home each day—in body bags or with broken bodies, minds, or spirits.

These crises changed the social paradigm in America forever, as well as the relationship that existed between The Salvation Army and the African–American community. Black Salvationists caught up in the struggle for liberty and justice in the United States prayed in the chapel on Sunday and in the streets on Monday as they wrestled

© Hulton–Deutsch Collection/CORBIS

Rev. Dr. Martin Luther King Jr., speaks to a crowd during the civil rights movement.

with conflicting priorities and emotions.

The Army and the Civil Rights Movement

In some cases, a lack of understanding within the black community about the Salvation Army's role in the racial and political struggle led to resentment toward the Army. Traditionally, the Army maintained a policy of political neutrality so that it could be of service to all people in crises. Longstanding bonds with police, the military, and emergency and rescue personnel, for example, made it difficult for Army volunteers to arrive at a riot scene and not offer food and drink to the weary workers—much to the dismay of the black freedom fighters.

In Washington, D.C., the reaction of Army leaders to the Civil Rights Movement alienated some members of the black community even more. In a paper entitled "The Poor People's Campaign and The Salvation Army," Brigadier W. R. H. Goodier, the National Capital divisional commander, stated the Army's official position—to "take no position"—in the campaign designed to force the United States government to act for impoverished African Americans. Although the paper stated that the Army was "sympathetic" to the goals of the campaign, the Army criticized the timing of Dr. King's march on Washington. The paper also questioned Dr. King's "wisdom" and said the campaign was "ill timed, weakens our [the United States] position in the family of nations, and provides propaganda which aids the enemy's [North Vietnam's] cause."[138]

However, white Salvationist leadership was anything but monolithic on the issue. Despite the Army's official policy, Commissioner Ernest R. Holz attended the March on Washington for jobs and freedom, which took place August 28, 1963. Attended by some 250,000 people, it was the largest demonstration ever seen in the nation's capital, and one of the first to have extensive television coverage.[139] Holz typified the many white Salvationists who disagreed with the Army's position to "take no position." In 1965 Holz wrote a scathing denunciation of the Army's policy in *New Soldiers*.

Brigadier Victor S. Wilson (left) and Commissioner Ernest R. Holz

> I saw banners and signs saying that Episcopalians, Presbyterians, Methodists, marched for full equality and rights for all. I did not look for the banner saying that my church, The Salvation Army, supported and marched for equal rights, for I know it was not there. I have been told that The Salvation Army supports full equality for all people, but I do not see it being declared in America today. The churches in America for the most part recognize their obligation in leading the drive to correct a

> moral wrong, a wrong which is a denial of Christianity itself. What is so very important is that these denominations now have leaders who take a public and unswerving stand on this issue.
>
> The Salvation Army, however, is remaining stagnant. Thousands of young people are unable to supply a definite answer to the question, 'What is your church's position on civil rights?' Black Americans are asking white Americans for respect and dignity as individuals. To deny them this respect and dignity is to deny whatever Christian philosophy is embodied in our original national thought and to deny the essence of Christianity.[140]

Black Salvationists, concerned about the Army's image in the black community, tried to develop a voice in Army policy but received little attention. During this time, the Army lost large numbers of talented, educated black officers, senior soldiers, and young people because of subtle and sometimes overt discrimination against them from within the Army.[141]

JFK assassination shakes the nation

On November 22, 1963, a gunman assassinated President John F. Kennedy in Dallas.[142] It was a tragic day for the United States. But the worst was yet to come. The nation continued to be plagued by racially motivated violence while getting more involved in an increasingly violent war in Vietnam. Ironically, at the same time government and community leaders urged black youth to refrain from using violence to express their rage and frustration over racial discrimination and segregation directed toward them in the United States, Congress passed legislation instituting a military draft that would put the same youth on the front lines of battle in Southeast Asia, a region they knew little or nothing about. The goverment's and the Salvation Army's mixed signals to the black community made Army ministry there even harder for black officers.

In The Salvation Army, black officers persisted in their effort to call attention to discrimination in the ranks. Several territorial committees met to discuss the status of black Salvationists and their future in the organization.

Ministry Milestones (1960–1962)

Abraham Johnson, at the time a young officer in the Eastern Territory, becomes Cleveland Superior Corps officer. That same year, Louise Hagler becomes the assistant corps officer. A year later, they marry and serve two years at the Superior Corps. They then assume command of the Cleveland Central Corps, which later becomes the Miles Park Corps. Their ministry together will soon be put to a great test. Cleveland's darkest days are coming, and they will be far worse than any James Jermy and James Fackler, Booth's early pioneers, had seen.[143]

Captain Dorothy Purser launches and becomes the director of the Booth Talbert Clinic and Day Care Center, named after Mary B. Talbert, a respected African–American woman in Cleveland. The clinic runs an exciting pioneering program

Dorothy Purser (seated left) at the Talbert Clinic

for unwed mothers. It serves 150 women a month, providing education, vocational training, medical care, and a day nursery for the women's children and infants. For her leadership at the clinic, Purser receives a citation for community service from the mayor. She also earns degrees in nursing from the University of Cincinnati Nursing College and Case Western Reserve School of Social Administration in Cleveland. One young mother named Linda sends Purser her high-school graduation photo with the following message inscribed on the back; "Without you accepting me into the Booth Talbert school and accepting my children into the Booth Talbert day care, I don't think I would have made it this far." God would continue to use Dorothy Purser in the troubling days to come.[144]

In the Southern Territory, in Washington, D.C., Captains Allan and Marjorie Wiltshire arrive to serve as as officers working alongside Brigadier Victor Wilson at the Washington Central Corps. He had assumed command of the Washington #2 Corps in 1949, (former name of the Washington Central Corps). A special bond develops between the Wiltshires and the Wilsons. Brigadier Victor Wilson had been Allan's former corps officer at the Panama Temple Corps in the Republic of Panama. Wilson was his schoolteacher and taught Allan the rudiments of music, taking him through the paces of the march entitled "Joyful Soldier." The Wilsons prepare the Wiltshires for what would prove to be a challenging urban ministry in the South—and beyond.[145]

Allan and Marjorie Wiltshire

In 1962, another Caribbean officer transfers to the United States after having served several appointments in the islands. Barbados-born Lilian Yarde becomes Harlem Temple assistant officer, a capacity she serves in for just two months before moving to Cleveland, where she will become a model officer and eventually earn the title "The Ebony Angel" during the riots that will take place there.[146]

Lilian Yarde

REX
THEATRE
WE DEMAND
VOTING RIGHTS NOW!
UAW SAYS
END SEGREGATED RULES IN PUBLIC SCHOOLS

Chapter 9
Saying 'no' to 'Jim Crow'

Army issues statement on 'racial justice'

IN 1964, THE FOUR U.S. TERRITORIES OF THE SALVATION ARMY ISSUED A JOINT STATEMENT on "racial justice," declaring that the Army and all of its programs would be offered to all people on an equal basis. The Position Statement read:

> The Salvation Army and Inter–Group Relations—The Salvation Army, as a branch of the Church, opposes discriminatory practices related to race or national origin at all levels of operation and administration, and seeks to promote inter–group understanding and give full support to the imperatives of human and civil rights, not only at the levels of housing and education and employment, but also in the areas of culture and religion, sharing that spiritual affinity which makes all men brothers.—Approved by The Commissioners' Conference, May 1964.[147]

Such a declaration took courage. Between 1865 and 1967, legislators in the United States had passed more than 400 state laws, constitutional amendments, and city ordinances legalizing segregation. These laws governed every aspect of people's lives, from education, public transportation, health care, and housing to the use of public facilities.

Signs from 'Jim Crow' days

Russell Lee/Library of Congress

In the days of "Jim Crow," black children, barred by authorities from attending school with white children, had to go elsewhere. Both black and white children found restrictions outside the classroom as well: Bus drivers forbade them to share seats; Pullman porters on trains kept white and black families in separate compartments; authorities and business owners denied blacks access to public parks and restaurants and, in some states, forced them to enter public amusements, such as the circus, through a separate entrance. Black theatergoers sat in the balcony in what was frequently called "nigger heaven" by white customers. On the job, employers forced African Americans to use separate entrances and bathrooms and to collect their paychecks at separate windows. Legislators ensured that, even in death, the races would remain separate. Several states prohibited hearses from carrying people from both races, and the law required cemeteries to maintain separate graveyards.

Miscegenation statutes—laws preventing racial "interbreeding"—were the laws most widely and strongly enforced, especially in the South. At least 127 laws in the United States prohibited interracial marriage and cohabitation. In Virginia, both whites and blacks who ignored the so–called "Racial Integrity Act" could receive sentences for up to 10 years of hard labor in a penitentiary.[148]

Against this backdrop, some African–American men, encouraged by the Salvation Army's official statement against segregation, took the plunge into officership and hoped God would make a way for them. In the East, Israel L. Gaither was one such officer. Commissioned as a member of the Heroes of the Faith session, Gaither, son of a Baptist minister, first attended The Salvation Army in New Castle, Pa., at the invitation of boyhood friends. Throughout his youth, his parents fostered in him a sensitivity to do God's will. So when, as a staff member at the Salvation Army's Camp Allegheny, he heard God's call to officership, he promptly responded.

In 1967, Gaither married Eva D. Shue, a white sessionmate who was a fifth–generation Salvationist from Sidney, Ohio.

As the first interracial couple to serve as officers in The Salvation Army, the Gaithers knew firsthand the potential for racism to impede the progress of both races and to hurt families. As Salvationists, the Gaithers could not marry without first obtaining written approval from leadership. Initially, they struggled but failed to gain support from the Army's territorial and national leadership.

Israel L. and Eva D. Gaither.

Despite these challenges, young Israel, 19, and Eva, 20, remained undaunted. During those stressful days, they found a friend in Brigadier John Waldron. Despite the hateful criticism he regularly received from other officers in The Salvation Army who were aware of his support of the couple, Waldron supported their campaign to change the Salvation Army's worldview regarding miscegenation.[149]

Israel also had the full support of his family. His father, a minister, spoke to him candidly about the risks involved in such a union. For Eva Shue's family from a small Ohio town that had virtually no prior contact with African Americans, the idea was harder to accept. However, in time, they did acknowledge Israel as their own.[150]

Help also arrived in the form of a landmark Supreme Court decision. The case of Loving vs. Commonwealth of Virginia, initiated in 1958, challenged the segregation laws. After several unsuccessful attempts made by another mixed–race couple, Richard Loving (a white man) and Mildred Jeter (a black woman) eventually brought a case that overturned the law. By unanimous decision, the Supreme Court struck down the Racial Integrity Act and similar laws in 15 other states, saying: "[There] can be no doubt that restricting the freedom to marry solely because of racial classifications violated the central meaning of the Equal Protection Clause.... Under our Constitution, the freedom to marry, or not marry, a person of another race resides with the individual and cannot be infringed by the state."[151]

The court's decision led to a chain of events that resulted in the Army's International Headquarters clearing the way for the union of Israel and Eva Gaither. Together, they served in their first appointment at the Pittsburgh Homewood–Brushton Corps. When riots broke out in Pittsburgh, the Captains Gaither sought to present a balanced picture of the Army's work in the black community. They and members of the corps provided groceries and encouragement to many black families after radical protesters burned local supermarkets to the ground.

Using their unique social credential, the Gaithers courageously ministered as husband and wife to racially torn communities and advocated understanding on both sides of the color line. Food stations, set up by the Army during the Pittsburgh riots, provided the Gaithers with an opportunity to counsel grieving families living in a hotbed of tension and violence and help them cope with the turmoil.

During this time, white officers such as Colonel Paul Seiler, the territorial men's social services secretary, offered support to the Gaithers. For instance, he collected all the spare trucks from 11 Army centers and used them for a massive relief effort.[152]

On February 21, 1965, former Black Nationalist leader Malcolm X, who had called for a "blacks–only" state in the U.S., was shot several times as he began a speech to 400 of his followers at the Audubon Ballroom just outside the district of Harlem in New York City.[153]

During those times when fires raged and blood literally flowed in the streets, the Gaithers, the Seilers, and other officers came to understand in a personal way the meaning behind the Army's "Blood and Fire" motto as they witnessed the sight of real blood and real fire.

Taking Brown vs. the Board of Education to heart

In the Central Territory, a young African–American man stepped onto a Salvation Army basketball court for the first time. Stephen Harper was only 16 years old when two white brothers invited him to their corps gym. After visiting the boys at their home, Harper, who lived in Rattlebone Hollow, a segregated section of Kansas City, learned that white people weren't all rich, as he had previously thought.

Stephen Harper

Harper's mom, Deloris, was the valedictorian of her high school class. She raised him and eight siblings while holding various other jobs. Her mother, a strong figure, helped Deloris with the child–rearing.

A determined woman, Deloris took the Supreme Court "Brown vs. the Board of Education" decision, based on a dispute in Topeka, Kans., to heart. She made sure her children received the best education available, even if it meant moving the entire family several times so she could stay within white school districts. (Political leaders redrew district lines to ensure elected officials retained their seats, but the exclusion of black children from the better schools was a common side effect.)

Harper's insistence that Stephen read music and play several instruments eventually paid off. Sporting an Afro, he gained acceptance at an all–white Salvation Army music event when leaders of three bands discovered he was the only person who could play the snare drum and read the music written for it.

Young Stephen played for all three bands that day. He

beat the drums with an enthusiasm he hadn't experienced before; deep in his mind, he realized that he had also found a way to "beat" racial segregation and discrimination by being "the snare drum player," not just "the black kid." Lawrence and Patrick McPherson, the two brothers who had invited him to play basketball, encouraged him to continue playing in the band. Among the best musicians in the band, one of the brothers played the trumpet; the other, baritone horn.

The Army's bandmaster helped Harper improve his sight–reading skills. As section leaders, Stephen, Lawrence, and Patrick organized the sheet music and prepared uniforms for events such as football games and parades. In contrast to the harsh treatment Harper and his five brothers and three sisters received in school from white children, white Salvationists treated them with respect and love.

Eventually, Harper met the expectations of his newfound Salvationist friends by becoming a uniformed soldier at the Bell Fountaine Corps in Missouri. By 1969, he was wearing a cadet uniform at the School for Officer Training in Chicago.[154]

Fighting on multiple battlefronts

During the Civil Rights Era, burning out was a monumental threat to many black officers. Riots and fires raged in urban centers across the nation as officers struggled to keep a balance between their service to God and the Army and their loyalty to the desperate people who marched in the streets.

George Evans

When riots broke out in Cleveland, Ohio, Captain George Evans who had recently opened a new work in Arlington Heights near Pittsburgh, did his part to present a balanced picture of Salvation Army ministry to the black community. He ministered to families amid intensive fighting between militant Black Panthers and local police. Colonel Giles Barrett, divisional commander, supported Evans and other black officers. He helped organize Salvation Army mobile feeding units from three cities and sent them into the "war zone" with orders to feed both police and community residents who were casualties of the violence.[155]

Lilian Yarde (see Milestones, Chapter 8, 1960–62) served on Cleveland's "battlefield." She fed residents amid utter chaos of flames, bullets, and even troops wielding bayonets. Yarde and other officers used the Addison–Superior Corps as a "battle station" where they prepared food and stored supplies.

Tirelessly, day after day, showing no regard for personal safety, Yarde drove back and forth through the burning city to deliver meals and manage the canteen (mobile food station). She ministered to junior soldiers (children), many of whom came to the corps for meals, refreshment, and rest. But she didn't stop there. Yarde also offered help to anyone who needed it—community residents, police of-

Lilian Yarde with National Guard troops

ficers, firefighters, and even National Guard troops.

The grueling work exhausted her at times. Once someone found her curled up, sleeping, on the corps chapel platform. But when she was awakened, instead of going to her quarters to rest, Yarde went right back to work in the streets, where she became known as "The Ebony Angel." In recognition of her selfless efforts, the city of Cleveland and The Salvation Army cited Yarde on two separate occasions for her work during the riots.

A warm–hearted woman, Yarde challenged people to believe that, when they submit their lives to Christ, He will take what they have and use it, regardless of their station in life.

Oliver Lee, a Cleveland State University administrator, is just one of the many people Major Lilian Yarde motivated to greater service to God and humanity during her 13 years in Cleveland. Yarde encouraged Lee to serve as a youth worker. After his day at the university, Lee would spend evenings helping young people at the corps with their studies. Under Yarde's ministry, Lee accepted Christ as his Savior. Eventually, he became involved in corps worship and his subsequent appointment as dean of continuing education at the university did not interfere with his corps work. Indeed, he became more committed and dedicated.[156]

Because of efforts by officers such as Evans and Yarde, the black community's view of The Salvation Army became more positive. Across the nation, Army officers, black and white, opened youth programs and provided practical support to families. As a result, despite the widespread vandalism that took place during the riots, Salvation Army centers experienced a modern–day Passover—they were typically spared during the window–breaking and looting rampages by protesters.

Ministry milestones (1965–1969)

Cleo A. and Carmen Damon

George Evans arrives for training at the SFOT's front gate on Andrews Avenue in the Bronx. His old address had been the Edgemont Corps on Locust Lane in Harrisburg, Pa. He enters the gate confidently and expresses himself articulately. The other cadets immediately notice his large Afro hairstyle. In time, they would also become keenly aware of the largeness of his heart for God.

In 1966, Evans meets Salvationist Carmen Garay. It wouldn't be long before George and Carmen would put their Christian faith on the line for a black community in crisis.[157]

In the Southern Territory, Cleo A. Damon, a Salvationist from Guyana, South America, comes to Atlanta, Ga., after having served as an officer in Jamaica and Belize. A graduate of the Pioneers session in Jamaica, Damon marries Carmen W. Pinnoch, a 1971 graduate of the Victorious session. Their ministry would take them to appointments in the South and as far away as Tanzania, East Africa.[158]

In the racially charged, post–Jim Crow era, Army officials in most places do not consider interracial corps a possibility. In Pennsylvania, for example, the Lehigh Recreational Center for black children begins as an extension of the white Lehigh Corps. Led by Captain Kenneth Abery, the well–equipped center offers neighborhood children various programs under the motto, "Recreation plus Christ equals re–creation."[159]

Hester and Robert Dixon

The Lehigh Recreational Center officially becomes the Philadelphia Germantown Corps. Hester Burgess and Robert Dixon are products of the Army's ministry there. Hester, who had started there as a Sunbeam at 6, had grown up and was well on her way to becoming an outstanding Salvationist. Robert had come to the corps as an adult and was employed as the custodian. They meet, fall in love, and marry in 1966. Bob hears God's call to ministry and becomes full–time director of the corps' community center.

Other blacks emerge from the Germantown Corps as successful professionals. Sharon McAfee, a nurse in Pennsylvania, describes in a letter what she had learned at "The Rec": "I was taught social and life skills such as cooking, house cleaning, sewing, personal hygiene, arts and crafts, games and sports," she wrote. "But most fulfilling are the values I learned: love, sharing, honesty, respect, and caring."[160]

Another black corps that was born from an all–white corps is the Brown Street Corps. Under the leadership of Captains Adrian and Eualee DaCosta, it starts in 1965 as an offshoot of the Philadelphia Temple. Although the buildings sat side by side, blacks could not worship in the Temple Corps.

Also during that year in the Southern Territory, the 9th Street Corps is born under the leadership of Captains Allan and Marjorie Wiltshire. The corps moves into the old Washington Central building and the Washington Central Corps moves and becomes the newly–opened Sherman Avenue Corps.

In 1966, young Maurice "Eddie" Smith enrolls in the Army's SFOT in Atlanta, Ga., as a member of the Messengers of the Faith session. In his second year, his colleagues votes him session president. Smith's achievement is a bittersweet victory for black Salvationists. As he marches across the platform to receive his diploma, a deep shadow looms over the event in the wake of national tragedies. Just two months earlier, on April 4 in Memphis, Tenn., an assassin gunned down Dr. Martin Luther King, Jr.; just three days before the SFOT commencement exercises, another assassin shot to death Robert F. Kennedy, the U.S. attorney general and brother of slain President John F. Kennedy. Three days later, June 8, 1968, as Lieutenant Maurice Smith marches across the School for Officer Training stage in Atlanta, he carries with him the weight of his new responsibility to God, family, his people, and the Salvation Army world. as the first black officer commissioned from the Southern Territory.[161]

THE SALVATIO
CHRIST
MY
MILES PARK
CLEVELAND
OHIO

Chapter 10

Change from within

McIntyre's 12-point plan

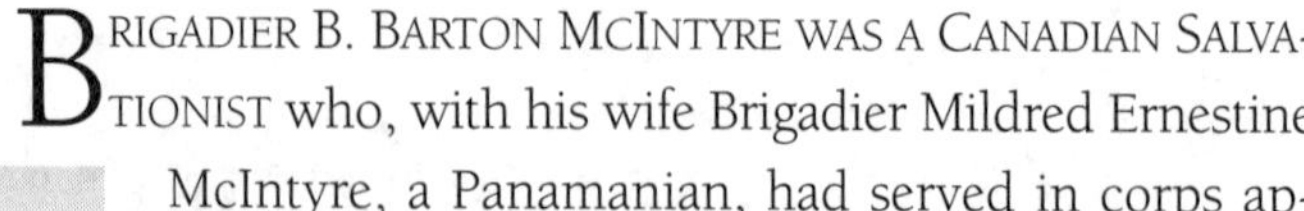

BRIGADIER B. BARTON MCINTYRE WAS A CANADIAN SALVATIONIST who, with his wife Brigadier Mildred Ernestine McIntyre, a Panamanian, had served in corps appointments in Harlem, Brooklyn, and Cleveland. In the Eastern Territory, Brigadier B. Barton McIntyre became the divisional secretary of the Metropolitan New York Division. In the current social and political climate, he decided to press the cause for racial equality within The Salvation Army. Two years earlier, concerned black Salvationists in the East had attempted to create an African–American Ministry Committee, but administration rejected their proposal. Now, McIntyre is ready to try a different approach. McIntyre was serving as divisional secretary in the Eastern Territory when he presented a paper entitled "Facing ghetto problems: as I see it." He wrote passionately on the plight of the African American:

B. Barton McIntyre

> The demand is NOW for immediate redress of three hundred years of abject subservience.
>
> Congress seeks sterner measures of restraint to bring 'respect for the law.' It could be translated into 'fear' and 'brutality' when the police seek to do the impossible and are driven to the abuse of their authority.
>
> This, in turn, translates itself into violent, uncontrollable rage when accompanied by no jobs, bad schools, closed unions, segregated housing, exploiting shopkeepers, prohibitive shopping and credit costs, and humiliating welfare costs. Suddenly they explode into a Watts or a Newark [sites of major civil rights riots].
>
> There have been sporadic riots and demonstrations in all areas in years past but today the medium of radio and television communications helps bring into focus almost every injustice from

South Africa to Rochester and centralizes every reaction from the Congo to Cleveland.

Countless remedies are being poured on this conflagration of divergent ideas by municipal, state, and federal governments. Monies, research, and manpower are poured out endlessly on the ghetto denizens, but these are only drops of oil in greatly troubled oceans.

The police force represents that structure and to many has become the butt of social abuse. This in itself should constitute a warning to the social agency who in its eagerness to recognize the law fails in its close linkage at times to see the need of the community and how it can best present its benefits to the people of the area. People who are being treated as wards of the state can quickly feel paternalism.

The second most–hated symbol of authority is the welfare caseworker. We must be careful to recognize people as individuals, recognize their needs, recognize our worth, and help direct our solutions to their needs.

The ghetto walls are more psychological than physical. And while the government can attack the physical aspects of poverty and deprivation, it has proven helpless to surmount the great barrier of human alienation and estrangement. We are on the spot, but it must be in love that we must begin the task of reconciliation.

We must not be lacking in imagination and will to discover the most appropriate way to deal with each local situation.

Then, too, we must remember that education, experience, and legislation, while important requisites, cannot take the place of a heart touched by Jesus' love. A completely altruistic approach is

> too much to ask for from the Christian Church that has been one of the chief contributors to the situation. But it is not too late nor too much to ask that it lead us on the way back. As an arm of that Church we, too, can be in the Vanguard.

McIntyre then listed a 12–point plan designed to address the issues he raised, calling for Salvationists to

1. Acquire knowledge of minority relations on an administrative and field level.
2. Speak out against groups practicing discrimination.
3. Practice fairness from the top down.
4. Organize interracial conferences with well–informed speakers.
5. Read books, newspapers, and magazines published by blacks.
6. Respect minority community leadership.
7. Establish Salvation Army humanitarian outreach without discrimination.
8. Invite people of lower economic status to corps worship meetings.
9. Open corps worship programs to community participation.
10. Conduct careful orientations for nonwhite Salvation Army officers.
11. Promote real love for freedom and fairness in Christ when training white youth for Salvation Army ministry.
12. Recognize that the radical fringe does not always represent racial groups. McIntyre said, "There are beautiful spirits in black and white filled with the love of God and man, wise in the ways of the world but dedicated to the task of brotherhood."

McIntyre's plan called for Army administration to address the issues that threatened to divide The Salvation Army and the United States itself. He asserted that the Army needed to speak out against the problem of discrimination and become an advocate for equality and justice on the race issue. He suggested the Army conduct its own self–evaluation and called for the Army to teach its youth, both black and white, the values of fairness and equality among the races.

McIntyre believed that his program would foster new ideas, lower barriers, and raise the education and understanding among people.[162] His plan, published in 1968, came in response to black oppression. But he acknowledged that no amount of education, legislation, or experience "...can take the place of a heart touched by Jesus' love."

As McIntyre expressed that love through his bold, prophetic ministry, he insisted on racial equality within the ranks of The Salvation Army. As the Army's highest–ranking black officer, he also served as the first black divisional secretary. His service would pave the way for other blacks

Open–air meeting in an African–American community

to earn appointments to administrative positions on divisional and territorial levels.

McIntyre put an instrument of peace and reconciliation into the hands of the Army's civil rights promoters. His 12–Point Plan led to discussion forums and debates about race–related issues significant to the Army and brought hope that segregation on Sunday morning would soon end in Salvation Army corps.

McIntyre's plan spoke to the broader issue of conflict resolution through education and the dissemination of accurate, compassionate information. But he made it clear that the "Jesus factor" must operate for any program to succeed. God's Word had warned him that, without love, the best intentions could result in the worst possible outcome. Only through love, he said, could righteousness and justice prevail.[163]

Black Commissioned Officers' Meeting of 1969

In the midst of the most racially turbulent period in United States history, black commissioned officers of The Salvation Army's USA Eastern Territory convened a special meeting to discuss race relations within the organization.[164] Some Salvationists voiced opposition to such a meeting. The black officers, who had wanted to bring down the walls of separation between themselves and the larger Salvation Army community, persuaded Army leadership that their intention was not to become "separatists" or "isolationists." Eventually, visionary Army leaders granted the black officers permission to convene for the purpose of assessing their future in The Salvation Army.

The meeting, the first of its kind in the Salvation Army's history, served to unite the voices of black officers concerning those issues. It had the support of Army leaders such as Commissioner Edward Carey, territorial commander; Colonel J. Clyde Cox, of Territorial Headquarters; Lt.

Colonel John Waldron; and Brigadier Charles Southwood, divisional commander.

Captain Israel L. Gaither, one of the officers responsible for planning the meeting, wrote that it encouraged the implementation of ideas and raised expectations for future meetings. The officers laid plans to publish a candidate recruitment brochure and suggested the Army hold a territory–wide forum with black youth on opportunities in The Salvation Army. Gaither wrote, "We are turning an important corner as far as Negro recruitment for officership is concerned, and I am anxious that the flow of [blacks], especially Negro young people in the ranks, will increase."

The minutes of the meeting implied that some critics were concerned that the black officers would later demand that the Army set up a "black division" within its ranks and become separatists or isolationists. However, level heads prevailed. Brigadier McIntyre, then divisional secretary for the Metropolitan New York Division, wrote to Cox with assurance that black officers "...did not want to be interpreted as a splinter group..."; rather, they were making an "...honest attempt within the Salvation Army framework to define objectives, expand relationships, and improve the general image of the Army in community services and opportunity. This is not to be interpreted in any way as separation," he wrote.

The long–range effect of this meeting was to force Salvation Army leadership to recognize its dual ministry both to black officers and to the broader black community served by the Army. Black officers held subsequent meetings and forums, which led to the formation of a territorial Multicultural Department in the East.

The hope was that young black Salvationists, disappointed thus far by the lack of opportunity, would be encouraged by watching their parents secure a better future when black officers would be able to play an influential role in shaping Army administration.

The black officers recommended that the Army devise new and effective methods to promote opportunities for service in the Army to blacks by

- Using posters, pamphlets, "specialing" groups, radio, and television.
- Adapting to its promotion campaign music to make it meaningful to all worshippers, black as well as white.
- Appointing black "specials" and inviting them to conduct weekend meetings at various corps, corps cadet rallies, or councils, and at camp meetings.
- Appointing black officers to the School for Officer Training staff.
- Preparing black officers for specific leadership positions.
- Introducing courses in black history, cooking, grooming, special music, clarinets, drums, and other programs relevant to the black community into Girl Guards, Boy Scouts, and young people's events.
- Devising methods at the corps and territorial level whereby soldiers from the Caribbean and corps nearest their residence or workplace could have communication with their home territories.
- Appointing a minority coordinator with department head status to serve at Territorial Headquarters.
- Submitting a proposal to the territorial commander requesting that black officers meet periodically for a full–day workshop in a central location in the territory.

The group also addressed longstanding cultural issues prevalent among black Salvationists. For instance, Caribbean officers typically found acceptance from whites more easily than did African–American officers. At the meeting, officers raised this issue and recommended that the Army spend more effort on developing black officers from the United States before tapping the Caribbean for "reinforcements" [new officers].[165]

However, such a task required that the Army first reconcile its internal differences and find ways to effectively bridge social and cultural gaps with the African–American community. According to one black leader of the day, the Army's tendency to embrace a neutral position on civil rights was an obstacle to achieving such reconciliation. The leader agreed with Dr. Martin Luther King, Jr., who had called the behavior of white moderates "the Negro's great stumbling block in his stride toward freedom."[166]

The Salvation Army of 1969 had changed since the radical days of Founder William Booth's early Army. Rather than engage in acts of civil disobedience, the Army opted to remain silent in most cases, even in the midst of an unjust status quo. Most men and women wearing the uniform were not expected to display the indomitable spirit of such legendary figures as Booth, who despite threats from the authorities, had protested in the street against the mistreatment and abuse of women and children workers in poisonous London match factories; or Joe the Turk in the United States, who had frequently endured the humiliation of incarceration for the sake of spreading the Gospel message. Although the Army supported the goals of civil rights in principle, it would not officially support the means being used to achieve those goals.[167]

However, Army administration did carry out several recommendations from the Black Officers' Meeting, such as allowing black officers to hold subsequent meetings and to convene forums on candidate recruitment. But the Army's social fabric was still tightly stitched to the larger society. Black officers continued to command only black corps, while white officers enjoyed more varied ministry opportunities.[168]

Ministry milestones (1969–1970)

Captains Abraham and Louise Johnson, counsel and encourage many families as they deliver food to them during the riots in Cleveland.

Abraham Johnson (in uniform) ministers to children on the streets of Cleveland.

In some areas of that city, black residents, identifying the Johnsons as the enemy, shout "nigger!" at them. Some black religious leaders and politicians accuse them of selling out because they serve as officers in a "white man's organization." The Johnsons are challenged to bring together various cultures and races within the community, including Caribbean, African, and white; urban and rural.[169]

Despite the heightened racial animosities perpetrated inside and outside the black community, a faithful core of white officers stand alongside the black officers during this struggle. Lieutenant James M. Knaggs is one such officer. When Abraham Johnson needed someone to help him teach music to at-risk children in riot-torn Cleveland, Knaggs responds to the call.

James M. Knaggs leads boys on a camping adventure.

One day, Johnson looks up and sees coming down the street a young, smiling white man dressed in a Salvation Army-blue uniform. Knaggs examines the handful of old brass band instruments in Johnson's inventory and gives them to the wide-eyed children who have gathered. He unfolds his music score and begins teaching them how to play the horns. It isn't long before the children are playing what actually sounds like music. Johnson watches and listens as the kids learn and improve under Knaggs' consistent, compassionate leadership.[170]

In the Central Territory, *hope* becomes the operative word for two African-American youths nurtured in the faith by white Salvationists. In 1969, Stephen Harper and Vivian Taylor enroll as cadets in the School for Officer Training in Chicago. Soon the rioting will be over, and as new officers, they will take their places as participants in a second "reconstruction."

The rebuilding begins in Cleveland, where the Army erects its first multipurpose center. Located in the Hough section of the city, it quickly becomes a symbol of hope for community residents who had been emotionally decimated by poverty and racial conflict. The Army appoints Majors Henry and Marjorie Gariepy, two white officers, to be the center's first administrators. Attending the dedication ceremony is James Farmer, the first black U.S. assistant secretary for the Department of Health, Education, and Welfare; Mayor Carl B. Stokes of Cleveland, the first black mayor of a major city in the United States; and Commissioner J. Clyde Cox, territorial commander of the USA Eastern Territory.

The Hough Center includes a gym, swimming pool, clubrooms, a roller–skating rink, a billiard room, and a gathering space. The Salvation Army's Booth Talbert Clinic and day care, run by Major Dorothy Purser, also operates out of the center.

Its designers equip Hough well for the task of providing recreational, medical, religious, and social services to the community. But the center, in and of itself, does not guarantee success in a community where people have lived with oppression, disappointment, neglect, and despair for so many years.

Many hard–working Salvation Army officers, employees, and volunteers reach out and gain the trust of Hough residents.[171] Major Henry Gariepy develops rapport with Army and civic leaders, high–profile benefactors, and national celebrities. Cadets Timothy and Grace Thomas, African Americans who had entered the School for Officer Training in 1969, serve as interns and help develop relationships with local residents.

Together, the Gariepys, Thomases, employees, and volunteers of the center encourage people from all walks of life—the famous and infamous, rich and poor, black and white, young and old, athletes and scholars—to support the reconstruction effort. When the Thomases graduate from the School for Officer Training in 1971, the Army appoints them to the Hough Center as its first corps officers. (Hough is officially recognized as a corps within the center that year).[172]

The Gariepys encourage Olympic track champion Madeline Manning Jackson and heavyweight boxing great George Foreman, among other celebrities, to promote the multipurpose center. The Army secures the trust of the Hough community and, with their involvement, develops

Commissioner Paul J. Carlson, territorial commander (at podium), installs Lieutenants Grace and Timothy Thomas as officers responsible for the first Hough Center Corps, assisting Major Henry Gariepy, Hough Center director (far right). Lt. Colonel Richard Atwell, divisional commander (left), looks on.

a program that brings over 1,000 people a day through its doors. In its first six years, it registers over 10,000 people as members of the center.

In 1972, evangelist Billy Graham requests to visit the center. After seeing a 5,000-volume library and tutorial program, a public school program, clinics, and crisis-intervention programs, he remarks, "This is Christianity in action."[173]

The Salvation Army's efforts at fairness toward blacks have not gone unnoticed by the black community. In 1968, The Cincinnati Medical Association (CMA), the black counterpart of the American Medical Association, recognizes the Army's attempt to make Martin Luther King's dream a reality. In a letter to Gerald White, editor of the *Cincinnati Enquirer,* Dr. Alvin H. Darden, Jr., president of CMA, expresses appreciation to the Army's Catherine Booth Hospital (CBH) for the significant contribution it has made toward improving the status of African-American physicians in that city. "This institution," Darden wrote, "stood alone in recognizing the capabilities of Negro physicians in the second and third decades of this century." Indeed, since the Evangeline and Catherine Booth Homes and Hospitals merged in 1940, CBH had been the only hospital in Cincinnati caring for the African–American unmarried mother, the only hospital in which the black physician could work, and the only institution caring for expectant single mothers—both black and white.[174]

Chapter 11

New momentum, greater challenges

Black officers in inner-city ministries (1971–1989)

"The real tragedy is, of course, that there is a great deal of material on black people in The Salvation Army, but there are not enough hands to bring it out now and use it. There are so many areas of the Army's history that are lying dormant, just waiting to be brought to light; this is but one example."

—James E. Beane, Historical Commission, June 18, 1974

IN THE 1970S AND 80S, CORPS APPOINTMENTS GAVE BLACK OFFICERS GREAT INFLUENCE in the United States through Salvation Army ministry. Such positions of community–based leadership offered opportunities for them to think globally while reaching people locally and making a difference in individuals' lives and in communities. In the aftermath of the civil rights struggle, the Army spent millions of dollars—both government and private funds—on social programs and facilities designed to rebuild inner cities across the nation. Some of the black officers commanding these programs launched successful corps ministries and served in administrative appointments.

Commissioning an African–American family

But a lack of racial equality persisted. Although many black officers loved corps work, some who had come from suburban or rural communities felt stereotyped and pigeonholed in urban ministry. Still others aspired to work in administration on the divisional, territorial, or national level, but were given no opportunity to do so. Although white officers were often assigned to lead black corps, few black officers led predominantly white corps.

African–American officers did not typically minister overseas either. Only Caribbean–born black officers had served in South and Central America and in Africa. As Harmon Tate had articulated years before, some African–American officers felt frustration that ministry to people of other cultures and races did not appear to be an option for them.

Moving pains: going to a new appointment

The commissioning of new officers traditionally takes place in June, with great pomp and fanfare. They stand at attention on the stage at the School for Officer Training before the territorial commander and an audience of family, friends, and other officers. Typically, each cadet salutes and waits for the commander to say, "You have been appointed corps officer of the (name) Corps!" The audience shouts "Hallelujah!" and "Praise the Lord!" as the new officer shakes the commander's hand and receives "marching orders." Some new officers are made corps commanders; some are appointed as assistant officers; others as Adult Rehabilitation Center administrators and assistant administrators; a few may receive appointments at divisional or territorial offices.

The retirement from active service by some seasoned officers helps make room for the new officers coming out of the school. With the appointment of the new officers comes a domino–like effect of moves for other officers in the territory. Anticipating the June moves becomes a national pastime among Army officers and soldiers alike. This is a time when officers can expect that they might have to relocate their entire family to another city, state, or territory in response to the call to service.

Black traditions clash with Army policy

In the black community, however, a minister often serves as pastor in the same church for 25 years or more; some spend their entire career in one church. This cultural expectation made it considerably difficult for blacks to understand the mentality behind the Army's annual June moves, which often took officer/pastors away from corps after as little as a year or two of service.

Timothy Thomas

Such was the case in Cleveland in 1972 when residents of the Hough community learned that the Army would reassign Lieutenants Timothy and Grace Thomas to Springfield, Mass. They had served as interns and then as corps officers at the multi–purpose center and had gained the respect and confidence of the community residents. "We love [the Thomases] and they love us and Hough," said Anne Whitt, a corps member. She and her neighbors circulated a petition to document the widespread support for keeping the young officers at the center.

At a hearing to resolve the matter and quell the many protests, James Alexander, Jr., president of the local Hough Community Council, said, "My phone's been jumping off the hook. People are really concerned." The Salvation Army's regional director for the area, Brigadier Walter C. French, explained that Army officers are accustomed to and must expect moves and transfers.

"We do this for the Army's good and for the officer's good," French said to the crowd, adding that three competent persons would replace the Thomases. But French's response did not address the question satisfactorily for the community. The people asserted that the Thomases had "filled their need completely" and that their abrupt removal would "damage the center's programs and break the hearts of children that they had so greatly impressed."

Although French conceded that the Army should have more adequately prepared the people, he stood firm on the Army's officer transfer policy. "The people in the community are to be respected in their wishes. We are not cal-

Salvationists gather to remember outstanding people of color.

lous," he said, "but The Salvation Army cannot relinquish its right to move officers." Whitt, not satisfied with the answer, said, "When there were riots in Hough, [the news traveled] all across the nation. But when we are trying to do something good for our children, no one hears us—not even in this room!"

Unable to extract a definite answer on whether the Army would reconsider the case, Alexander told the group they would meet among themselves to determine what to do. Mason Hargraves, a resident and community activist, asked rhetorically, "What shall I tell my son?"[175] Eventually, the political and social turbulence calmed, and the waters of ministry again flowed under new leadership.

In those days, officers typically served from three to five years in an appointment, so similar scenarios repeated themselves as residents of African–American communities experienced conflict, misunderstanding, sadness, and apprehension about the future when they learned their officers were being reassigned. Would the new officers continue or cancel programs? Would the ministry remain effective? These and other questions emerged each time the Army reassigned officers.

The advantage to the system, however, was that the Army could easily replace ineffective corps leadership.

The moves also created openings for newly commissioned officers to serve at established corps.

Ministering in an African–American community: what are the needs?

The Army's transfer policy raised a broader question: Would the black urban community ultimately accept the Salvation Army lifestyle? In September 1972, a committee convened in Washington, D.C., in the Southern Territory to study the Army's approach to inner–city needs. The committee included Colonel Paul Thornberg, Major Vivian Scale, Captain Allan Wiltshire, James H. Bryant, Milt Servias, Captain Raymond Cooper, and Doris Chandler. Rev. Walter Cox chaired the two–day meeting. Discussions focused on the Army's ministry to people of color.

Trust—or the lack of it—between African Americans and The Salvation Army emerged as a theme. Bryant emphasized that there was a real need for American–born black officers, "...but we cannot expect successful recruitment until internal racial problems are reconciled and some of our white officers improve their attitudes toward the black community." He suggested that the training school include more intensive studies in human relations in its curriculum. Wiltshire said that white officers were not the only Salvationists African Americans looked upon with suspicion. Raised in the Republic of Panama, Central America, he said, "A foreign accent can affect an officer's relationship and effectiveness in a community." Another obstacle to developing trust rested on the perception that The Salvation Army was a "white man's organization." Major Scale said most black men had this view of the Army

Children engrossed in Bible Study

and, due to prejudice and discrimination, "... [they are] suspicious, afraid, insecure, frustrated, and exploited."[176]

This conference, the first of many such meetings, helped open the door to more substantive discussions that would result in real change in Army policy. Many issues raised in conference for the first time resulted from a national climate that demanded that such discussions take place throughout the country, and not only in The Salvation Army. The committee raised challenging questions: How could The Salvation Army be more effective in its varied ministry to soldiers, adherents, and social service recipients? How could the Army dispel the image or reputation it had in the black community as a white organization? How could the Army provide a forum for frank discussion of race–related problems and point the way to solutions? According to the Servias papers, these and many other questions remained unanswered. But the committee would address them in future meetings.

Ministry Milestones (1970–1974)

In 1970, Brigadiers B. Barton and Ernestine McIntyre become territorial evangelists in the Eastern Territory.

Lieutenant George Evans, also an Eastern officer, attends the Brengle Holiness Institute in Chicago in the Central Territory. The institute, held annually, celebrates Commissioner Samuel Logan Brengle's strongest suit, his pursuit of holiness, and brings Salvation Army leaders together for short, intense periods to sharpen and refresh their spiritual sensitivities, especially their understanding of holiness.

When Evans returns from the institute, the Army assigns him to New Jersey to open the Newark Westside Corps.[177]

In the Southern Territory, Allan and Marjorie Wiltshire return to full–time service as corps officers of the Sherman Avenue Corps in Washington, D.C., the city where they had served under Brigadiers Victor and Latrude Wilson.

In 1971, the Wilsons retire from active service and move to Cleveland, where Victor Wilson serves as interim officer at a corps there. He also conducts revival services in New York.

In the East, Captains Israel and Eva Gaither become commanders of the Brooklyn Bedford Temple Corps and form a spiritual bond with the people there.

In the Central Territory, Stephen Harper is commissioned as a member of the Victorious session. His first appointment is as assistant officer at the St. Louis (Euclid) Mo. Corps. There he meets Ray Wert, a black Salvationist who becomes a father figure to this new lieutenant who had grown up without a dad.

Originally from Pennsylvania, Wert came to the Great Lakes region when he joined the U.S. Navy for military training. But after his Navy service ended, he landed on hard times and became an alcoholic.

One day, while Wert was drunk on a street corner, The Salvation Army found him, and he was miraculously saved. With the nurture and love of Salvationists, Wert refocused and dedicated his life to serve God. People knew Wert as an outdoorsman who loved to hunt and fish. He was dubbed "Nature Boy Wert" because he could name the flowers, trees, fish, and other woodland creatures with ease.

Wert's determination and dedication to ministry impresses Harper. One snowy Sunday afternoon, when Harper is busy driving his congregants home from a morning Holiness meeting, he hears someone say, "It's snowing outside. I don't think we're coming back tonight for the meeting at 6." At about 4 p.m., Harper phones everyone to determine who will actually come to the evening meeting. No one says they will.

Harper tries to reach the Wert family, but they are on their way to the corps. That evening, Ray Wert conducts the entire service for his own family and Lieutenant Stephen Harper. Undaunted, Wert preaches for 45 minutes.

Vivian Taylor, a Victorious sessionmate of Harper, experiences her own memorable moments during her first appointment as a Salvation Army lieutenant. She is surprised to find herself at a predominantly white corps. Although the neighborhood of the corps is mostly black, its members

Salvationists march in honor of Harlem Temple Corps dedication, 1987

who had moved to the suburbs still travel back into the city for church.

Taylor realizes that her mission at the corps is to "bridge the gap" between her white congregation and the surrounding black community. Her strategy is to go door–to–door, visiting neighborhood families. She starts a senior citizens group consisting of corps and community residents, and she also opens a community center. Gradually, the black youth in the community begin to believe the Army is "there" for them.

In 1972, Captains Abraham and Louise Johnson are appointed to the Harlem Temple Corps. They envision a new corps building with better facilities and capacity to serve the community. With the help of a supportive advisory board composed of influential local business people, political leaders, celebrities, and Salvation Army divisional leaders, the Johnsons eventually build a 40,000–square–foot building at 138th Street and Lenox Avenue. It is the largest corps community center in the United States at the time.

Using mobile feeding trucks called canteens, the Johnsons establish a thriving food program that, at its peak, serves approximately 400 Harlem residents each night. In time, many inner–city religious leaders who had previously rejected the Johnsons call upon them to speak from their pulpits and to serve on political and civic committees. As community leaders accept the Johnsons, they ultimately begin to see The Salvation Army as a positive spiritual and

HARLEM
CORPS
N.Y.C.

Chapter 12

Salvation Army music and the African–American community

"When your song was sung before an audience of over a thousand people in Congress Hall, the impression was so great, it touched us in spots which words of eloquence rarely reach."

—Commissioner John McMillan to Thomas Ferguson

As early as 1869, blacks made music in London's streets during Christian Mission open–air meetings. As part of William Booth's army, they helped give momentum to the fledgling denomination. In the United States, African Americans sang hymns and praise songs in meetings held by Army pioneers James Jermy and James Fackler in Cleveland (1872), Eliza Shirley in Philadelphia (1879), and Commissioner George Scott Railton in New York City (1880).

However, trends in music took the momentum in a new direction. During the 1870s in London, brass banding became the modern music of the day. It eventually emerged as the Army's official musical expression in worship. In 1878, William Booth published *Songs of The Salvation Army* and formed its first brass band.

In 1879, *The War Cry*, the Army's official publication, introduced new songs weekly. And a year later, as Railton and his seven "hallelujah lassies" stepped off the boat onto New York City streets, Booth issued a General Order in *The War Cry* encouraging Salvationists to develop more brass bands and Salvation Army music.

Booth knew that passersby could easily hear the sound of brass and percussion instruments outdoors, where the Army held numerous open–air evangelistic meetings. Moreover, the brass bands fit perfectly into The Salvation Army's military motif.

In Booth's *Second General Order on Regulations and Rules for Brass Bands*, published in 1881, he appointed composer

A typical open–air meeting in Harlem, New York.

Fred Fry to produce brass arrangements for Army bands. It took him just a year to release his first band tune arrangements.

In 1883, the Army released its *Publication of Salvation Music, Volume II*, and the first music book with original material by Salvationist authors and composers. The Army also formed its first music department under Herbert Booth's supervision.

In 1884, the Army released its first *Band Journal*. And in 1885, another General Order published in *The War Cry* stated that "henceforth Army bands must use only music published by The Salvation Army."[178]

The Army's policy of using European music exclusively, however, made it more difficult for the African–American community, steeped in a Gospel music tradition, to accept the Army's ministry as it once had. Blacks gradually withdrew from the Army as a place of worship.

Most African Americans loved Gospel, a style of a cappella music that they had originated during slavery. It had become the chief means of covert communication among the slaves in America as early as 1760 and continued to be the music of choice for African Americans.

Gospel music served an important role in rebuilding African–American unity, identity, and spirituality after slavery. According to Rev. Wyatt T. Walker, Gospel music historian, its role was:

> To give the community a true, valid, and useful song
> To keep the community invigorated
> To inspire the uninspired individual
> To enable the group to face its problems
> To comment on the slave crisis
> To stir each member to personal solutions and to a sense of belonging amid a confusing and terrifying world
> To provide a code language for emergency use[179]

The African Methodist Episcopal Church, founded by Rev. Richard Allen, and having already been in existence for 100 years, offered the "liberation music" that appealed to African Americans. The growing presence of black Baptist, Presbyterian, Episcopal, and Congregational churches in the United States helped widen the worship–style gap between The Salvation Army and the African–American community.

Bridging the gap

African–American singing groups in the United States, such as the Fisk University Jubilee Singers helped bridge that gap. The group's successful tours, beginning in 1875, introduced black cultural songs to whites in both the United States and Europe. They helped make the "Negro spiritual" a permanent American art form.

However, the manner in which the Fisk singers pre-

The Fisk University Jubilee Singers

sented the antebellum songs of faith was far from their original rendering in the praise houses and the cotton fields of the South. The domestic and international tour audiences heard a "concertized" form of the spirituals, written (or arranged) for ears trained in the discipline of European music.

The Fisk Jubilee Singers and other black university choirs of that era enjoyed much success and inspired many other organizations to form similar groups. The Salvation Army was no exception.[180]

A *War Cry* article published in 1894 focused on the musical contribution African Americans could make to Army ministry. Entitled "The Colored Work," it featured a four–point rationale for evangelistic outreach:

1. The power of the Salvation Army's song: We are assured that the colored people love song. They sing naturally; they sing well; they sing with volume and yet with sweetness.
2. The Salvation Army's life: The colored race loves that which gives evidence of freedom, and when free with them, they are free with you.

3. The Salvation Army's power of music: The moment an instrument of music appears in their midst, their faces, their expression, their attitude, their very being changes, and their natural instinct and love of music calls forth their sympathy, and at once, we have a ground into which to sow our seed.
4. The Salvation Army believes in the crowd: That is, believes in laboring among densely populated centers, and in this country, especially in Southern cities, there are thousands, if not tens of thousands, of this class populating vicinities which would ensure the Salvation Army a crowd every time it appeared in their midst.[181]

Tom Ferguson

The Army's campaign to attract musically talented blacks resulted in the emergence of a Salvationist composer and musician who possessed an ear for both European and traditional black ethnic music.

That person was Thomas Ferguson, a Jamaican–born Salvationist living in Boston. In 1898, when Scott Joplin, the American ragtime pianist and composer, became known for such tunes as "Maple Leaf Rag" and "The Entertainer," Ferguson was hearing the beat of a different drummer. Widely acclaimed as a composer, writer, and poet, Ferguson was among the most famous of Salvationists.

He wrote both the music and lyrics to more than 40 popular Salvation Army songs. Often accompanying himself on guitar, he always performed with the enticing rhythm and movement characteristic of Caribbean music. Salvationists worldwide still sing his most famous song, "By the way of the cross."

Commissioner John McMillan once said to Ferguson,

"When your song was sung before an audience of over a thousand people in Congress Hall, the impression was so great, it touched us in spots which words of eloquence rarely reach."

McMillan was referring to the 1914 International Congress in London. Evangeline Booth, so strongly impressed with Ferguson's singing, featured him there as lead singer in "The Commander's Own," an elite group of 13 African–American singers who offered a powerful ministry.

More than 20,000 Salvationists dressed in national costumes, representing 54 nations, and speaking 34 languages, felt spiritually touched by Ferguson's songs.

"Goodbye, Pharaoh, Goodbye" became the "song of the Congress." Delegates sang it until someone said, "none but a cynic could have sat quietly and refused to make the movements which go with the song!"

The War Cry's July coverage of the Congress showed a large photo of "The Colored Brigade," also part of Ferguson's contingent. The following month, *The War Cry's* cover photo showed Ferguson's contingent among the many Salvationists who attended tea on the tennis court of the Astor Estate, where General Bramwell Booth addressed the delegates.

Despite having received international acclaim as a musician, Ferguson served the remainder of his life as "chief engineer" at the Boston Palace Corps, where his highest position was corps sergeant–major (lay leader). Although Salvationists hold such corps appointments in high esteem, there is no record of his receiving further recognition for his music, in either the United States or abroad.

Fifth I. C. C. Number

WAR CRY

No. 1713 Official Gazette of The Salvation Army in the United States Price, 5 cents

NEW YORK, SATURDAY, AUGUST 1, 1914

A *War Cry* cover showing the arrival of Tom Ferguson's contingent at the Astor Estate

Nevertheless, Ferguson continued to write both poetry and music in books published by the Ernest C. Mackness Company of Boston. *Visions in Song* has the words and music to 100 songs he wrote. He published 74 poems in *Thoughts of the Silent Hour: Poems, sacred and secular*. Not all of Ferguson's entries were poems, however. In a short essay entitled, "Courage: What is it?" Ferguson shared the following story.

> During the Spanish–American war, a colored soldier was mortally wounded on the field of battle. The chaplain informed him that he could not live, and said to him: 'Are there any requests that you would like to ask?' 'Yes, chaplain,' he said. 'Put your hand in my inside coat pocket.' The chaplain did. The soldier said, 'Chaplain, what did you find?' The chaplain said, 'A Bible.' 'Chaplain,' said the soldier, 'Open it.' Again the chaplain complied with his request. 'Chaplain, what did you find there?' The chaplain said, 'Five dollars.' 'Chaplain, hold it up and let me see it.' The chaplain held it up. 'Chaplain,' he said, 'I bet you five dollars I am going to live.'
>
> We often sing a chorus in our prayer meetings which runs: 'Courage to love thee, Courage to serve thee, Courage to come to thy footstool and bow. Dear loving master, I will take courage, I will take courage and come to thee now.'
>
> Courage: What is it?

In June 1998, the USA Eastern Territory opened the Heritage Museum on the first floor of Territorial Headquarters. At the center of the museum, to convey the passion and commitment that has characterized Salvationists during the Army's rich history, designer Julie Chesham Wittington placed dramatic displays featuring mannequins

William Edmunds stands beside the Tom Ferguson exhibit at the Heritage Museum, USA Eastern Territory

dressed in exquisite period uniforms.

Wittington honored Thomas Ferguson with a display in the exhibit. The Ferguson mannequin wears an Army gray uniform, a USA flag draped across his chest, and a bright red "wide–awake" hat similar to the one Ferguson wore as an American delegate to the 1914 International Congress. Wittington placed a photo of Ferguson, holding his guitar, on the wall behind the mannequin. Another photo shows the "Commander's Own," the brigade of black Salvationists invited by Commander Evangeline Booth to sing at the Congress. A guitar leans against the wall under the photos near the mannequin.

At the display, Wittington also included an audio recording of Ferguson's most popular song, "Goodbye Pharaoh, Goodbye," sung by Major Yvon Alkintor, an Eastern Territory officer. Museum visitors can hear the music by pushing a button.

Burt Mason as Tom Ferguson

Wittington's display is the first memorial ever built anywhere in the world to honor a Salvationist of African descent. It stands next to memorials for other great Army icons: a World War I doughnut girl, National Commander Evangeline Booth, and Joe "the Turk" Garabedian, the legendary street evangelist, to name a few.

In 1999, the Army dramatized Ferguson's life story on stage in New York City at a Friday Evening at the Temple meeting. Burt Mason, a young Salvationist of Jamaican descent, like Ferguson, portrayed him before a capacity crowd on "African Heritage Celebration Night" at Centennial Memorial Temple. Seated on stage was the Reverend Bernice King, guest speaker and daughter of the Rev. Dr. Martin Luther King, Jr.

Wearing an Army gray uniform, red "wide–awake" hat, and carrying a guitar, Mason said, as Ferguson:

> I was a teenager when the Army first 'opened fire' in Jamaica. I was fascinated by this 'religion with fiddle and drum!' All the churches had to close their doors that evening as everybody went to see these strange people.
>
> Soon after, I ran away from home and engaged a position on a fruit steamer trading between Jamaica and Boston. One night, while sleeping on the deck, I had a vision. I dreamt that I saw a crowd of people in the open air enjoying themselves, when suddenly the trumpet of God sounded and there was a cry of the judgment.
>
> I saw a great fire burst forth and sweep the hills. The people were running in confusion everywhere. I remembered all my teaching and opportunities and yet I was not saved. I stood there and wished a thousand times that I had never

been born. Just then, I awoke and found the tears rolling down my cheeks.

Something unusual had happened to me for I was now anxious about my spiritual welfare. On reaching port, I found that the churches did not hold meetings on weeknights so after going around I found The Salvation Army on the job. I went into the meeting and there on August 15, 1898, God spoke to my soul!

I joined my ship again and in the spring, left my ship at Philadelphia. I attended the meeting held that night at the largest corps in the city. Twenty souls came forward that night. Two days afterward, I left for Boston. With my heart aglow with the hallelujah fire, my fiery zeal won me the name of 'Jamaica Ginger.'

It's time for your soul to catch fire! It's time for you to write and sing your song for Jesus! What is your name? What do people call you? What is your testimony? Tell it! Sing it! Shout it! All day-long! Be a witness for Jesus![182]

New Sounds for Christ

During the 1970s, third–generation Salvationist Kenneth Burton helped bridge the gap between traditional Salvation Army and African–American music. Burton was the grandson of Senior Major Lambert and Estava Bailey, who had served as Harlem Temple corps officers from 1929–41. Burton's mother, Doris Bailey–Burton, directed choirs for more than 30 years. She also directed a group called the Melotones that ministered at Army and civic events. As a euphonium player, she studied at Star Lake Musicamp under Erik Leidzén, a famous Army composer and bandmaster. The camp exposed Doris to the best young musicians from England and other parts of the world. Her contact with them taught her to appreciate good–will; she enjoyed taking her international friends on sightseeing tours of New York City, and the campers exchanged ideas and addresses. The correspondence with the visitors continued for many years.[183]

Despite having experienced a failed marriage,[184] Bailey–Burton encouraged her son Kenneth to hone his skills on baritone horn at the Harlem Temple Corps. Under the leadership of Eldon (Donny) McIntyre, Jr., Kenny grew in knowledge and skill. He also received fatherly advice from Corps Sergeant–Major Don Ricketts, who took him under his wing.

Kenneth, along with several other Harlem Temple bandsmen, attended New York City's celebrated Music and Arts High School. He also joined the Army's Metro Youth Band, conducted by legendary cornet soloist Derek Smith.

Kenneth and his twin brothers Brett and Bart exposed youth of African descent to both band and Gospel music. Arnold (another Burton who became a concert singer in five languages: English, French, Italian, Spanish, and German, and performed in many European countries) worked with his brothers in helping young people.[185] The effective outreach of the Burtons helped many young black Salvationists stay in the corps when a flood were leaving the faith altogether.

In 1976, Kenneth's brother Brett and E. Lewanne Dudley formed a Gospel group called the New Sounds for Christ. When Brett and Lewanne entered the School for Officer Training in 1978, Kenneth became the group's leader. Today, it is the longest–standing contemporary Gospel group in The Salvation Army. New Sounds has traveled throughout the United States and the Caribbean, ministering through a medium sometimes misunderstood by Army traditionalists. More than 65 young people have been with the group.

"I'm one of those few people who love brass band music

Early members of New Sounds for Christ, circa 1978

and contemporary Gospel music," Burton once said in an interview for *Priority!* magazine, a national Salvation Army publication produced by the USA Eastern Territory. "I really like to go back to my roots and listen to Gospel music." Burton, who has a deep love for both traditional and contemporary music, believes contemporary music is greatly needed to reach African–American youth.

Growing up in the Bronx while attending the Harlem Temple, Burton felt drawn to secular artists such as Phyllis Hyman, Patti LaBelle, Stevie Wonder, and the Delfonics. "I used to go to the Apollo [Theater] all the time," he once said in a *War Cry* article, "spend four dollars and see a great concert. That was something we took for granted." He also found the music of Christian artists such as Kirk Franklin and the Brooklyn Tabernacle Choir appealing.

At the same time, notable Salvation Army composer Erik Ball and New York Staff Bandmaster Derek Smith left their mark on Burton.

In 1992, Burton received the "Man of the Year" award during the Army's historic International "Celebrate Christ"

Congress. General Eva Burrows and Commissioner Robert Thomson, then leader of the USA Eastern Territory, presented the award to Burton at a men's rally. At other times, he also received the Musician of the Year award from the Greater New York Division, and the William Booth Award.

In June 2004, during the BridgeBuilder's session commissioning exercises, Burton was admitted to the Order of the Founder (O.F.), the highest honor that the organization can bestow on a member. To become part of this distinguished group, Burton had to be recommended by the territory and accepted by General John Larsson. Commissioner Lawrence R. Moretz, territorial commander, and Colonel James M. Knaggs, chief secretary, presented the award to a surprised Burton following a New Sounds for Christ performance.

Moretz called Burton an "exemplary individual with an unquestionable commitment to helping others," particularly in the Harlem community where he has long been a "tremendous influence and stabilizing force."

In his remarks, Moretz recognized Burton for being successful inside the Army as a musician and mentor of many young African–American Salvationists and for serving as bandmaster, music director, and corps sergeant–major for more than 28 years. Calling Burton "the personification of Salvationism," Moretz also pointed out that he had succeeded in the business world as an assistant vice president at the Bank of New York.

General Eva Burrows presents the 'Man of the Year' award to Kenneth Burton in 1992.

Lt. Colonel Abraham Johnson called Burton a "moving force in the corps … deeply spiritual and a mentor, especially for the young folks."

Burton chaired the first Ter-

Burton leads the New Sounds for Christ and the Vasa Gospel Choir during a concert in 1998.

ritorial Black Ministries Committee in 1977 and helped develop an inner–city curriculum at the School for Officer Training and a Black Ministries event for the Friday Evening at the Temple series.

Burton was overcome with emotion when he responded on stage to becoming a member of the O.F. He talked about the guidance of the Spirit and the love of his family that has enabled him to do what he has done. He also expressed his gratefulness for the award and for The Salvation Army and what it has done in his life. Ever the evangelist, he addressed the crowd, saying, "I pray that if you don't know Jesus, you will meet Him here tonight." He urged young people to study the Word of God and get to "know Him."[186]

William L. Rollins

Bill Rollins, another black Salvationist, has also helped bridge the gap between traditional Army and ethnic music styles. Born and raised in the mean streets of north Philadelphia, Rollins managed to avoid gangs, street fights, and other negative influences. Raised in a single–parent home, Rollins got his first big break when he attended a new public school for talented youth.

His mother had tried to create a wholesome but secular environment for Bill and his brother, Nathan. However, Bill decided early that he wanted a different life for himself. His first church experience occurred when a soldier of the Army's Germantown Corps invited his mother to a Sunday meeting. Bill was awestruck by the corps band music and began attending the corps every Sunday.

Brigadier Adrian DeCosta, a cornet player and legendary Army missionary to Africa, gave Rollins a baritone horn. Bill devoted himself to music, eventually studying music education at the University of Cincinnati. He played in the orchestra, sang in the chorus, and worked with professors. While in school, he attended the Cincinnati Citadel Corps and later took a job as divisional music director at the Southwest Ohio & Northeast Kentucky Divisional Headquarters.

In 1986, he married his friend Valencia, whom he had met at the University of Cincinnati. A year later, Bill accepted a job as divisional music director in Massachusetts and moved his family, which now included a 6–week–old son, to Boston, where they attended the Boston Roxbury Corps.

The Rollins family in 1994.

The Rollinses had two more children and became one of the corps' most influential families under the guidance of Corps Sergeant–Major Edward Gooding, like Burton an Order of the Founder recipient.

The Rollinses took on several roles. Bill became the corps bandmaster, Songster leader, and a Sunday school teacher. Valencia took part in worship meetings as well as community activities.

As an African American, Bill pushed the creative envelope of Salvation Army music, always exploring new ways to make his ministry relevant and effective. He did not limit his approach to simply band or even Gospel music. Rollins discovered power in drama, mime, dance, storytelling, clowning, poetry, and art to communicate God's word to people of all races.

In 1999, as the Massachusetts Divisional Music Director, Bill Rollins compiled *Praise Choruses* to preserve "the oral tradition." In 2005, he became director of the Eastern Territorial Songsters.

In 1994, Rollins joined forces with Captain Richard Munn, then the divisional youth secretary. Together they wrote a musical entitled "Lord of the City," a dramatic portrayal of the Army's work in an intense urban setting. It incorporated reggae, rock, Gospel, and Latino music styles. Munn wrote the lyrics, and Rollins set them to music.

Captain Janet Munn, Richard's wife and associate divisional youth secretary at the time, helped Rollins transform the divisional music camp program. He broadened the curriculum from the standard brass and vocal emphasis to include a wide range of other expressions. Under his leadership, the Massachusetts divisional music camp became a fine arts festival.[187]

Allan Wiltshire, Jr.

Allan Wiltshire, Jr.

Allan Wiltshire, Jr., was yet another young Salvationist who helped build bridges between traditional Army and contemporary music styles. The son of Army officers, Wiltshire received his first training in music from his father, then–Captain Allan Wiltshire of the Washington, D.C., 9th Street Corps.

Wiltshire learned more about music as he passed through numerous band camps on the divisional and territorial levels, including the USA Eastern Territory's Star Lake Musicamp. He then took his place on the cornet and then vocally on the soprano bench of the National Capital Area Band.

Despite his training in the most traditional settings, Wiltshire had a passion for modern music that eventually took priority. Before he entered the Berklee College for Music as a jazz composition and arranging major, Allan ministered internationally and visited more than 15 countries while sharing a special blend of piano and vocal styles.

Wiltshire completed his collegiate music training at the University of Maryland, earning a degree in trumpet performance. He met Sherry on the marching band field of the University of Maryland. As an interracial couple, they bridged yet another gap.

Allan worked several years as a freelance musician and composer in the Washington, D.C., area under the company name Monzae (MOHN–zee–hay) Productions. Monzae is the African ancestral name of the Wiltshire family.

Allan's credits include recording projects for the Salvation Army's Cross Roads label. He also contributed to an innovative project spearheaded by Army composer Stephen Bulla entitled *Contemporary Songbook Volumes 1 & 2*. Other credits include projects for Island Records, DC Disk Records, educational media projects, and other commercial recordings.

In 1991, the Wiltshire family moved to Norfolk, Va., where Allan served as the minister of music for the Norfolk Corps. Allan and Sherry founded the Norfolk School for Music, the Salvation Army's first weekly music conservatory on the corps level.

In 1992, Allan became the assistant music director and arranger for Fortress, the USA Southern Territory's first full–time contemporary music ministry. He later became director of Onward, considered "phase two" of the territory's contemporary music ministry. The groups ministered at 20 Salvation Army Youth Council meetings, reaching more than 20,000 people and traveling an estimated 45,000 miles.

Upon completing the Onward ministry, Wiltshire became the Southern Territory's contemporary music consultant. He used modern arts in Army worship, working with local music leaders to train them in new worship styles.

As a consultant, Wiltshire worked with many well–known artists and ministries, including Babbie Mason, Nashville's Gospel Music Association, Dr. Charles Stanley, and Pastor Bill Hybels.[188]

The Traditionalists

Many black Salvationists also embraced traditional Salvation Army music and even mastered European classical music. The Salvation Army Heritage Hill Band in Grand Rapids, Mich., was the first commissioned Army band in the United States. Launched in 1884, it was composed of approximately 30 members. As part of the band's 110th anniversary celebration in 1994, it released two photographs showing the original group. As many as five women are

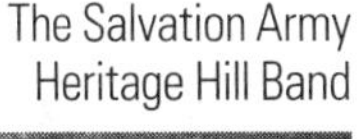

The Salvation Army Heritage Hill Band

shown among them, and at least two African–American men are seen playing euphoniums.

As the work of the Army developed in the United States, it designated the Grand Rapids Corps as part of the USA Central Territory. Through the years, the corps changed location several times because community residents did not always accept the Army's evangelistic fervor. In those early days, authorities often jailed members of the band and persecuted them for their outspoken evangelism.

Despite these setbacks, the beat of the Army's drum reverberated during countless open–air meetings and attracted seekers to the mercy seat, where they had an opportunity to accept Christ. The band's record of continued and uninterrupted service in Grand Rapids still stands today.[189]

Margaret Wiltshire Davis

In the 1980s, another Wiltshire immersed herself in classical music. Her instrument was not the cornet, piano, or baton. It was her voice that launched Margaret Wiltshire–Davis's ministry into the stratosphere of Salvation Army music. Widely recognized as a classical singer "par excellence," Davis traveled throughout the United States singing praises to the Lord at numerous high–profile events.

Margaret Wiltshire Davis.

A fourth–generation Salvationist, "Meg" came up through the ranks, including Sunbeam, Girl Guard, Corps Cadets, Singing Company, and corps band. From age 13 to 23, she played cornet in the National Capital Band of the National Capital and Virginia Division in Washington, D.C.

However, it was at Star Lake Musicamp that Wiltshire sang her first solo during a concert and recital. While a college student at the Catholic University of America, Wiltshire continued her association with The Salvation Army, playing with the National Capital Band and serving as songster leader of the National Capital Songster Brigade. After earning a Bachelor of Music degree in general choral music education, she taught music for three years in Washington, D.C., to children on all grade levels.

Wiltshire led choral groups, gave private voice lessons, and taught general classroom music. She particularly enjoyed the annual elementary school musicals. All the while, Wiltshire shared her faith.

A highlight of Wiltshire's musical career occurred in 1985 when she sang before an audience of more than 2,000 people in the National Cathedral in Washington, D.C., on the occasion of Salvation Army General Jarl Wahlstrom's visit during the International Youth Congress.

In 1989, Wiltshire moved to New York and began work in the Greater New York Division's Community Relations Department at Divisional Headquarters. She responded to the call to officership and together with her husband, David Davis, a former officer who had served 10 years in the Youth Department as Camp Bureau director for Star Lake Camp. They entered the School for Officer Training—Margaret as a cadet, and David as a cadet spouse—and both became officers after graduation.

In 2003, the Army released Margaret's first CD recording, entitled "My Lips Will Praise You."[190]

Patrick Morris

Patrick Morris

Another musical traditionalist, Bandmaster Patrick Morris of Arlington, Va., served both The Salvation Army and the U.S. Army.

The son of Jamaican–born Salvation Army officers, Brigadier and Mrs. Hugh (Beryl) Morris, Patrick served as a bandmaster of the Arlington, Va., Corps and trombonist in the Army's National Capital Band. He also served as a euphonium player for the U.S. Army Band.

The Harlem Temple Corps Band

Morris's father, Brigadier Hugh Morris, moved from Trinidad to Guyana and then to Jamaica before The Salvation Army transferred him to the Harlem Temple Corps in New York City.

Brigadier Morris taught his son to play the alto horn, and, ever since, music has been a constant in Patrick's life.

While attending high school, Morris took his first music course taught by a professional music teacher. But his most significant early exposure to music occurred when the Army's New York Staff Band admitted him at age 16. He also played solo in the "Carnival of Venice" with the Goldman Band at the Lincoln Center Band Shell in Central Park in New York City.

A short time later, he became bandmaster at the Harlem Temple, where he gained valuable leadership training. He later became bandmaster at the Brooklyn Bedford, Philadelphia Roxborough, and Arlington, Va., corps.

In 1983, Morris joined the U.S. Army and entered its band program. He took assignments at the 19th Army Band at Ford Dix, N.J.; the U.S. Continental Band at Fort Monroe, Va.; and at Fort Myer, Va.

As the premier band of the U.S. Army, the Fort Myer Band is the official band for diplomatic and state functions and performs musical honors for the arrivals of foreign heads of state, diplomats, and high–ranking military officials. Since 1925, the U.S. Army Band has also led the Inaugural Parade of every incoming U.S. president. "Pershing's Own," as the band is known, performs more than 5,000 times each year, including at more than 1,000 funerals and ceremonies at Arlington National Cemetery.

The U.S. Army selected Morris's composition entitled "The Blessings of Liberty" as the official march of its Training and Doctrine Command.

Morris has also served for several years as a member of the Salvation Army's Star Lake Musicamp faculty, which encourages young Salvationists to sharpen their music and leadership skills. Morris also met his wife, Cyndy, at Star Lake.

Morris, who served during the Gulf War's Operation Desert Storm, once said he felt able to serve in two armies under two flags because of his attitude. He said he made it his goal to avoid negatives and to be as much like Jesus as possible.[191]

Eric Dina

Eric Dina began playing a toy piano at home in Cleveland, Ohio, in 1979. At age 3, "He played over and over," his mom remembers, "and every time he played, he played the same song. He made it up in his head—the same little melody." Eric perfected that melody on his little dinosaur–shaped piano. Soon, people began using the word *prodigy* to describe the little boy. Eric recalls his family's reaction.

"They realized I had perfect pitch, the ability to identify frequencies and that sort of stuff. I could figure out the melody line of most hymns." Hymns were the songs that Eric heard most. That's because his mom, dad, and grandmother were Salvation Army officer/pastors who led thriving congregations. But at the tender age of 4, Eric experienced a difficult setback; his parents, who were serving as pastors in Philadelphia, divorced.

"I moved back to Cleveland with my mom and grandmother after my parents' separation," Eric recalls. "I spent summers with Dad, and the rest of the time with Mom in Cleveland." Despite emotional turmoil, Eric kept focused on his music. Mary Alice Vogel, a music teacher, saw great potential in him. As a result, at age 5, Eric entered the Cleveland School of Music, where he studied piano and theory for several years. His formal lessons, which included a year of learning about Gospel music, lasted four years.

"Music played a huge role in my life," says Eric. "It is the one gift that I know God gave me. It is something that defines me.... I couldn't imagine Eric Dina without music. That's just something I can't even fathom."

At age 7, Eric was introduced to Salvation Army brass banding at the Army's Camp Ladore in Waymart, Pa. The young boy was quite taken by Harold Burgmayer, a well–known Salvation Army bandmaster and music teacher. Eric says, "I started going as a 'staff brat,' but later began going on my own. I worked there for a couple of years." Eric didn't realize that his exposure to Army music was also deepening his spiritual life.

After his parents' divorce, Eric relied more strongly on his grandmother, Major Dorothy Lykes. "The role of the grandmother in the African–American family is huge," says Dina. "I had a super mom, but I also had a super grandmother!" It was Lykes, a Canadian–born Salvationist, who spoke words that became music to Eric's spiritual ears. One Sunday morning in 1984, when Eric was 8, he heard her preach a sermon that changed his life. That day he responded to the call of Christ and knelt at the altar.

Eric quickly points out that becoming a Christian was purely his decision.

"My mother, father, or grandmother didn't force me," he says. Eric chose Christ at a time when his peers chose cursing and alcohol. "I knew about Jesus and the Bible through my mother and father," says Eric. "So I thought, this is something I want to do. This is the life I want to choose for myself." His new stand soon became well known among his friends. "They understood that there are things that you just don't approach me about," Eric says.

Eric Dina

Then came two summers of trauma for Eric. In 1985, when he visited his father in Philadelphia, he witnessed firsthand an explosion of political violence. Just a few blocks from the west Philadelphia corps where Captain Winston Dina was pastor was the house of a radical organization called MOVE. After severe conflict between MOVE members and residents in the neighborhood, Philadelphia Mayor W. Wilson Goode ordered MOVE members arrested. The conflict escalated and erupted in riots; a massive fire destroyed the MOVE house and 61 other homes. Two hundred sixty community residents were suddenly homeless. Many sought shelter at The Salvation Army, which became the focus of media attention.

The following summer, 1986, was an even more difficult one for Eric. His father became very ill. A once-robust man at 300 pounds, Eric's father began losing weight rapidly, eventually dropping to 140 pounds. That summer, 10-year-old Eric spent most of his time with Ervin McKoy, a close friend of his father and a fellow Salvation Army pastor. Although McKoy had his own family to care for and ran a day camp, he still took Eric in.

"Dad was in the University of Pennsylvania Hospital, just down the street from the corps," Eric recalls. Although he knew his father was ill, Eric didn't realize how serious the situation was.

At the end of summer, Eric returned to Cleveland to be with his mother. Three weeks later, just before the Sunday praise meeting, Eric saw his mother burst into tears. After the meeting, she told him his father had died. "I was shocked," Eric says. "I didn't see it coming."

Eric says retreats to the Salvation Army's music camps in Ohio and New Jersey became very important following his father's passing. He spent quiet evenings at camp writing about his feelings until he could get a handle on them. What Eric couldn't put into words, he expressed in music.

One day, following a performance at Star Lake Camp, Phil Smith, a Salvationist and principal trumpet soloist for the New York Philharmonic, entered Eric's cabin to congratulate him. "You did a good job," Smith said. Eric was thrilled. When Eric heard Smith play a trumpet solo at a large Salvation event, he remembers thinking, "Wow, this is really nice. This is what I see myself doing."

That same year, Eric tested for entry into University School in Shaker Heights, Ohio, one of the highest-ranked private schools for boys in the United States. His family and his public school teacher expected he might qualify to enter the school in the seventh grade. To their surprise, he was offered admission and a partial scholarship so that he could start in fifth grade. Eric dove into the school's liberal arts curriculum, studying math, language, history, and science. And the door opened for him to study trumpet. "I performed a lot of trumpet literature that I wouldn't have had an opportunity to perform elsewhere. They really featured me there," he recalls.

Kerry P. Brennan was headmaster of University School and Eric's choral conductor. According to Brennan, Eric quickly distinguished himself as an "impressive student in all ways." Brennan said that not only was Eric a "fine musician, a tuneful singer, virtuosic trumpeter, and inspiring pianist, he was also a dedicated scholar and fine citizen."

Eric went on to the University of Cincinnati College Conservatory of Music, graduating magna cum laude in 1998. Now, at age 26, he uses his musical gifts in service to others and to the Lord.

At his University School, Eric teaches beginning string; fourth, fifth, and sixth grade chorus; fourth grade general music; and beginning brass programs. "He has committed his significant gifts to teaching and to giving a new generation of University School boys the kind of experience that helped form him as a teacher, musician, and man," says Brennan. "I couldn't be prouder."

For The Salvation Army, Eric serves as divisional music liaison in the Army's Northeast Ohio Division, and he collaborates with the Army's youth band in the Eastern Pennsylvania and Delaware Division and with other Army groups.

Eric is also a music teacher for the Cleveland Municipal City School District. He performs as co-principal trumpet for the Suburban Symphony Orchestra and has won top honors in statewide and national trumpet competitions. He dreams of playing professionally with the Cleveland Orchestra, touted by many as the best in the world.

In 1999, Eric married. Like Eric, Rebecca Dina is a former Star Lake camper, a public music schoolteacher, and the child of Salvation Army officer parents.

Eric admits that balancing the responsibilities of music and marriage can have its arpeggio and even staccato moments. "It can be tough," says Eric. "Before marriage I would practice two to three hours daily. But now, I need to find the right balance. I need to listen to Becky more. I could practice five to six hours a day, but if I'm miserable, then it's not much good." His priorities these days are, "God, Becky, then career. God is honoring these priorities so that time spent is more productive," he says.

Eric's mom, Charlene L. Fawcette, who runs the Army's Superior Avenue church in Cleveland, is still amazed by Eric's ability to focus. For example, when the divisional youth band threatened to disband, Dina stood up and made a commitment to keep it alive. "He felt that it was his calling, his ministry," says Fawcette. "He said he didn't care if the Army paid him. He just had a strong calling and conviction and commitment to the young people and to the music."

Fawcette realized then that something special was coming from deep within her son's character. "When I visited him at rehearsal, I was just in awe," she says. "The way he stood up and explained the piece they were playing, and then found references in Scripture to support the music—I said, 'What is all this?' " Eric explains, "I try not to hide from being a Christian. I am a Christian first, then a trumpeter or pianist, or whatever the case may be."

That attitude is what will continue to provide Eric Dina with perfect pitch, not just as a musician, but as a man of God.[192]

The New York Staff Band and others

Several instrumentalists of African descent have been members of the New York Staff Band, beginning in 1965 with Eldon (Donny) McIntyre, Jr. He was the first of three sons of Ruby and Eldon McIntyre, who served as Times Square Corps and Bedford Temple bandmaster for many years and was the brother of Lt. Colonel B. Barton McIntyre.

Donny also sat first chair, solo cornet, in the Star Lake Band that year. He had been the Harlem Temple Corps bandmaster during the late 60s and early '70s. During that

Early Salvation Army Band in Michigan

time, he took the band's skill level and ministry to new heights. The band was well known throughout the Eastern Territory and traveled to many cities including Cleveland, Niagara Falls, and Pittsburgh.

Donny's life outside The Salvation Army was as illustrious as it was in the Army. He earned a Ph.D. in mathematics and was an engineer for Bell Labs. He also served as a professor at New York University, and he was a major influence and a great friend to many of the young people in the Harlem Temple Corps.

During this era in the Eastern Territory, there were several black bands. Among them were the Harlem Temple, Manhattan Citadel, Jamaica Citadel, and Bedford Temple bands. Theirs was a close fraternity that enjoyed close fellowship every summer at the annual youth councils.

Other blacks followed Donny's example and became members of the New York Staff Band. They included Vernon Morris, Derek Saunders, Kenny Davis, Robin Davis, Michael Davis, Michael Anglin, Henry Reid, Aly St. Fleur, Ephraim Lopez, Rodney Harris, Burt Mason, and Adam

Burton. Many have gone on to become doctors, lawyers, actors, and professional musicians. Obba Babatunde, who played cornet in the Jamaica Citadel Band, has appeared in many films and on television. Earl McIntyre, brother of Donny McIntyre, became a professional trombonist and has appeared with many stars and performed with Broadway plays.[193]

Army groups abroad echo Gospel sound

Just as a metronome's pendulum swings, so has the momentum of Salvation Army music shifted from time to time; from Gospel singers to the big bands and back again.

Although traditional African–American music had influenced early Salvation Army worship in the United States, a period ensued during which the Army generally preferred traditional brass band music. However, the growing popularity of Gospel music abroad, particularly among Army youth groups in the 1990s, resulted in a brief but notable return of such music at official Army meetings in the United States.

Vasa Gospel Choir

Army choirs from as far away as Ireland, Sweden, and Iceland visited the United States, bringing with them the familiar sound of African–American Gospel music, albeit in a radically different–looking package.

As the first all–white Gospel choirs ever to minister in the Salvation Army world, the enthusiastic presence, impressive sound, and rhythmic moves of these choirs stunned and delighted both black and white audiences. The singing groups effectively used music to challenge cultural norms and longstanding assumptions that have kept the Christian community divided along racial lines.

In 1998, the Vasa Gospel Choir arrived in the United States from Sweden to tour Army corps in the Eastern Territory. The group made its debut at Centennial Memorial Temple during the Forward 2000 Cadet Welcome program. The choir is made up of young Salvationists and non–Salvationists; this deliberate crossing of denominational lines was one way the choir could reach the unchurched with the Gospel of Christ.[194]

Northern Ireland Youth Choir

That same year, 50 members of the Northern Ireland Youth Choir, a mix of Protestants and Catholics, also made their USA debut at Centennial Memorial Temple with a sweet harmony rarely, if ever, heard in Ireland. Their "Harmony Tour" took them to several venues, including the Harlem Temple Corps. Their "Hallelujah Windup" brought people to their feet and brought tears to the eyes of many. With hands raised high, chorus members marched around the chapel, proclaiming the love of God.

Youth from Harlem and Ireland knelt shoulder to shoulder at the altar and prayed for world peace. Adrian Madden, Ireland divisional youth officer and keynote speaker, said, "We want to proclaim to the people of New York and wherever we are, that the young people of Northern Ireland want peace. They want to work together and show the rest of the community that there needn't be war and strife—it can be unity and togetherness."[195]

In 2001, the Moss Gospel Company (MGC) arrived from Norway and joined forces with the New Sounds for Christ to tour several venues, including the Central Baptist Church in Manhattan and Seton Hall University in New Jersey. Several of the 32–member group and others who heard them expressed how the tour ministered to them personally. One MGC member, Thor–Erik Fjelivang, said he would remember the tour for the rest of his life. The Seton Hall University campus Christian youth group leader, Andre Brown, said, "We have white people, we have black people, and everybody in between. And when students walk by this room, they are going to look inside and say, 'That's cool.' "

Kenneth Burton, New Sounds for Christ director, said his most memorable moment occurred during a rehearsal. "When we sang the benediction together, I got a feeling of the presence of the Holy Spirit. Just seeing and hearing the two choirs together—from both ends of the world and being in one accord at that one moment—in touch with God."[196]

Chapter 13

Building relationships; tearing down barriers

In the USA Western Territory, Gwendolyn Holman entered the Army's training college. Like many African Americans called to officership, she had somehow pierced the racial, psychological, and cultural barriers put up by society that typically kept African Americans from considering The Salvation Army as a ministry career.

Growing up, Gwendolyn had no African–American Salvation Army officers to serve as role models. Their numbers in the Western Territory were few. Nevertheless, Gwendolyn felt at home at The Salvation Army corps in San Francisco, where she began attending at age 3. As she grew older, her time at the corps increased to the point where her parents jokingly suggested that she take her bed down there. It was a multicultural corps before the termed had even been coined. There were Filipino, African–American, and Caucasian families attending. She saw firsthand how people of different ethnic backgrounds could love one another and worship together in harmony.

At the training college, Gwendolyn heard rumors about the many discussions at Territorial Headquarters about who would be her roommate, what kind of house duties she would have, and where she should and should not go. However, she never sensed this tension from the training school staff or sessionmates. She always felt that she was being treated the same way everyone else was treated.

Majors Brian and Gwendolyn Jones

However, despite the Haight–Ashbury, "flower child," "love everyone" reputation of California during the 60s and 70s, there were moments when racism reared its ugly head. One such moment came during the Christmas season when a group of cadets went caroling in a wealthy neighborhood. When a black woman answered the door of a home, some of the cadets assumed she was the maid; she was not. During a visit to a clinic, some cadets expressed surprise to see a black doctor in residence.

In these moments, Gwendolyn felt compelled to use her "black militant" approach to correct the misconceptions and to let everyone know, for example, that "African American" and not "colored" was the preferred way to address people of color in the 70s. She challenged those who openly expressed their belief that blacks could dance and sing but not play tennis or golf. She had already earned a B.A. in Christian Education from Azusa Pacific University with a minor in early childhood education and had been a director and teacher of a preschool. Little did she realize at the time that her lessons on racial attitudes in the West were just beginning.[197]

Gwendolyn Holman was commissioned as a member of the Followers of Christ session. She served as an assistant officer in Inglewood; Van Nuys; and Glendale, Calif.; and as Christian education officer before being appointed commanding officer in Compton, Calif. She also served in Las Vegas as an assistant officer. Regardless of the appointment, she tried to correct racial injustice. For instance, at one corps, the leaders had been conducting two sets of meetings for all youth programs. They told her they were doing this to accommodate the young people who could not attend the earlier Sunday school program and the Tuesday night youth activities. While this may have been true, to Gwendolyn, the arrangement seemed racially motivated; one group of children were white and the other black. Gwendolyn and the corps leaders discussed the racial tensions, concerns, and problems created by the separate programs and how the groups could be reconciled. Although some members of the corps offered strong resistance to the final proposal, Gwendolyn and the other leaders merged the youth groups successfully.

The young officer also learned a few lessons about cross-cultural ministry—even within the African-American community. At another appointment, where the corps population was about 90 percent black, Gwendolyn wasn't seen as "their people." Something about her was significantly different. "You talk funny, you walk funny, you eat different foods than we do," they reminded her at every opportunity. Although she was as black as they were, her multicultural perspective was foreign to them. That was when Gwendolyn learned that "it takes more than being black to reach black people—it takes relationships." The corps grew, not because Gwendolyn was an African American, but because she had learned to listen, understand, and love this particular body of Christ.[198]

Holman married Dr. Brian Jones, who was white. In 1985, the Army sent the Majors Jones to serve in Hawaii, Oregon, Arizona, and eventually at the College for Officer Training. At one appointment, the Joneses served a small rural community where the population was 98 percent white and was not ready to accept an interracial officer couple. The residents were shocked to learn that Gwendolyn held a college degree. They called Brian "a traitor to his race" and many other hurtful names for marrying a black woman. They stared at the Joneses as they tried to minister, shunned them, and refused to invite them to social events.

One day while driving through the neighborhood, Gwendolyn was pulled over by a police officer, who asked what she was doing in that part of town. The few minority citizens lived in another section. The police stopped her a second time before she and her husband eventually requested that the Army move them to another community. The Joneses realized that it would take years before the people there would be able to hear the Gospel message from a mixed–race couple. As long as the residents saw them as the enemy, they would spend precious time fighting racism, rather than meeting human need.

When the Joneses asked their territorial leaders why

they had sent them to such a place, the reply was, "We never thought about it." They said they knew the Joneses had accommodating attitudes toward all people and believed they could love "the whosoever." For the Joneses, it was wonderful to realize that their leaders had seen them simply as officers and not as black or white officers. However, that distinction also contributed significantly to who they were. From that day on, Army leaders gave careful consideration to the Joneses' appointments.

Ministry Milestones (1974–1980)

In 1974 in the East, Captain George Evans is appointed as the first Brooklyn Brownsville corps officer. However, he is not alone. Shortly after opening the Newark Westside Corps, he had married Lieutenant Carmen Garay, an officer of Hispanic origin. This appointment would prove to be their longest and most rewarding and a special source of spiritual strength and encouragement to them for years to come.

Captains George and Carmen Evans launch an online prayer ministry.

~

Captain Maurice "Eddie" Smith is transferred from the Southern to the Western Territory, where he reopens the work in Compton, Calif., a city near the riot–torn Watts, in South Los Angeles. Smith supervises the building of a million–dollar corps center there.

~

Glenda Marie Law is commissioned an officer in San Francisco and assigned to a corps in Adam County near Denver. The daughter of social worker Helen White, known among Salvationists as a compassionate, outgoing giver of love to the sick and shut–in, Law continues that legacy by becoming a League of Mercy volunteer. She conducts two women's groups, a reading program, and Bible study classes, assists in ministerial duties, and comforts the elderly and sick.

Law had spent 10 years as a soldier of the Van Nuys, Calif., Corps. She had also worked as a counselor at the Army's youth camp in Calabasas and participated in Girl Guards, a youth group modeled after the Girl Scouts. After high school, she had studied law at Pierce College in Woodland Hills, Calif., for a year before enrolling in the Army's training college.

Diane Lorick is commissioned in the Central Territory as a lieutenant. She serves at the Midland Divisional Headquarters but later moves to the Milwaukee (West) Corps. After marrying Lieutenant Stephen Harper, she returns to the St. Louis (Euclid) Corps, her home church, as corps officer with her husband.

Dorothy Purser

Brigadier Dorothy Purser is appointed chief secretary, or second in command, of the Caribbean and Central American Territory. She had been serving in the Eastern Territory in Cleveland. The appointment makes her the first woman to hold the post in that territory's history and the highest-ranking woman officer in territorial leadership in the (then) 51-territory Salvation Army world.

Purser says she feels fulfilled in her mission and desire to be an officer; being in charge and helping others solve their own problems makes her very happy. Despite opportunities, she never marries. Purser, like most other women, says she would certainly not mind having a husband "to have and to hold till death they do part." But she is never in any doubt as to her ability to make it on her own.

Purser retires from active service in 1979 as a lt. colonel and moves to New York City, where she remains engaged in life and ministry as well as attending college classes and pursuing reading as a hobby.[199]

Colonel B. Barton McIntyre's most recent campaign as territorial evangelist in 1974 is highlighted in the *Call and Post,* a black newspaper in Cleveland. The article describes his 20 years of ministry in Cleveland. The paper also details the ministerial career of the McIntyres and covers their retirement from active service in 1975 during a ceremony held at divisional headquarters on East 22nd Street. "Twenty-three years were spent in the Central area of the city," the article states. "They are the first black leaders in The Salvation Army in the U.S. to achieve the rank of colonel and the only black officers to retire at this rank from a territorial administrative position in this organization."[200]

Captains Israel and Eva Gaither become divisional youth leaders in the Greater New York Division.

Captain Lilian Yarde assumes command of the Bedford Temple Corps in Brooklyn, N.Y. Opportunities for pulpit ministry came easier to single Salvation Army women officers, including black ones such as Yarde.

Captain Dorothy Lykes preaches three sermons on Sunday at Cleveland area churches and teaches Sunday school to children aged 2–16. Lykes, a widow, is also mother of two adult children, one a lieutenant at the Central Corps in Cleveland and the other, the director of spiritual services at the Hough Multipurpose Center. Born in Canada, Lykes shares equal status with men in the officer corps, performing marriages, and funerals and counseling families facing hard times.[201]

In 1976, the Eastern Territory administration approves the formation of the Territorial Black Ministries Committee. The committee addresses important issues, organizes heritage celebration nights and conferences, and encourages the recruitment of black officers. Kenneth Burton, a young member of the Harlem Temple Corps, serves as committee chairperson. The committee works toward the day when the Army's sensitivity to the needs of people of African descent would be heightened to such a degree that they would be attracted to the organization in greater numbers.

Two years later, in 1978, the committee begins to see results when 20 percent of the young people attending the Army's annual officer recruitment seminar are of African descent. Captain W. Todd Bassett serves as Candidates Secretary and is responsible for the Youth and Candidates Seminar. He writes to Lt. Colonel Stanley Ditmer, the white Program secretary, "It is with pleasure that I give you wholehearted endorsement to the proposal from the Black Ministries Committee that prospective black candidates be encouraged to participate in the Candidates Seminar."[202]

Lieutenant Maurice "Eddie" Smith transfers from the Western Territory to the Central Territory to serve as the assistant officer at the Milwaukee (West) Wisconsin Corps. The Army also promotes him to corps officer the following year. Smith does not serve alone. In 1979, he marries Lieutenant Ana Rosa Flores, originally from the Manhattan Temple Corps in New York City.

That year, members of Flores's home corps hear Dr. Martin Luther King, Sr., speak at a Black Heritage Night event. The newly formed Black Ministries Committee sponsors the event, which takes place during a Friday Evening at the Temple (FET) meeting in Centennial Memorial Temple (CMT) in New York City.

© Flip Schulke/CORBIS

Dr. Martin Luther King, Sr.

"Daddy King" says that God has given him a vision that has kept his family going despite the tragic loss of several members. He had co–pastored the Ebenezer Baptist Church in Atlanta with Dr. Martin Luther King, Jr., from 1960 until his assassination on April 4, 1968; another son drowned in a swimming pool; and a crazed man had stabbed Daddy King's wife to death as she played the organ during a Sunday morning church service. His passion and love for God moves many people in the audience to the altar for prayer that evening.[203]

Robert Dixon, director of the Salvation Army's Germantown Community Center, in the Eastern Territory and his wife, Hester, a clerical supervisor at the County Board of Assistance in Philadelphia, leave their comfortable middle–class life in 1979 to become cadets at the Army's School for Officer Training, now located in Suffern, N.Y. The Dixons immerse themselves in the intensive curriculum, learning Salvation Army religious doctrines, preaching and business techniques, and social work skills.

Grace Cumberbatch enters training in the Southern Territory as a member of the Joyful Evangelists session. Born in Barbados, Grace had grown up in a Salvation Army home. Joseph, her father, had been on board the *HMS Lady Drake,*

which survived a German U Boat torpedo attack in 1942. His near–death experience focused his efforts on the important things in life. Joseph and Enid, his wife, eventually moved their two daughters to Bermuda where they received their primary and secondary educations. Grace enrolled as a Salvation Army soldier and participated in various corps activities. When she arrived in the United, States, she continued her education, attending Morgan State College in Baltimore and Howard University in Washington, D.C. As a student at Howard, she maintained her affiliation with the Army by attending the Sherman Avenue Corps. From there, she entered the College for Officer Training in Atlanta. She would begin her officer career as an assistant at the Blue Field and Covington, Va., corps.[204]

Patty Richardson is commissioned as a Salvation Army officer from the College for Officer Training in Chicago in the Central Territory. Two years earlier, she had heard God's call to ministry. Richardson was a college student at the University of Nebraska on a four–year scholarship when she left the university to enroll in the CFOT. She already held a bachelor's degree from Cornerstone University and was pursuing a master's degree in organizational leadership. Richardson had been introduced to the Army as a child in Nebraska when someone invited her to Sunday school.

Major Norma T. Roberts, an officer from the South working with the USA Eastern Territory, authors a book entitled *The Black Salvationist,* the first work ever written on the history of people of African descent in The Salvation Army. The idea for the project had originated during the "Candidate Recruitment Among Minorities" conference, held in April 1972. Officers attending had been inspired by the civil rights movement and expressed a desire to document the role of blacks in the Salvation Army in the United States.

That same year, officers attending the Territorial Evangelism Commission executive sessions offered further encouragement for the project.

However, finding a writer and researchers to complete the project proved a daunting task. During the seven years that followed, various people attempted the project. Finally, Roberts was asked to synthesize the material that had been gathered by others, add to it, and produce a record of black involvement in the organization. She soon learned it would be no easy assignment. She had only scant written material from which to work and was able to conduct only a few personal interviews. Some information conflicted with other sources, which meant she had to do extensive checking and cross–checking. She called the result "a preliminary study; a beginning of a great adventure."

Then–Captain Israel L. Gaither, chairperson of the steering committee, acknowledged that he had mixed feelings regarding the project. On the one hand, he was disappointed that there wasn't more information after so many years in the making. But he also realized the quality of the small quantity of information in hand. "Despite my feelings of great disappointment in the outcome," he wrote, "I do believe we have 'a beginning.' Its preservation, even in this form, will someday be valuable, due to its content." His words would prove to be prophetic.[205]

Chapter 14

Fighting the enemy on all sides

Overcoming social disillusionment and an imploding black community

THE 1980S BROUGHT NEW CHALLENGES TO THE UNITED STATES AND ITS BLACK COMMUNITIES. The year 1980 began with most Americans gravely concerned about the plight of 52 hostages held in Iran. In November 1979, Iranian revolutionaries had stormed the U.S. Embassy and taken the hostages, many of whom were American citizens. Despite efforts by various agencies, Iran remained adamant and held the hostages as prisoners of the state.

An attempt by the U.S. military to rescue the hostages failed when eight servicemen were killed as the two helicopters they were riding in collided during a dust storm. In addition, a gasoline embargo against the United States put Americans in long lines at the pump and shortened their emotional fuses. The Iranian standoff, the fuel embargo, and the botched rescue attempt seriously damaged Democratic President Jimmy Carter's re–election bid that year. Republican Ronald Reagan, the former actor and governor of California, won the election in November by capturing 51 percent of the popular vote.

The change at the White House reflected a political shift toward conservatism. The trend was also reflected in a new and unsympathetic view of the plight of blacks living in urban communities. The phrase "black–on–black crime" came into vogue as newspapers across the country used it to describe the random violence members of the black community perpetrated against themselves. According to social experts, a "subculture of violence" had emerged.

Suddenly, statistics about blacks killing blacks were everywhere. Op–ed pieces cited homicide as the leading cause of death for black men and women between the ages of 25 and 34; black men from 25 through 44 years old were 11 times more likely to die as homicide victims than were white men of the same age category. Although one of every nine Americans was black, one of every two male murder victims was black, and one of every two people arrested for murder was black. Blacks were two and one half times more likely than whites to be victims of rape or robbery.

With such statistics in the news, the issue exploded on the national scene as the conservative press vilified black children and black families as the cause of their own tribulations. Articles written by noted sociologists described black parents as "dysfunctional," "welfare mothers," "absent fathers," and "on–the–dole" parents. Writers described black youth as "hardened teens" who had been "decimated by three decades of destitution programs, welfare bailouts, and affirmative action." The press, politicians, and pundits concluded the black family was unraveling. It seemed the nation was undergoing another period of disillusionment regarding the effectiveness of its social agenda for the poor, and particularly blacks living in inner cities.[206]

Not highly publicized during this time was the fact that homicide rates in the United States for *all* people between 18 and 34 years old had spiked in the 1980s. From 1985 to 1993 the increase among 18–to 24–year–olds alone was 150 percent.[207] Nevertheless, the focus remained on African Americans and so did the blame.

The nation's attention shifted from President Lyndon B. Johnson's "Great Society" reforms, set forth in the 1960s and designed to eliminate poverty and racial injustice, and focused on President Reagan's "Trickledown Economics" strategy, designed to cut taxes to the wealthy and leave the burden of helping the poor up to the wealthy. As the U.S. government abandoned its commitment to helping the underprivileged, The Salvation Army broadened its ministry to blacks and other ethnic groups during the 1980s. Since Commissioner Railton proclaimed in 1880 that the Army would get "American Africans…fairly started," it had tried to maintain its focus on the poor and, in particular, the African–American community down

Inner city youths

© David Turnley/CORBIS

through the years, despite setbacks caused by external and internal opposition.

Fulfilling Railton's promise

Sometimes, moving black officers across territorial borders was necessary to revitalize an officer's ministry. As a member of the National Capital Area Band, Captain Allan Wiltshire found his ministry frustrated in the 1980s by policies of racial segregation in the South. On one occasion when the band went to a town to minister, a little black boy helped him unload the brass instruments from the bus. "See you at the concert," Wiltshire said to him after they had finished the task. "Is it for coloreds?" the boy asked in earnest.

Allan Wiltshire, Sr. and children

On another occasion, the band, scheduled to perform at an annual appreciation dinner at a popular restaurant in the Washington, D.C. area, met the bandmaster at the entrance of the restaurant. After the bandmaster had explained to the attendant that Wiltshire and the other blacks were members of the band, they were finally escorted to the dining room.

That year, the Wiltshires requested a transfer from the Southern to Eastern Territory. They accomplished this through the kindness of then–Captain Israel Gaither who took the Wiltshire's request to Lt. Colonel Walter French, Greater New York divisional commander. Not long after, the Wiltshires assumed leadership of the Brownsville Corps and then the Bedford Temple Corps in Brooklyn, N.Y. Their situation, although not perfect, improved considerably.[208]

'We cannot all sing and dance'

With a spirit reminiscent of Lt. Colonel McIntyre, Captain

Allan Wiltshire, Sr., Bedford Temple corps officer in Brooklyn, N.Y., presented a paper entitled "Cultural Awareness and Minority Ministries" during the Army's National Social Services Conference in Kansas City, Mo. Wiltshire said: "The future of The Salvation Army hinges on its ability to respond sensitively, effectively, and in the spirit of Jesus to the needs of those who inhabit the inner cities of this great nation." He called on the Army to divest itself of its preconceived notions and stereotypical attitudes toward blacks.

> We cannot all sing, dance, and play sports. We are not all immoral and lecherous. We are not all lazy and shifty. We do not all try to get on welfare. Many coming to our establishments may be considered amongst the 'walking wounded' with some emotional hang–ups, or victims of our stressful society.
>
> Many have seen better days, but because of the economic crunch, they need help with the utilities, the rent, or groceries. There are those who come with deep–seated spiritual problems looking for the Balm in Gilead that will make the sin–sick whole. What do we do? Well, let me see. He is black. Let me deal with him from the richness of his blackness. Let me first engage him in one of those handshakes that take all of three minutes to complete. Let me compliment him on the tightness of his Afro haircut. Let me congratulate him on the progress of the Rev. Jesse Jackson's bid for the presidency. Maybe I should turn on Michael Jackson's tape, 'Thriller'; it should set the mood.
>
> I should be careful as I rap with him in his native dialect—ghettoese—the urban language. I will call my secretary and send out for some soul food. It is a pity I do not smoke because a joint

> and a beer would relax him and we would really get this interview going. A bit overdone—on purpose. But, you see, we can go overboard with this culture bit.

Wiltshire quoted several noted black sociologists, writers, and activists to support his ideas, such as Thomas Sowell, James Baldwin, Dr. Martin Luther King, Jr., and Air Force Brigadier General Daniel "Chappie" James, among others.[209]

On June 16, 1980, at the Salvation Army's International Congress in Kansas City, Mo., Corps Sergeant–Major Edward Gooding received the Order of the Founder, the highest honor given to a member of The Salvation Army. A panel of senior leaders at International Headquarters had carefully scrutinized his nomination for the award, which is rarely given. As a recipient, Gooding received special status and a place in history for having modeled the values and ideals that exemplify true Salvationism. The Army recognized him for more than 47 years of distinguished and memorable service and outstanding Christian witness at the Boston (Roxbury), Mass., Corps. While receiving the award, Gooding flashed his irrepressible smile. His audience in the vast auditorium stood on their feet and listened as the man warmly known as "Sarge" and hailed as a model lay leader by members of The Salvation Army accepted the honor.

Edward Gooding receives the Order of the Founder award from General Arnold Brown in 1980.

Gooding had served as a foreman for the U.S. Navy

working in the Panama Canal Zone before coming to Boston where he had displayed a fearless attitude as he confronted dangerous men on city streets with the Christian message. Gooding earned his living as a factory manager. But he also became known as a community evangelist who attracted new soldiers to the Roxbury Corps and essentially stopped it from closing as the population of the neighborhood shifted from white to black.

Gooding's house–to–house visits led to his setting up Boy Scout, Cub Scout, Girl Guard, and Sunbeam troops at the corps. The corps also offered music lessons to the community and eventually formed a youth singing group and brass band. Gooding put the young Salvationists to work at open–air meetings in the park, where their music, singing, and evangelizing skills went to good use.

During the turbulent '60s, Gooding and his wife joined the National Association for the Advancement of Colored People (NAACP) and became active in the local chapter. They also took part in the National Urban League and marched in civil rights demonstrations. Through the years, corps officers came and went. But the community could always depend on Gooding to be there for them and to help provide the continuity and stability needed through unavoidable transitions in leadership.

Gooding understood the meaning of discrimination. Limited opportunities for people of color in the Canal Zone had led him to immigrate to the United States. And as plant production manager at the Gorton Corporation in Gloucester, Mass., his second job after arriving in the U.S., he faced stiff resistance from 50 employees, who resented being supervised by the only black in a corporation of 500 workers.

But amid the challenging civil rights era, Gooding remained focused on his primary purpose: proclaiming the Gospel of Jesus Christ to all people. As part of his witness, he also preached the gospel of love, pacifism, and nonviolent response to injustice. Despite the prevailing political climate, Gooding continued to connect with the spirit and soul of people around him. He always stressed his personal conviction: "In the final analysis, God is the answer. Only our love for one another will make a difference."

Many people confessed faith in Christ through the ministry of this kind, calm, but courageous man. A gifted evangelist, Gooding used *The War Cry*, the national magazine of The Salvation Army, as his best tool for reaching others with the Christian faith. "One day, I decided to give the plant manager one," he remembers. Gooding subsequently gave copies to other managers and left some magazines in the company cafeteria. Eventually, plant employees began asking for copies every week, and Gooding accepted a small donation to the Army for each copy.

He was also eternally grateful for what the Army had helped him avoid in life. "[The Army] saved me from many problems and troubles people are going through in the world. I've never known what it means to be down in the gutter with no direction in life. I thank The Salvation Army for that blessing," he said in 2000.[210]

Ministry Milestones (1980–1984)

In the Western Territory, Lieutenants Victor and Rose–Marie Leslie arrive from the Caribbean, where they had been commissioned as Salvation Army officers. Although he was the son of Caribbean officers Majors Cameron and Embla Leslie, Lieutenant Victor Leslie was no stranger to the United States. He had lived in Madison, Wisc., before enrolling in the Army's training school in Jamaica, W.I., where he joined his fiancé, Lieutenant Rose–Marie Campbell. Victor was not the only Leslie to be commissioned. Clement Leslie, Victor's older brother, had enrolled in training in the USA Southern Territory in 1978. During the commissioning

Victor and Rose–Marie Leslie

events of 1980, the Leslie family had the distinction of having two sons commissioned, within a week of each other and in two different territories, into the "Proclaimers of Salvation" session by then–General Arnold Brown.

To come to the United States, Lieutenants Victor and Rose–Marie Leslie had to resign their officership, which was the Army's policy for Salvationists immigrating from the Third World. After the Army reinstated them in the United States, they served as corps officers at the Phoenix South Mountain Youth Center in Arizona, and in San Francisco and Oakland, Calif. They helped community leaders design and implement social programs aimed at helping at–risk children in minority neighborhoods. The California State Assembly awarded the Leslies certificates of recognition for exceptional work in the minority community.[211]

The following year, Captains Maurice and Ana Rosa Smith transfer from the Central to the Eastern Territory. Their first child, Marcus, was almost a year old at the time. They assume command of the Homewood–Brushton Corps in Pittsburgh. A daughter, Erika Fabiana, was born a short time later.

In 1981, Lieutenants Robert and Hester Dixon, former Salvation Army and U.S. government employees, graduate from the School for Officer Training as ordained ministers and qualified social workers. Their first appointment is in Newark, N.J.

That year, the Territorial Black Ministries Committee sponsors another Heritage Night at the Temple in New York City. The event features Tom Skinner, a black evangelist and motivational speaker who was legendary for having organized a highly successful evangelistic crusade in Harlem's Apollo Theater in 1960 when he was only 18. An estimated 10,000 people had attended Skinner's weeklong campaign back then, including Salvationist Clarence Barry–Austin, a 12–year–old immigrant from Guyana, South America.[212]

Clarence Barry–Austin

Although Barry–Austin had been attending the Harlem Temple Corps with his parents every Sunday, he knelt with some 2,200 people one night in the Apollo Theater after hearing Skinner's message and committed his life to Christian service. Barry–Austin grew up to attend Rutgers University and become an attorney. Later, he served as a civil court judge in the Township of South Orange Village, N.J.[213]

At the Heritage Night celebration, Skinner, who had spent time at the Army's Brooklyn (Bedford) Temple Corps as a young man, delivers a passionate message urging Salvationists to reach youth with the Gospel message and build indigenous leadership from within its ranks. The author of four books challenges the Army to pursue racial reconciliation and salvation for a new generation by teaching youth how to manage and lead ministries. "The totality of your energy should be obsessed with loving God," he says.[214]

In 1982, the Dixons transfer to the Brownsville Corps and Community Center in Brooklyn. As officers, their income is less than what it had been when they worked in Philadelphia as employees. But now they are living happier and more fulfilled lives as corps officers (administrators and pastors). The Army provides them with a home, vehicle, stipend, and private school tuition for their three children. This is a blessing because the schools in Brownsville are crime–ridden. The Dixons work eight hours a day, six days a week.[215]

Lilian Yarde, the "Ebony Angel" of riot–torn Cleveland, is promoted to Glory in 1982. Her favorite Scripture passage had been Psalm 37:37, which reads, "Observe the perfect man, and consider the just for the end of that man is peace."[216]

Delilah Collier

That same year, Commissioner John D. Needham, national commander of The Salvation Army, issues an official statement that "the creation of cross–cultural models and the identification of existing programs must have priority, as should the development of the corps community center, to reflect an indigenous profile in terms of ethnicity, need, and language." A special minorities ministries committee reports to the national commander for two years. It is dissolved in 1983 when the commissioners reaffirm that the special minority emphasis should be conducted on the territorial rather than the national level.[217]

In the Eastern Territory, Delilah Collier, a local officer from the Hartford Citadel Corps in Hartford, Conn., becomes the Black Ministries Committee's new leader. Committed to "serve God with every fiber of her being," she manages to run a household, work part time for the local school district, and graduate from college with a teaching certificate. Her ministry as a Bible teacher, and mentor to young people would become legendary in The Salvation Army.[218]

In the Central Territory, Stephen and Diane Harper become the first African-American officers assigned to Territorial Headquarters in the United States. Stephen Harper is appointed as an assistant to the Candidates Secretary. His subsequent appointments include territorial director of boys' activities and assistant candidates secretary. Diane Harper is appointed as assistant Territorial Student Fellowship secretary. Although the Harpers recognize the need for the Army to have people of color in territorial administration, they miss corps work. "We missed the congregation—watching children grow, helping families through crises," says Major Stephen Harper years later.

Stephen and Diane Harper

When someone tells Stephen that Methodist ministers were required to go back to pastoral work after serving five years in administration, he says jokingly, "What a great idea!"[219]

Lonneal Richardson

Also in the Central Territory that year, Lonneal Richardson is commissioned as a Salvation Army officer. He had begun attending The Salvation Army in Memphis, Tenn., at age 9, when his mother enrolled his youngest brother in a Salvation Army day-care program. Lonneal's mother later becomes an employee at an Army shelter for battered women, where she works for 35 years. He earns a bachelor's degree in business and leadership from Cornerstone University. He also marries Patty in June.[220]

In 1984, the Army looses another icon when Lt. Colonel B. Barton McIntyre is promoted to Glory. At his home–going service, friends, family, and officers reflect on the way in which he courageously pushed to have black Salvationists moved to the front lines of ministry in The Salvation Army.

Commissioner Norman S. Marshall II, then national commander, formally proposes to International Headquarters that The Salvation Army overturn its policy of not allowing officers who had immigrated to the United States on their own initiative to join the denomination until they had spent at least five years in this country. To address a shortage of black officers particularly in inner cities, his proposal asks that the Army reinstate these officers into active service immediately. "We desperately need leadership to help with our establishment of beachhead operations in these ethnic groups,"" Marshall argues. The Chief of the Staff is sympathetic, but Marshall's request is rejected. International Headquarters fears that too many officers would leave developing countries to pursue the fabled American Dream. The Army decides that if the work among African Americans is to grow in the United States, more black officers must come from local communities.[221]

SALVATION

Chapter 15
Courage in the trenches

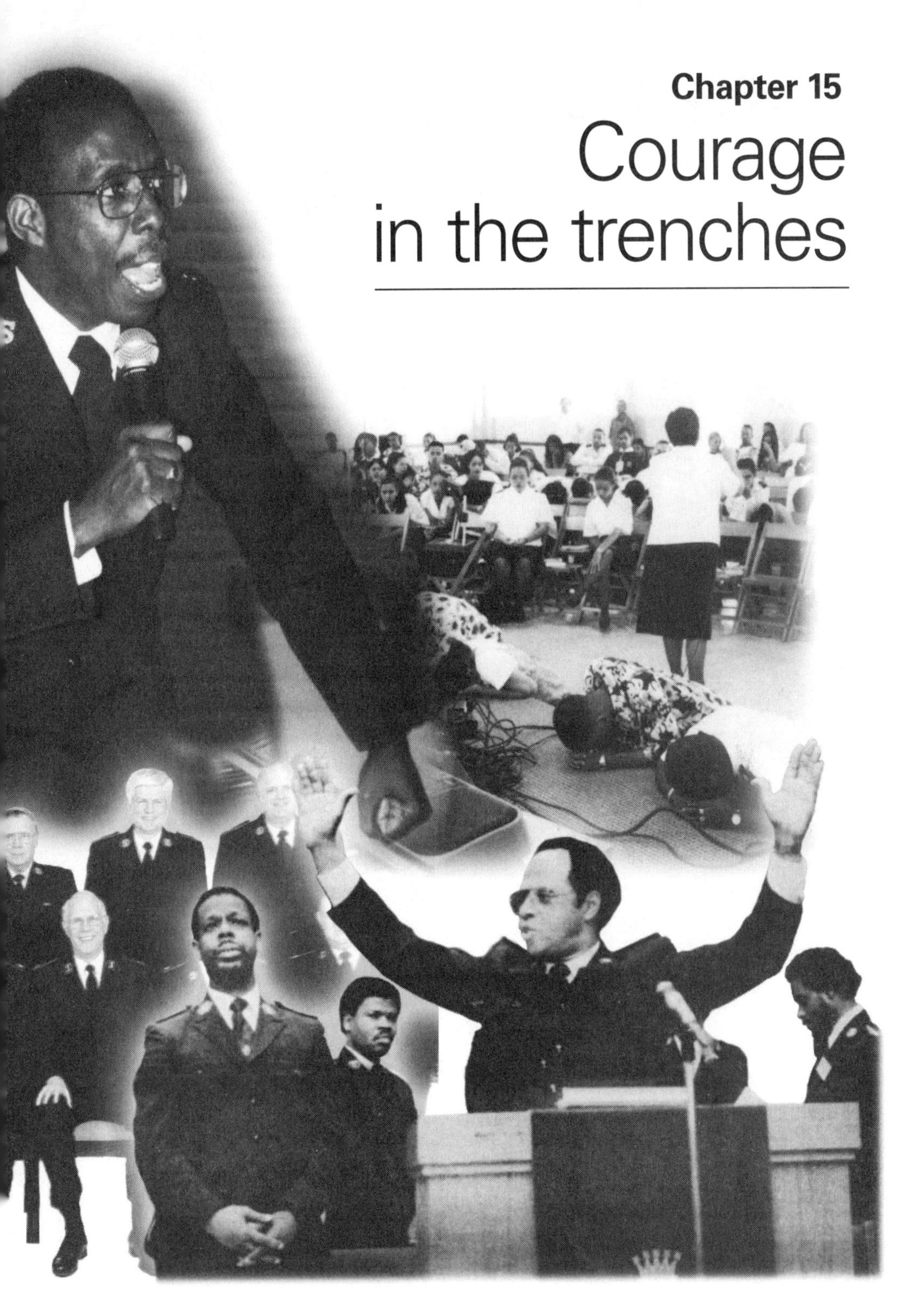

IN 1985, LIEUTENANTS ROBERT AND HESTER DIXON, two African–American officers who were homegrown, agreed that of the 19 years they'd been married, the past six had been the best. They had worked as bell ringers in front of Bloomingdale's department store in Manhattan. Hester said, "Some people give us donations. Others stop to chat, and some even stay to sing awhile with us (although once, when Bob was once in the middle of a chorus of 'Rudolph the Red–Nosed Reindeer,' a man offered him five dollars not to sing!)." The Dixon children, Robert, 17, and Heather, 15, were in Salvation Army camps in New Jersey, where they worked and participated in camp activities. Heather was the star singer in the songster group.

Robert and Hester Dixon

Brownsville, Brooklyn, with its grassed–over, graffiti–covered walls, was a poor community where the Dixons were corps officers. Ninety percent of the residents lived on welfare. Prostitution and drug deals happened in the streets every day. But Bob and Hester's social programs and religious services offered people a refuge from the poverty. The after–school program, day–care center, summer camp, Girl Guards and Boys' Adventure Corps, Songsters, and Timbrels provided something for people to do from morning to night. "Sometimes people say to me, 'How do you do it?'" said Hester. She worked constantly. People would sometimes call her at home at two in the morning. She traveled all over Brooklyn, caring for people. "Don't you ever get tired of it?" people would ask her. But she always answered, "I am deeply grateful for it."

Bob and Hester believed that when they could give another person a little joy, a little faith in God, a little gratitude, then they knew they'd had a successful day. "It's a comfort to share the trials as well as the triumphs with my husband," she said. "He always says, 'We can do together what neither of us could do alone.' " They agreed that the best time of year for giving was at Christmas. In addition to the caroling and bell ringing in front of Bloomingdale's, they distributed more than 1,000 carefully wrapped gifts to children in Brownsville. These were toys donated by manufacturers and individuals. The women's groups also helped make Christmas memorable for families in unfortunate circumstances. Many women were single heads of families struggling in the midst of negative influences to bring up children on welfare payments. Working together in women's groups gave the moms opportunity to share stories and not feel so alone. The corps Christmas parties changed the way some women celebrated Christmas at home. They realized the most important gifts to their families were themselves. "Just do the best they can and celebrate the warmth and joy of being a family together. When I hear that they've done that, I know I've received the greatest Christmas gift of all," Hester said.[222]

The Wiltshires in Panama

'They know me by my uniform'

Majors Allan and Marjorie Wiltshire were appointed as divisional leaders to the Central American nation of Panama. In 1988, they were caught in the crossfire between 24,000 American troops and the forces of General Manuel Antonio Noriega. The United States had invaded that nation to oust Noriega from power. The conflict between Noriega and the U.S. Army's "Operation Just Cause" put thousands of innocent Panamanian lives at risk. Despite the war that threatened to tear the country apart, the Wiltshires continued their work. One day, an American tank gunner, who saw Major Alan Wiltshire wearing epaulettes on his white shirt, shouted, "Halt!" Thinking Wiltshire was an officer in Noriega's army, the gunner aimed his weapon at him. When Wiltshire told the soldier that he was with The Salvation Army, the young man shouted, "Take off that shirt before you get fired on!" But Wiltshire didn't take off the shirt. "I wasn't going to take off my uniform," he said. "People in the community knew me by my uniform. They understood what it meant." That day, the gunner stood down and the uniform stayed on.

The fighting raged in Panama City as helicopter gunships bombed suspected enemy strongholds. The city was on fire. Infantrymen conducted door–to–door searches of buildings, including divisional headquarters. In the midst of physical fighting, the spiritual war against poverty and want continued. Food and supplies stockpiled by Noriega's soldiers as a safeguard against economic sanctions were confiscated by American troops and given to The Salvation Army for distribution to the poor.

Holiness meetings flourished during the crisis. People were coming to The Salvation Army in large numbers for prayer. Captain Marjorie Wiltshire invited them into the sanctuary of the refugee camp. The U.S. "Operation Just Cause" succeeded in deposing Noriega. The conflict came to an end as suddenly as it had begun. But the work of helping hurting people in the aftermath was only beginning. For many months, The Salvation Army continued to bring comfort to families who had lost their homes and, in some cases, their loved ones.[223]

Soldier extraordinaire

In August 1989, in an impressive ceremony conducted by Commissioner James Osborne, the commander for the Southern Territory, Clara Paige, the Young People's Sergeant Major (YPSM) from Norfolk, Va., received the Army's prestigious Order of the Founder award posthumously during Commissioning Weekend in Symphony Hall in Atlanta. The ceremony took place just days after her promotion to Glory. Catalina Gooding, a sister, and Corps Sergeant–Major (CSM) Edward Gooding, O.F., of Boston, Mass., her brother–in–law, received the citation from Osborne, who presented it for General Eva Burrows.

Clara Paige

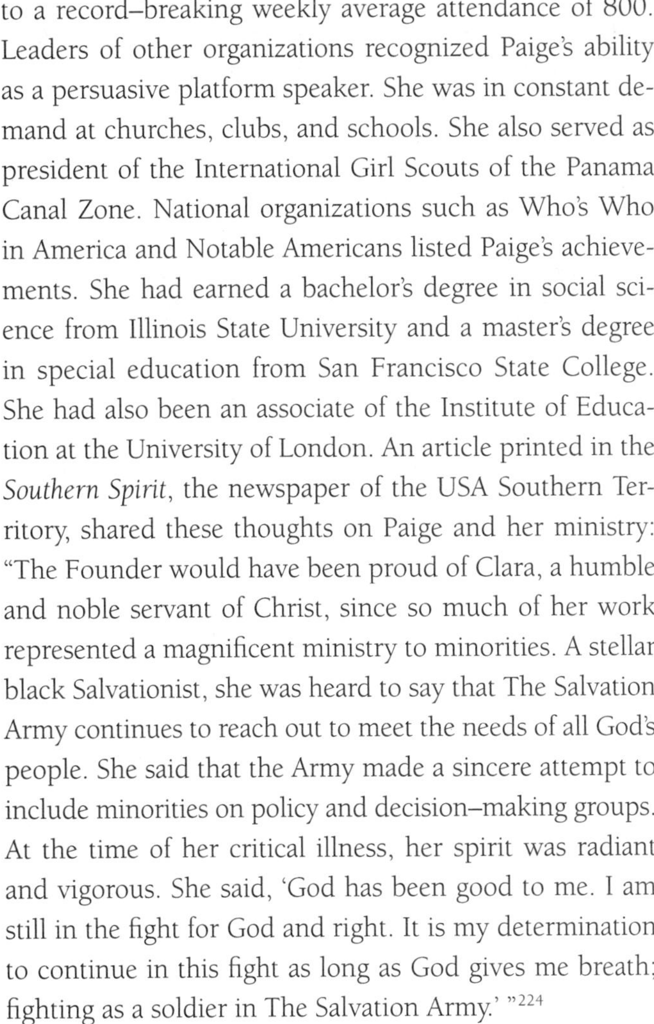

Described as "God's Extraordinary Soldier," Paige led the Norfolk Corps' Sunday school to a record–breaking weekly average attendance of 800. Leaders of other organizations recognized Paige's ability as a persuasive platform speaker. She was in constant demand at churches, clubs, and schools. She also served as president of the International Girl Scouts of the Panama Canal Zone. National organizations such as Who's Who in America and Notable Americans listed Paige's achievements. She had earned a bachelor's degree in social science from Illinois State University and a master's degree in special education from San Francisco State College. She had also been an associate of the Institute of Education at the University of London. An article printed in the *Southern Spirit*, the newspaper of the USA Southern Territory, shared these thoughts on Paige and her ministry: "The Founder would have been proud of Clara, a humble and noble servant of Christ, since so much of her work represented a magnificent ministry to minorities. A stellar black Salvationist, she was heard to say that The Salvation Army continues to reach out to meet the needs of all God's people. She said that the Army made a sincere attempt to include minorities on policy and decision–making groups. At the time of her critical illness, her spirit was radiant and vigorous. She said, 'God has been good to me. I am still in the fight for God and right. It is my determination to continue in this fight as long as God gives me breath; fighting as a soldier in The Salvation Army.' "[224]

Ministry Milestones (1985–1989)

In 1985, the Army commissions Lydia Pearson as a member of the Guardians of Truth session. She had entered training in 1983 from Geneva, N.Y., a small town in upstate New York where she had been a member of the only black family at her corps. Indeed, young Lydia had never even seen a black officer in the Empire State Division.

Then one summer as a teenager at camp, she met Captain Anita Brown. Lydia was moved by the good she saw Captain Brown and other concerned Salvationists doing in the lives of people. Their example inspired Lydia to accept God's call to service as an officer in The Salvation Army. As a cadet, she had been the only black in her session. This had not been a problem for her. But ministering to and working with people of her own race would present a new challenge.[225]

Lt. Colonels David and Doreen Edwards take their first appointments outside the Caribbean, in the USA Eastern Territory as assistant chief secretary and director of the Overseas Child Sponsorship program. David was from Guyana, and Doreen was from Barbados. They had served in corps appointments, she in Jamaica and Trinidad, he in Trinidad. Together, they had served in a number of corps appointments throughout the Caribbean. They had also served in social services on divisional headquarters. David had served as training school principal and Doreen as the finance officer at the training college before being appointed to Territorial Headquarters in Kingston, Jamaica.

The Black Officers' Hall of Service is dedicated in 1986 to honor officers, both active and retired, who had shown outstanding dedication in service to the Army in the USA Eastern Territory. The Bedford Temple Corps in Brooklyn serves as the venue for the hall, whose walls are lined with large photos of each honoree. A biographical sketch describing each individual's accomplishments accompanies each photo and career highlights. During the dedication ceremony, Major Abraham Johnson reaches up and removes a Salvation Army flag to unveil a photo of him and his wife, Major Louise Johnson. Their photo hangs next to that of Senior Majors Lambert and Estava Bailey. Among the honorees are Lt. Colonels McIntyre, Lt. Colonels Edwards, and the Majors Gaither. "There are over 130 black and Hispanic youngsters regularly attending the community center," says Silvina Jarvis, the center director and overseer of the Hall of Service. "It is our hope that this will inspire them to become active in the Army as officers or local officers (lay leaders)." To be admitted to the Hall, a person had to have served at least 20 years as an officer. Jarvis' vision of black officers inspiring Spanish–speaking people of color would be realized in the next millennium.[226]

Eastern Territorial leadership expands the scope of the Territorial Black Ministries Committee to include other ethnic groups, such as Hispanics and Koreans, and renames itself the Ministries to Minorities Committee. A year later, by recommendation of the committee, administration changes the name again to the Ethnic Ministry Committee. The reason for the change was that members had decided that the word "minority" had a negative connotation. Delilah Collier returns to lead the committee. The Army's leadership sends delegates to the National Convocation on Evangelizing Ethnic America and to the National Black Evangelical Association Convention. The Army is prepared to increase its "commitment to the people of the new ethnic America." The Army in the East officially announces its strategy to make this effort its number one priority, without diminishing the importance of traditionally established corps.

By 1987, all four territories establish cross–cultural ministries bureaus. In the East, Major Richard Shaffstall, a white officer, directs the bureau, and the Ethnic Ministries Committee becomes part of it. Shaffstall conducts a territorial demographic survey, and the bureau uses the statistics from the survey to formulate its goals and objectives.[227]

Also in the East, the Army continues to move the Lt. Colonels Edwards up the leadership ladder by appointing them as New Jersey divisional leaders (David as divisional commander and Doreen as divisional director of Women's Organizations). A year later, the Army moves them again, this time to posts at International Headquarters, where he serves as undersecretary for the Americas and Caribbean and she as zonal secretary and Women's Ministries secretary for the Caribbean. Seven years later, they again serve at IHQ, he as international secretary and she as zonal secretary for

Women's Ministries for the Americas and the Caribbean.

In the Southern Territory, The Salvation Army's ministry to Haitian immigrants begins in a section of Miami known as "Little Haiti." The Miami Edison Corps had originally been an Anglo corps, and when whites moved out of the community, the Army seriously considered closing the corps. The Army attempts to save it by appointing a Haitian couple, Captains Jonas and Gelina Georges, as corps officers. Although they leave Army officership soon after, the corps remains open and active as Haitians continue to move into the community. The Army transfers Majors Ernest and Christine Mills to the corps from Jamaica, and they serve an exclusively Haitian congregation for three years.[228]

In 1988 at the International College for Officers in London, Major Israel L. Gaither is elected session president. In each of the four refresher courses held annually, a group of 24 Salvation Army officers, representing as many as 20 countries, spend six weeks studying a range of subjects relating to the program and purpose of The Salvation Army in the world.

Also that year, the Eastern Territory holds a Black Ministries Consultation to examine issues and strengthen solidarity among black Salvationists. Captain Wilfred Samuels speaks on the Gospel and the essence of Salvationism. Major William LaMarr, a white officer and general secretary for field

Leaders gather at the Black Ministry Consultation (l–r) Major Lyell Rader, Major Israel L. Gaither, Lt. Colonel Dorothy Purser, Major Paul M. Kelly, Major Abraham Johnson, and Major Allan Wiltshire.

The Johnsons receive recognition from (l–r) Commissioner Stanley Ditmer, General Eva Burrows, and Commissioner Andrew S. Miller.

operations in Greater New York, deals with church growth issues, and Major George Evans, who had just earned a master's degree in theology from Ashland Theological Seminary in Ashland, Ohio, shares methods for equipping and mobilizing the laity for mission in the black community.

In his paper, Evans shares key words he believes will assist in effectively meeting the spiritual needs of people of color. These words are: *concern, compassion, commitment,* and *involvement.* Lt. Colonel Dorothy Purser presents issues confronting black Salvationists. Daniel Diakanwa and Joseph Lloyd, young Salvationists involved in social work, conduct discussions on the role of blacks in Salvation Army leadership. Major Israel L. Gaither presents a paper entitled "Toward the 21st Century: Choices and Responsibilities." He challenges delegates to do their part in promoting the mission of The Salvation Army. Major Abraham Johnson speaks on affirming diversity and building unity in the Army.[229]

That year, General Eva Burrows recognizes the Johnsons for their faithful service to The Salvation Army by presenting them with a special certificate during the Eastern Territorial Congress held in Ocean Grove, N.J.

Michel Christel and his family move to New York City after pioneering The Salvation Army's work in French Guiana. Christel, with the help of former Haitian Salvationists residing in New York, starts a ministry to French–speaking immigrants while pursuing a doctoral degree at the Theological

International Seminary Extension Program. This ministry expands to include the Army's Bushwick Corps in Brooklyn under the leadership of Yvon Alkintor, another former Haitian Salvation Army officer who migrated to the U.S.[230]

Stephen Harper, from the USA Central Territory, tours Zimbabwe as a member of the Chicago Staff Band. He and wife Diane enjoy 15 days in the former Rhodesia, but they are surprised to see black African officers, who had recently moved into leadership, provide for their underlings the same meager quarters they had suffered through during the years of President Cecil Rhodes's oppressive regime. The Harpers realize that culture dies hard and that new faces—even black ones—don't necessarily change old systems right away. The Harpers also travel to South Korea, the Philippines, and Europe with the band.[231]

In 1989, Robert Watson, a white employee and son of officers, becomes leader of the Cross-Cultural Ministries Bureau in the USA Eastern Territory. In addition to his regular duties, he coordinates the Scandinavian Congress, the oldest annual ethnic Salvation Army gathering. He also launches City Lights, a program designed to send 12-member urban mission teams to urban corps for eight weeks of cross-cultural training.[232]

That same year in the East, the Army assigns Major Maurice E. Smith to the New Rochelle, N.Y., Corps, after he had spent three years leading the Philadelphia Temple Corps. Smith serves as New Rochelle corps officer for the next six and one half years and receives his 25-year service badge. His creation of new programs and remodeling of old facilities brings appreciation from the community and growth to the corps.

Chapter 16
Crossing cultures, elevating subcultures

"[Black officers] have the capacity to lead in any community, not just black communities."

—Commissioner David Edwards

OVER TIME, BLACKS HAD PROVEN THEMSELVES COMPETENT AND CAPABLE corps officers, divisional leaders, and administrators. They had served during the most challenging and dangerous periods in United States history. And, because so many urban communities desperately needed social service programs, corps in these communities where black officers served were the Army's largest in terms of personnel, facilities, and budget. What could possibly be the next frontier? Where would black officers find new challenges on The Salvation Army horizon? New appointments would address social and cultural issues within The Salvation Army as they never had before.

Since the Army's Commissioners Conference of 1983 (a national board of leaders from all four territories, which meets annually to discuss policy), the creation of cross–cultural models and the identification of existing programs had been relegated to the territorial level (see Ministry Milestones 1980–84). These bureaus helped keep cross–cultural ministry on the agenda and provide implementation strategies for Salvationists engaged in such work. In 1991, Daniel Diakanwa became the Cross–Cultural Ministries Bureau director at Eastern Territorial Headquarters. Diakanwa had served as a social worker for The Salvation Army in New York City for seven years. Born and raised in the Republic of Congo as the son of the territorial commander, Diakanwa brought a unique understanding to his position at the bureau as its African Heritage consultant. He attended the Harlem Temple

Corps and conducted ecumenical Bible studies and prayer meetings for French–speaking African immigrants and students in New York City. He also counseled Adult Rehabilitation Center beneficiaries in Mt. Vernon, N.Y.

Charlotte (Kimbeni) and Daniel N. Diakanwa

In 1993, Diakanwa conducted a workshop during a symposium on African–American recruitment and preparation he helped organize. At that event, he told a story about an African–American man who had been a resident of the Bronx Adult Rehabilitation Center. During a group therapy session Diakanwa conducted at the ARC, the man suddenly stood and said, "You don't understand what this nation did to black people. You don't know nothing, man! So don't tell us what we can do to improve our conditions because there ain't any job out there for an uneducated nigger like me!"[233]

After Diakanwa shared the story, symposium delegates paused to reflect on problems such as this one facing many black men. As a trained social worker, Diakanwa had counseled many men to help them manage their anger, grief, and subsequent depression and feelings of hopelessness. In the ARC were men of all races who suffered from deep depression, which, in some cases, had spiraled downward into psychosis. Many had exacerbated their psychological problems by attempting to medicate themselves with alcohol or drugs, thus becoming candidates for "dual diagnosis" treatment. Others had resorted to domestic or physical violence. Fortunately, through the ARC, many of these men finally received counseling they so desperately needed to help put them on the road to hope and recovery.

In 1994, the USA Eastern Territory established its first Cross–Cultural Ministries Department (CCMD) and

Translation Bureau (a smaller organization within the department), under the leadership of Commissioner Ronald G. Irwin, territorial commander, and his cabinet. Irwin appointed Major Allan Wiltshire to head CCMD and Major Marjorie Wiltshire as Translation Bureau director. Daniel Diakanwa became African heritage consultant (he had served as Cross–Cultural Ministries Bureau director in 1991). Wiltshire soon announced plans to appoint consultants for Salvationists of Hispanic and Asian heritage. Having been born in Panama, he spoke English, Spanish, and French. Ethnic Army leaders applauded the department's formation, believing it would place the USA Eastern Territory on the cutting edge of cross–cultural ministries in the Army world. This effort was a sign that a new approach to racial reconciliation was on the horizon.[234]

In October 1995, Daniel Diakanwa organized the Regional African Heritage Convocation under the theme "Stand and Withstand" at the Harlem Temple Corps. The Territorial Cross–Cultural Ministries Department sponsored the event. Among other topics, delegates discussed issues of race and equality in The Salvation Army—issues that had been part of Diakanwa's life even before he left his home in the Congo (formerly The Democratic Republic of Congo, formerly Zaire) to live in the United States. Many years ago when his father had been a young officer, he had desired to go to Europe to continue his education. But when his father suggested the idea to a white European territorial commander, that commander slapped him across the face. The elder Diakanwa kept this humiliating experience from his wife and children for many years. Those had been difficult years, when nationals were not permitted to hold positions of leadership.

Times eventually changed, however. As more African leaders insisted upon having their own people lead nongovernmental organizations operating in their countries, the doors of opportunity opened to officers such as the elder Diakanwa, who eventually stepped into the position of commander himself. On the day of his installation as territorial commander of Congo–Kinshasa, he told the story to a shocked audience about literally being slapped in the face. As he delivered his installation message, the family, hearing the story for the first time, held each other and cried. Memories of humiliating racial injustice became a driving force behind young Daniel's desire to see cultural and racial equality and understanding prevail in the Army's ranks. Diakanwa and committee members attempted to make such regional convocations an important part of territorial ministry.[235]

For Captain Lydia Pearson, a young black woman from a small white town in upstate New York, being a member of the committee became a defining moment. In appointments as a corps officer, most of her friends in the Army had been white. But in 1987, the Army transferred Pearson to the Greater New York Division and expected her to blend into a community of black officers she had never met. She said they looked at her curiously when she mingled with white friends. That scrutiny caused her to take a different perspective. She began to question them, saying, "We're all one Army." During the Territorial Committee for Salvationists of African Descent (TCSAD) committee meetings in 1993, Lydia participated in ongoing discussions about 20–year old issues yet to be resolved, such as the lack of black officers in divisional and territorial leadership. She also realized that black Salvationists come from a variety of backgrounds: American, Caribbean, African, and others who were a mixture of ethnicities and nationalities. These revelations, she said, would later help her become a better teacher during her appointment at the School for Officer Training during the late 1990s.[236]

In the Central Territory in 1999, Captain Janet Love's grandmother reached her 93rd birthday. Love noticed the familiar patchwork quilt wrapped around her grandmoth-

Janet Love

er's legs. The history of African–American women in quilting is almost as old as the history of the United States. In the time of slavery, slave owners needed black women to spin, weave, and sew quilts for the opulent beds in their massive plantation homes.[237] Unnoticed by the slave owners were other quilts these women spun for their children's freedom. Embroidered in those quilts were maps used by the Underground Railroad to lead escaped slaves to Canada.[238]

Most of the brilliant colors of Love's grandmother's quilt had faded. But it evoked vibrant memories for Love. And from those memories, she caught a vision for the future of multicultural relations in the Salvation Army's Central Territory. As Multi–Cultural Ministries Bureau director, she articulated to the territory her vision for success, "... to attract and disciple people of varied ethnic and racial backgrounds and build cultural sensitivity and relationships among officers, soldiers, employees, and volunteers." To achieve this mission, she and her staff visited Army sites, conducted workshops, and participated in worship services. Love hired a full–time English/Spanish translator to meet the needs of a growing Hispanic Salvation Army community. "That quilt [her grandmother's] is like the body of Christ," she said. She quoted the Apostle Paul, who said, "Here there is no Greek or Jew, circumcised or uncircumcised, barbarian, Scythian, slave or free, but Christ is all, and is in all. Therefore, as God's chosen people, holy and dearly loved, clothe yourself with compassion, kindness, humanity, gentleness and patience" (Colossians 3:11–12). "If a square or two were missing from that quilt," Love continued, "its effectiveness would be hindered. If five or more squares were missing, its look would be distorted and incomplete, its comfort and warmth diminished. If we in our corps ignore or do not value those who look, speak, or worship differently from the way we do, we limit ourselves. We cannot see the full beauty of God's patchwork quilt. Our witness and ministries to the world will lack the vitality that could draw people to the Creator."[239]

Elevating a subculture

In 1991, in the Central Territory, Kendall Mathews launched a ministry designed to reach an urban subculture. He was commissioned a lieutenant of the Servants of Jesus session. Previously, Mathews had earned his bachelor's degree in social work and psychology in 1985 from Greenville College. He and his wife, Katrina Diane, were appointed to the Detroit Harding Corps. They encouraged steady growth by improving social programs. While meeting the physical and social needs of the people, the Mathews also ministered to their spiritual needs. Lieutenant Kendall became known for telling people that salvation is free and that every need can be met through Jesus Christ. The Mathews' goal was to empower people of this poverty–stricken community to have more pride and confidence, which would lead to more productive lives. The Mathews committed the corps to introducing individuals to a brand of holistic urban ministry that provided services and programs for individuals and community. The Mathews looked at the spiritual and social programs as one continuous ministry. "One cannot be totally effective without the other," Lieutenant Kendall Mathews had said.[240]

Katrina and K. Kendall Mathews

In 1994, Mathews, who had committed himself to a philosophy of helping others, earned his master's degree in theology and doctorate in Christian psychology from Andersonville Theological Seminary. Three years later, Mathews earned his Certified Social Work Manager

(CSWM) certificate. While attending the Central Territory's first "African–American Council of War," Lieutenants Kendall and Katrina D. Mathews presented a paper entitled "Urban Corps and Institutional Social Services: How we are perceived, bridging the gap from client to soldier." They outlined strategies by which Salvationists could empower entire communities through "Upward Mobility Stages of Development." They wrote about the steps needed to walk an African–American social service client through the process of becoming a member of The Salvation Army. They quoted General Arnold Brown, once the Salvation Army's international leader, who said, "For the Salvationist, social work is never an alternative to the Gospel, rather, an expression of it." The holistic ministry at the Detroit Harding Corps, where the Mathews served as corps officers, resulted in several ARC men becoming members of the corps. While receiving treatment for substance abuse, many had made the corps their home of worship and spiritual renewal.

The Mathews also focused on youth ministry. They formed the Youth Enrichment Institute (YEI), a program designed to help area high school students develop life skills. For children aged 5 to 13, the corps instituted an after–school program. Through the program, children improved their academic and Bible study habits, developed literacy skills, and enjoyed recreational outlets. The Mathews used basketball tournaments, which drew as many as 500 residents and participants, to attract neighborhood youth. The YEI and after–school programs served nearly 450 youth. Emergency food and utility programs helped 150 families.[241]

In the Eastern Territory in 1993, Auxiliary Captains David and Betty Pate launched the New Hope Recovery Corps (Church) in Albany, N.Y. David had been a "good Southern Baptist boy from Florida" when he met Betty Turner, 12. She knew instantly that one day she would

Captains Betty and David Pate

marry the charismatic young man with an infectious laugh. But after getting married and moving to Manhattan, David got involved in socializing with so–called "friends" who were drinking. Soon, he slipped into an alcohol addiction that lasted 10 years. During that time, Betty, who had given her life to Christ at age 8 and who later earned a doctorate in theology, spent many hours on her knees praying and relying on her supportive Christian family. Now, after 32 years of marriage, in their 50s, and as officers in The Salvation Army, their sights were set on ministering to men and women with substance–abuse problems. Their dream was that the New Hope Recovery Church would provide a way for them to minister to whole families, not just individual recovering addicts.

The Army's Adult Rehabilitation Center in Albany had been the place where David had found help, but it was available to men only. "What about the women?" asked Betty. "The way I saw it was, there had to be a fellowship that would include women and their children." Before New Hope opened its doors, the Pates had a group of 60 people [families of addicts] coming to a drop–in center to receive peer counseling. At a corps planter seminar held at Territorial Headquarters, David Pate presented a brief talk on "catching the vision." He revealed how, by using a choir as a vehicle, he and Betty had developed a rapport with Albany's African–American community that resulted in significant growth. In just three weeks, the corps sprouted to 115 members. Pate recommended that the seminar delegates catch the vision: "Find the vehicle God has for you and ride it!"[242]

Ministry Milestones (1990–1998)

In 1990 Lt. Colonels David and Doreen Edwards return to the Caribbean Territory with the rank of colonel to become the first nationals appointed as its leaders in the Army's history, breaking longstanding color and national barriers.

~

The Majors Wiltshire return to the USA from Panama to serve in the Massachusetts Division, Allan as divisional secretary and Marjorie as assistant Home League secretary at the Boston headquarters. She is also appointed as the Eastern Territory's first social issues secretary.

~

Mrs. Brigadier Latrude Wilson is promoted to Glory in July 1990.

~

Sr. Major Pearl Hurdle, is promoted to Glory. She is remembered for being a great open–air campaigner, and cornet and triangle player, and for extending the Lord's Kingdom in many ways. Her congregations had loved her because she was dedicated to serving and loving people.

~

In the Southern Territory, Captains Onal and Edmane Castro transfer from Haiti to command the Maimi Edison Corps and Community Center in the Florida Division. While serving in that corps, they start a gym program and soccer team, which brings many young people and their parents to the corps. In July, Majors Metelus and Adeline Charles, another Haitian couple, take over leadership of the corps.[243]

~

In October 1992, the Army transfers Colonels Franklyn and Joan Thompson to the United States to serve as assistant chief secretary and assistant territorial Women's Auxiliary secretary in the Eastern Territory. The Caribbean–born officers had just finished two–year appointments as assistant chief secretary and territorial Outer Circle Home League secretary in the Australia East and Papua New Guinea Territory. Prior to those appointments, Colonel Franklyn had served as field secretary and as chief secretary for the Caribbean Territory, responsible for Army administration in Antigua, the Bahamas, Barbados, Belize, Cuba, Grenada, Guyana, French Guiana, Haiti, Jamaica, Trinidad and Tobago, Surinam, St. Vincent, and St. Lucia. Colonel Joan served as Territorial

Home League secretary. Franklyn, who was born in Nassau, the Bahamas, had become a Christian in 1955 and joined The Salvation Army a year later. He was commissioned in August 1958. Joan entered training from Speighstown, St. Peter, in Barbados and was commissioned in 1965. She served in Dunsville in St. Ann and the Havendale Corps in Kingston, Jamaica before marrying Franklyn in June 1966.[244]

~

In the Eastern Territory in 1992, Harlem Temple celebrates its centennial with the theme, "A Cherished Past, A Challenging Future." An estimated 300 people attend the weekend event. Members of the corps and divisional leaders in full Army uniform parade down Lenox Avenue (Malcolm X Boulevard) marching, singing, and playing band music "to the glory of God." Major Timothy Thomas, corps officer; Lt. Colonel Raymond L. and Mary Wood, divisional leaders; and Commissioner Orval Taylor led the march that drew the attention of Harlem residents.

As part of the celebration, the corps honors six of its most faithful soldiers: Mary Nicholas Blackmore, Clarence Matthews, Mildred Christian, Inez Henry, Madeline Edgehill, and Lucille J. Austin. Major Thomas presents them with plaques and says, "I want to thank each of you for your dedication and your love for God in His service." The Honorable Percy Sutton, former Manhattan borough president, chair of the Apollo Theater Investment Group, and friend of the Army, brings greetings from New York City Mayor David N. Dinkins and Congressman Charles B. Rangel. Major Abraham Johnson, former corps officer of 17 years, gives a dedicatory prayer.

The corps had begun in 1892 as "New York Eight" in Greenwich Village. Its relocation to midtown's West Side and then to 138th Street in the heart of Harlem, reflected the migration of the black community in New York City.[245]

~

In the Western Territory, Captains Victor and Rose-Marie Leslie become the first persons of African descent to be appointed to a divisional headquarters in that territory.

~

In 1993, Lt. Colonels Israel L. and Eva D. Gaither are appointed to Territorial Headquarters in the USA East. Lt. Colonel Israel Gaither becomes field secretary for personnel and Lt. Colonel Eva is appointed as territorial League of Mercy secretary. Prior to these appointments, the Gaithers had served as Southern New England and Western Pennsylvania divisional leaders.

Also in the Central Territory, Lieutenants Lonneal and Patty Richardson receive the "Nonprofit Minority Leadership Achievement Award" in 1994 for "outstanding nonprofit leadership in the city of Grand Rapids." Four years later in the city of Detroit, the Richardsons receive the "Spirit of Detroit Award" for "recognition of excellent achievement, outstanding leadership, and dedication to improving the quality of life for the citizens of Detroit."[246]

In the Southern Territory, Major Grace Cumberbatch attends the International College of Officers in London, England. Upon her return, she transfers to Territorial Headquarters to assume the position of administrative assistant for the secretary for personnel. Prior to this, she had served, among other administrative positions, as divisional secretary for the Georgia Division.[247]

The Army's ministry in Long Island rode the wave of Haitian immigrants into the United States. On October 30, the Army's Haitian outpost in Westbury becomes the first Haitian corps in the USA Eastern Territory. Lt. Colonel Raymond L. Wood, divisional commander, put a Haitian couple, Brother Luxene and Sister Islande Claircius, in charge. "Make the word of God the centerpiece of all that you do," Wood says at the dedication ceremony as the Army and American flags wave above his head. "And preach the word of God with certainty and great confidence."

As Wood speaks, the Clairciuses stand at his right side holding their Bibles. Captain Yvon Alkintor, who serves as translator during the bilingual service, stands to Wood's left. Alkintor, commanding officer of the Bedford Temple Corps in Brooklyn and coordinator of the Westbury Haitian Community Project, reflects on how Westbury had been but a dream back in 1989 after he had resumed his officership (he was subjected to the Army's ruling on officers immigrating to the United States from the Third World) and taken command of the Bushwick Corps.

The new Westbury Corps, which occupies part of the second floor of a small office building on Urban Avenue, holds

50 people. "This is the headquarters for Haitians on Long Island," says Alkintor. "The Salvation Army is very strong in Haiti ... we're looking forward to getting membership."

Nine months later, Alkintor's words proved prophetic; the corps moved to a larger building on Maple Avenue to accommodate the growing church. Between 1994 and 1997, it was the fastest–growing corps in the Eastern Territory.[248]

~

In 1994, Nelson Mandela, a black African attorney and freedom fighter, is elected president of South Africa. This event sends ripples of racial reconciliation throughout the world and will eventually have a profound effect on race relations in the U.S. Salvation Army.

~

In February of 1994, the Colonels Franklyn and Joan Thompson become Northeast Ohio divisional leaders. During their tenure, they help improve the management of social workers by corps officers. They also help improve ministries in Greater Cleveland and in some 40 corps community centers throughout the division. They study for two years at the Alliance Theological Seminary in Nyack, N.Y., and travel overseas to tour the Holy Land as a way of enhancing their own spiritual understanding and ministry effectiveness. In May of the following year, the Thompsons return to the Caribbean Territory to serve as territorial leaders. But this appointment would not be the end of their officer service in the United States.[249]

Franklyn and Joan Thompson

~

Lt. Colonel Israel Gaither is named chair of the National Cross–Cultural Task Force. This appointment puts racial issues on the Army's national ministry agenda. He also serves on numerous other national and territorial commissions. In 1997, he appears in *Emerge,* a magazine for the upwardly mobile African–American community. His snapshot and caption announce that he is the first African American and youngest officer to serve as a territory's chief secretary (second in command) in the Salvation Army's history.[250] Rarely had promotions within the Army received such attention in the secular world.

~

That same year, Colonel David Edwards, the Caribbean territorial commander, participates in a series of discussions among international Army leaders in Hong Kong on another important topic relevant to the Army's global ministry. These discussions would give birth to the Spiritual Life Commission, which was later held at the International Conference of Leaders (ICL) in Melbourne, Australia. The focus of the discussions was the Army's position on the sacraments. Edwards later wrote, "We felt that a thorough study of the issues involved was necessary. We felt that any decisions taken should be as a result of theological considerations and not for pragmatic reasons." When the ICL took place three years later in 1998, Edwards was there as the USA Western Territory leader. After the meetings, he returned, not to his office in USA West, but to the Georgetown, Guyana, Citadel Corps to pay tribute to his Aunt Dora, the woman who led him to Christ. "She was the first person my wife and I thought of, following the announcement of my appointment to the USA Western Territory," he wrote. "[My brother Douglas and I] were twice blessed. We knew the unconditional love of a mother and our Auntie Shaw. The only difference was that while my mother might have had reason to love us, not so my aunt. Hers was a love without reason. Here were two boys she made her own when she did not have to."

Edwards returned to the USA Western Territory, reaffirmed in his resolve to serve the Lord Jesus and The Salvation Army. When Commissioner Robert A. Watson, a former national commander, installed the Edwardses as Western territorial leaders on July 1, 1997, they become the first Salvationists of African descent to lead a territory in the United States. The ceremony was well attended; many wanted to get to know the West's new commander and president of Women's Organizations. Those attending the ceremony met two people many later described in the territory's newspaper *New Frontier* as "intelligent, well–read, contemporary people, who were excellent communicators, able to relate effectively, in touch with the tempo of the times, with an engaging sense of humor, a deep passion for souls, and with strong commitments and devotion to God and the Army...." At his installation, Edwards says in his deep, booming voice, "God calls us all to serve Him and to live our lives in service to others." Pointing to the newly arrived cadet session named the "Faithful Intercessors," he continues, "God has not stopped calling young people to be officers of The Salvation Army. He does not call all, but he does call some. If God calls, make yourself available."[251]

In the Eastern Territory in 1996, Cadets John and C. Anita Stewart graduate from the School of Officer Training not as lieutenants, but as captains. This is only the second time in the territory's history that cadets had graduated as captains; the exception came because a regulation stated that promotion was based on the service of the spouse who served the longest. In this case, it was Anita's previous appointment as captain that necessitated the ruling. Their first appointment together is as corps officers of the Atlantic City, N.J., Corps.

John and C. Anita Stewart

They had been attending the School for Officer Training as members of the "Messengers of the Truth" session. John, who was born and raised in Hartford, Conn., had overcome many years of drug and alcohol addiction, thanks to the Army's Adult Rehabilitation Center in Springfield, Mass.[252] Stewart, the son of the first black to head a fire department in New England, felt a spiritual fire burning in his bones. He realized it was God's call to officership in The Salvation Army and entered training in 1994. As a single officer, Anita Turlington had already gone through training and had attained the rank of captain before she married John. Youth ministry had been her passion, and she looked forward to continuing her work with young people in future appointments. But while her husband was in training, she was appointed at Territorial Headquarters. In 1996, during the PowerPoint Word and Witness Congress in Niagara Falls, N.Y., as many as 5,000 people, including General Paul A. Rader, world leader of The Salvation Army, witnessed Commissioner Ronald G. Irwin, territorial commander, commission the Stewarts as captains.[253]

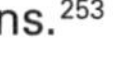

In 1996 in the USA Western Territory, Major Victor Leslie is appointed divisional secretary for the Intermountain Division. He had recently returned from the Brengle Holiness Institute. Major Rose–Marie Leslie, is appointed as the divisional

Women's Ministries secretary for the Intermountain Division. Just two years earlier, Victor, who had been a banker before becoming an officer, had served as divisional finance secretary for the Northern California Division, overseeing 70 corps. At that same time, Major Rose Marie had expanded her duties as League of Mercy/Silver Star/Medical Fellowship secretary by using her training as a registered nurse to provide hospice care in the San Francisco Bay area.[254]

In the USA East, Major Maurice "Eddie" Smith receives a citation from the mayor of the City of New Rochelle, N.Y., for outstanding achievement and an award from the Inter–Religious Council of New Rochelle.[255]

In October of 1996, Salvation Army General Paul A. Rader visits South Africa and participates in the nation's "Day of Reconciliation" by launching the signing by Salvationists of a special Book of Reconciliation. The following year, the international Salvation Army publicly acknowledges its failure to "stand up and be counted" during the years of apartheid and states its commitment to develop programs and policies to "combat racism and strengthen what reconciliation has already taken place while aggressively partaking in our mission to reach the world for Jesus Christ."[256]

Captain E. Lewanne Dudley, the assistant Eastern territorial youth secretary, publishes her testimony of reconciliation, "Blessing Overcomes Insult," in the *War Cry* magazine. Dudley, who had grown up in a predominantly white suburb of Poughkeepsie, N.Y., attended a black Baptist church before becoming a Salvationist. As she grew older, she became firm in her belief that God had given her the same confidence to endure racial persecution as He had given her ancestors. "Throughout my school days," Dudley wrote, "I had an inner confidence only God could give. I am sure that it was God's steadfast love sustaining me. The same God who gave my ancestors the strength to endure great persecution and prejudice helps me handle negative situations that come my way."[257]

Within the next two years, at least four black officers attend the International College of Officers (ICO). In 1997, Major Victor Leslie from the Western Territory is appointed to attend

ICO; then in 1998, Captain E. Lewanne Dudley and Captain William Edmonds from the USA Eastern Territory attend. At the time, Edmonds was serving as assistant director of Cross–Cultural programs and was the home officer at the School for Officer Training. Major Lonneal Richardson from the Central Territory, who also attends ICO in 1998, is elected vice president of his session.

For Dudley, ICO is an eye–opening experience. It reminds her of her trip to South Africa in 1997, where she received her first exposure to global issues.

To qualify as an ICO delegate, an officer must be nominated by his or her territory and accepted by the ICO principal and international secretary. The recommendation is then proposed to the Chief of the Staff, who is second in command of The Salvation Army worldwide. The Chief then evaluates each candidate's proposal based on the criteria of spiritual maturity, desire to grow in holiness, ministry and leadership potential, potential for development, and other relevant considerations.

E. Lewanne Dudley stands before a sculpture of William Booth at the ICO

ICO gives Dudley a clearer picture of the Army's global ministry. One day, as she stands in front of The Salvation Army museum in Nottingham, England, before a statue of Founder William Booth, she realizes that she must stand for change. "First, I am willing to *be* changed," she said later, "to allow God's Holy Spirit to work through me. As others see that transformation in me, I believe change will catch on, like a fire, as people sense the Army's greater mission."

When Dudley steps into Coventry Cathedral and learns of its history, she sees the light of reconciliation. Years ago, at the end of WW2, young people from Germany had joined with British youth to rebuild the cathedral, which had been bombed by German warplanes. Dudley walks up to the wood altar and reads from the stone wall behind it the words of Jesus, who had said on the cross, "Father, forgive them, for they know not what they do." Dudley shares her thoughts about Coventry with her ICO delegate colleagues Captain Daniel J. Raj of India and Captain Beslom Hanunka from the Zambia and Malawi Territory.[258]

Conrad Watson, the Adult Rehabilitation Centers Command's (ARCC) director for program in the USA Western Territory, is among a group of officials who accept the Army's "Program Excellence and Achievement" award for the San Diego ARC at its national social service conference. The ARC is the first in the nation to create a six–month residential program, the first to add transitional housing, the first to implement an effective re–entry program, and among the first to add a women's rehabilitation component. The center emphasizes counseling and has a professional, well–trained staff under the direction of Dr. Ed Lataille, rehabilitation services director.

In the Central Territory, Captain Janet Love, multi–cultural ministries director, attends the territory's Youth and Leadership Councils. Approximately 140 officers, soldiers, and employees offer proposals that suggest ways the territory can more effectively minister in a multicultural society. They discuss recruitment strategies, how to translate Army literature into other languages to reach non–English speaking communities with the Gospel, as well as evangelism and leadership development. Love and the Cross–Cultural Ministries Department take the recommendations to heart and work to implement them throughout the territory.

That same year, Colonels Franklyn and Joan Thompson return to the United States from the Caribbean Territory to command the Army's Eastern Michigan Division in Detroit, with Colonel Franklyn serving as divisional commander and Colonel Joan serving as director of Women's Organizations. Among other projects, they initiate the Metropolitan Division's African Heritage Praise & Celebration Weekend in Chicago. The celebration includes prayer meetings, seminars, Bible studies, and a Gospel festival. "Crowns of grace are prepared for us so we could all be children of God," said Colonel Franklyn in his sermon. A united male choir sang "Ordering Our Steps in the Word." The Chicago Temple Choir sang "Christ is All" and "Perfect Praise" as men and women assembled at the foot of the cross in prayer, giving praise to God.

CADETS DENNIS YOUNG
& PATRICIA LOCH
SCHOOL FOR OFFICER
TRAINING

Chapter 17

"A warrior people"

Advocating reconciliation, locally and globally

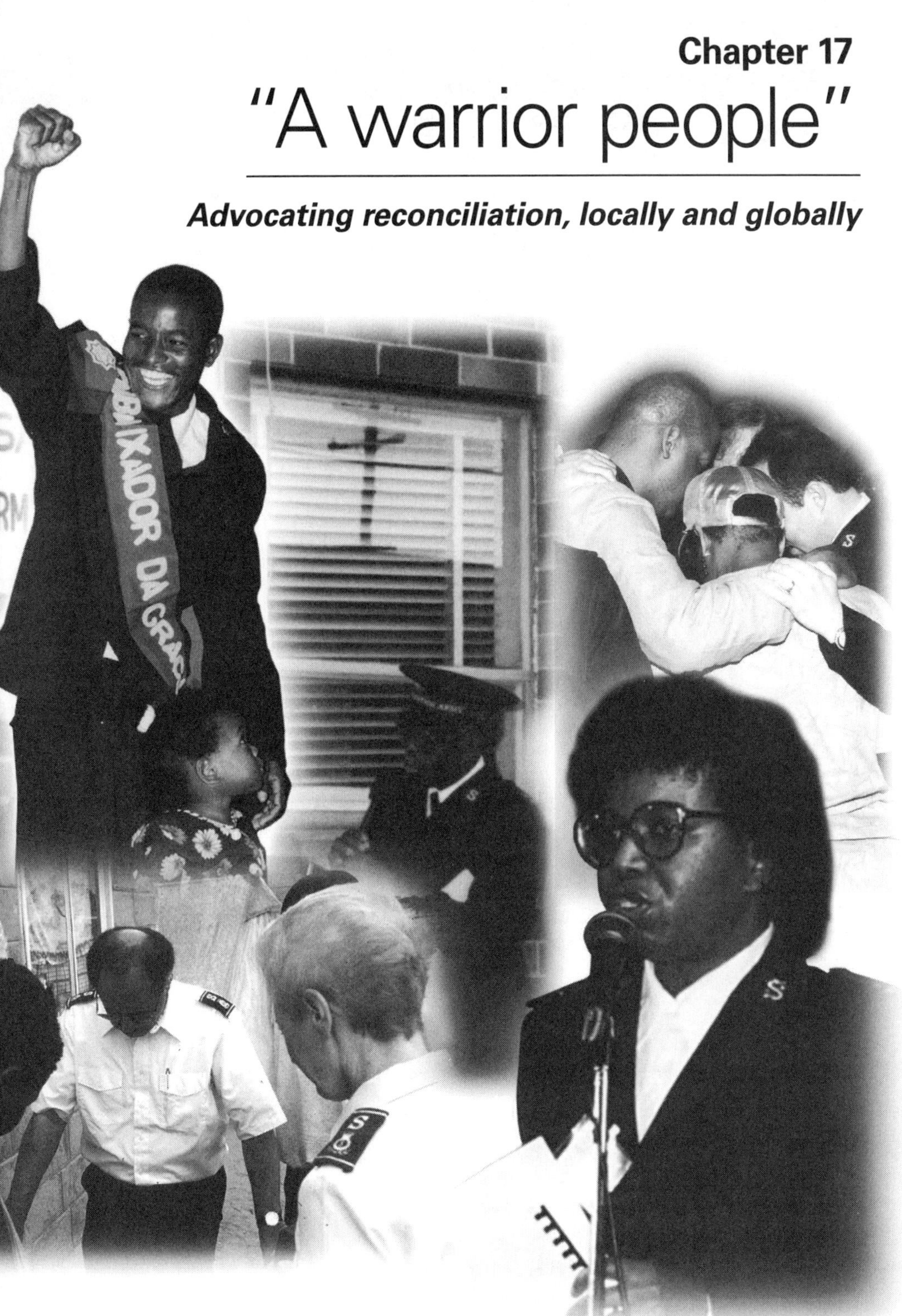

In the Eastern Territory, Salvationists gathered for an African Heritage Leader Development Symposium in October of 1997. Major Abraham Johnson shared his personal testimony and vision for the future of race relations in The Salvation Army. "Things can change for the better, even though they take time," he said. "We in the Eastern Territory are in the midst of change. I can see it and feel it and I am blessed and thrilled to be a part of the coming change in our Army's leadership's attitude." Johnson also shared his Six–Point Vision: 1. More officers of African descent commissioned with a variety of academic degrees; 2. Officers of African descent who will become better educated about the black experience in the midst of change; 3. Officers and lay Salvationists of African descent on major decision boards; 4. Advisory boards, corps planning boards, and advisory councils that reflect a diversity of cultures and expressions; 5. A time when officers of African descent will be appointed to corps other than inner–city corps, with Anglo officers appointed to corps that are populated predominantly by people of color; and 6. A time when ethnic names for corps will cease.

Abraham Johnson speaks at a symposium

In an oratory style reminiscent of Dr. Martin Luther King, Jr., Johnson said prophetically,

> I see Salvationists of color support each other through the ministry of the Army, regardless of their origin. I see the day coming when it will not be unusual to have colonels, commissioners, and international leaders as men and women of color coming from our territory. I also see the day when we as people of color will not have to explain that The Salvation Army is a church, a

> spiritual movement, living and teaching holiness. I further foresee the day when the black church will recognize our Salvation Army officers, both men and women, as ministers of the Gospel, desiring to accept us as part of the vital ministry of any mainline city or town.[259]

Praying for a valiant soldier

As Johnson spoke that night at a resort in the Pocono Mountains, one officer who sat in the audience may have been concerned about whether he would live to see that day come. Major George Evans felt something was physically wrong with him. Soon doctors diagnosed him as having a rare form of stomach cancer. They predicted he wouldn't live much longer. Evans underwent three surgeries. Many officers, both black and white, came to his side and comforted him. Majors Phil R. and Karen K. Satterlee, Majors Harold and Karen Gulley, and Evans's wife, Major Carmen Evans, were there the day Colonel W. Todd Bassett leaned over and said, "George, we're starting the prayer line again."

The ailing Evans heard the message but slipped into unconsciousness before he could answer. During those dark days, he nearly died twice, but the operations proved successful, and the cancer went into remission. Evans, although physically weak, found strength by reading Scriptures such as Jeremiah 17:14: "Heal me oh Lord, and I shall be healed" and Jeremiah 17:16: "As for me, I have not hastened to be a pastor to follow thee."; Exodus 15:26 also motivated Evans. "I am the Lord the healer, for I will restore health unto thee and I'll heal thee of thy wounds." Family, friends, and other officers showered him with many prayers and letters. These expressions of love encouraged him to continue his pastoral ministry.[260]

Ambassadors of reconciliation

Colonels Israel L. and Eva D. Gaither faced a different kind of challenge. General Rader, who had recently publicly admitted the Army's failure to "stand up and be counted" during the years of apartheid in South Africa, made another historic move in appointing the Gaithers as leaders of the Southern Africa Territory. The appointment of this interracial couple could not have happened there before the presidency of Nelson Mandela. The political climate had changed radically since apartheid ended, and the appointment of the Gaithers signaled to the world that the Army would now stand strong on racial equality.

The Gaithers with Nelson Mandela

Breaking racial barriers was nothing new for the Gaithers, who had opened the door for other interracial couples to step into Salvation Army training schools in the United States. Yet this appointment, the Gaithers knew, would be daunting.

Colonel Israel Gaither later said, "Following the initial shock on receiving word of the appointment, I experienced an overwhelming feeling of inadequacy. It was at that point, as it has happened on previous occasions when we have received our 'farewell orders,' we again gave ourselves to the Lord in renewal of our covenant and commitment." Colonel Eva Gaither described her conflicting emotions: "I am anticipating, with great excitement, the opportunities for ministries which will be mine; and yet, I cannot help but have feelings of sadness over leaving family and friends in this great territory." She also expressed her confidence in God's word. "I will enter my new responsibilities confidently believing that the same God who has equipped me in the past will continue to be with me in the future."

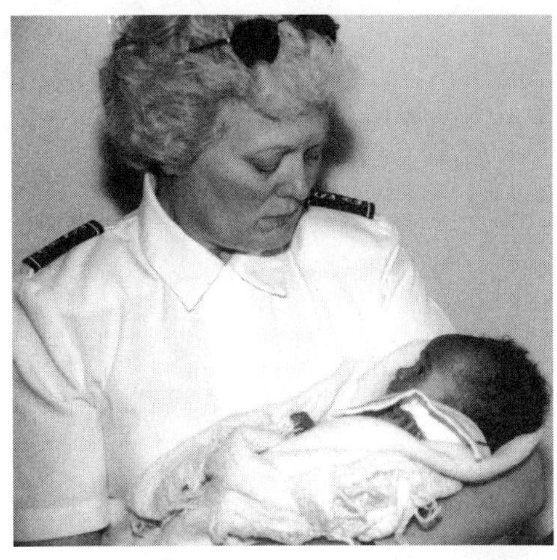

Eva Gaither holds a HIV/AIDS baby at Etembeni, a Salvation Army home for orphaned children in Johannesburg.

Commissioner Eva took strength from the book of Jeremiah, as Major George Evans had. "'For I know the plans I have for you, declares the Lord, plans to give you hope and a future.'" Eva Gaither added, "And I believe it!" (29:11).

"I will be candid with you," said Israel Gaither to hundreds of soldiers and officers at his farewell service in New York City. "We prefer not to leave. We haven't finished our work. But we have to yield to the will of the Lord. We cannot deny that this is what He would have us do." During Gaither's farewell address, he did not allow soldiers and officers to believe reconciliation was something necessary only in post–apartheid South Africa. He called on the USA Eastern Territory to continue its own movement toward racial healing. "You must not allow forward movement to become strangled! I call on you to come together in unity and in love. Let reconciliation really happen in this territory!" It was clear Gaither's message resonated with many Salvationists facing their own struggles. People came forward in a steady stream to the mercy seat.

The Gaithers, in obeying the call to go to South Africa, set an example of what it means to, as a Salvation Army song says, "Go in the strength of the Lord." They prepared themselves to enter a land of rich diversity, where people had come from a variety of ethnic backgrounds, including Zulu, Bantu, Xhosa, and Afrikaner. The Afrikaners were white descendants of Dutch, German, and French settlers. The Gaithers would soon learn that in the Southern African Territory, which includes the nations of South Africa, Mozambique, Lesotho, St. Helena, and Swaziland, the Gospel is preached in 11 languages. Israel, serving as the

Army's first American–born black territorial commander, said, "Day by day we are being confirmed and affirmed that this is what the Lord wants us to do."[261]

On Oct. 29, 1998, Bishop Desmond Tutu's Truth and Reconciliation Commission presented its report to President Nelson Mandela. The report was the result of nearly three years of exhaustive investigation. The wave of racial reconciliation that resulted rippled across the ocean and crashed against U.S. shores. Salvationists began writing letters to their corps, divisional, territorial, and national leaders asking the Army to initiate a day of reconciliation in the United States. In July, at the Builders of the Kingdom session commissioning ceremonies, Commissioner Ronald G. Irwin, USA Eastern territorial commander, called for every Salvationist in the territory to repent of the sin of racism. The "Journey of Hope" program followed a two–day multicultural conference. Commissioner Irwin said the timing was especially fitting because of "our long record of organizational and personal prejudice; our overt and subtle discrimination against other cultures and races, and particularly against people of color; our penchant for stereotyping, for making sweeping generalizations, for making judgments about people of other races and cultures; our ready tendency to give glib lip service to equality for all people and love for one another while harboring hatred in our hearts—all of this is shameful, a disgrace which cannot be tolerated, for it is blatantly unchristian, an embarrassment to God, and grieves the Holy Spirit!"

Commissioner Ronald G. Irwin

Irwin concluded, "And so I call upon Salvationists to join me in repentance, that we might be reconciled to God and to each other in Christian love so that our Army can be sacrificially involved in the creation of a world free of racism and strife, making our Army an example of a communion of spirits in which such barriers no longer exist."

Some Salvationists thought Irwin had overreacted, gone too far in his statements. Others applauded him and said he had hit the mark. In any event, Lt. Colonel R. William Hunter, then secretary for program for the East, said "'Journey in Hope'" was "the beginning, not the destination." Many actions arose out of the evening program and the multicultural conference. For instance, the territorial commander introduced intentional steps designed to confront and correct racism and encourage reconciliation and unity among Salvationists. "Our 'Journey in Hope,' " Hunter said, "... has begun with a single step. We affirm that it is a journey that will not end with that single step."[262]

To keep the journey going, Hunter engaged Dr. Glandion W. Carney, a noted African–American writer and spiritual formation expert, to help develop pilot reconciliation programs for Salvation Army officers and employees. He focused his work on the USA Eastern Territory's Eastern Pennsylvania and Delaware Division.

Black Salvationists: descendants of 'a warrior people'

That year the USA Eastern Territory produced a video entitled "Soldiers of Uncommon Valor," which highlighted the contributions of people of African descent in The Salvation Army. Narrated by Colonel Israel L. Gaither, chief secretary when the documentary was filmed, the 30–minute video recounted, in words and in pictures, more than 100 years of Army work in the African–American community. In addition to displaying images and accomplishments of the past, the video also portrayed the Army as an organization in which, as the script read, "the spectre of racism which caused so much personal sorrow and distress to our beloved Army is a vanishing nightmare," and in which "candidates for officership who are of African descent are welcome and urgently needed."

Shot in studios and on location, the story of Army soldiers and officers of African descent as a "warrior people" drew a connection between ancestral heritage, rooted in the world's earliest civilizations, and the potential for officer candidates of African heritage to achieve significant progress in modern times. "In our veins flows the blood of kings and priests, of saints and martyrs, of great people and humble people," said Gaither.

The project was a joint venture of the Community Relations and Development Department, headed by Major Carl L. Schoch, a white officer; the Cross–Cultural Ministries Department, led by Major Allan Wiltshire; and Jeffrey Schultz, director of the Media Ministries Bureau, who is white. Wiltshire said of the project, "I share in the excitement and anticipation of seeing the involvement and contributions of Salvationists of African descent affirmed and documented. These valiant soldiers have been faithful to their God and the Army down through the years. We can all benefit from their example in godliness, purposeful living, and tenacity in spite of insurmountable odds."[263]

The Eastern Territory also held its first multicultural conference for Salvationists of Korean, Hispanic, African, and European descent (not to be confused with previous symposiums, which had been for only people of African descent) featuring guest speaker Commissioner Earle A. Maxwell, Chief of the Staff (second in command) of the worldwide Salvation Army.

In the USA Western Territory, Commissioner David Edwards, territorial commander, was busy with efforts designed to move reconciliation forward. In April, he spoke in Melbourne, Australia, at the International Conference of Leaders on cross–culturalism and the future of the races. "Recent immigration statistics from around the world indicate that as the movement of people and shifts in population continue, [all parts of the] the world [are] becoming increasingly multicultural. Much of that movement is from the developing world to the developed," he said. "This blending of people, however, does not automatically mean that the realization of the vision of the Kingdom lies within our grasp. The fact that people for whom I have had little value or respect while they lived halfway across the world have come to live across the street from me in no way suggests that I am prepared to value and respect them any more than I did before. As society intermarries, it will gravitate toward a variegated mix of white, black, and brown, and the 20st century will have gone the way of the horse and buggy. When this occurs, the words *black*, *yellow*, and *brown* will be relegated to the trash can of bigoted history."[264] Later in October, Edwards held a Youth Forum in California to discuss cross–cultural unity.

Major George Evans continued to respond to God's call, despite an ongoing battle with cancer. He participated in the Eastern Pennsylvania and Delaware Division's online prayer initiative. He said, "God is the nearest and dearest part of my life ... When I am at my lowest, I need a source of strength that is beyond who I am. That is when God lifts me up and helps me stand." He made his final public appearance at the territory's first Men Officers' Conference held in May 1999 in Hershey, Pa. Dressed in casual clothing, 600 officers of various races, cultures, and ages assembled for several days, on a first–name basis, to celebrate their common identity as brothers in Christ.

The spiritual embers they had been fanning were now ready to ignite among these men. All the praise meetings, messages, Bible studies, and times of fellowship had set the stage for one remarkable moment when there was nothing else left to do but just be. The breakthrough came as Evans, who had struggled many months with his illness, stepped up to the platform. Speaking simply and from his heart, Evans delivered a moving testimony describing how God had healed him from a condition that, from all accounts, appeared hopeless. When he looked to the audience and said, "I am a living miracle this morning," tears filled his eyes, his voice broke, and every man in the "Red Room"—be he black, white, and brown—stood together and praised God in a loud voice. They were ready to enter into His presence.

Colonel W. Todd Bassett, chief secretary for the USA Eastern Territory, asked each man to search his heart and reflect on what he hoped to take home from the conference. The request opened the floodgates of response that led to men praying together, one–on–one and in small groups, and worshipping the Lord. The outpouring of love and camaraderie was, by all accounts, so amazing that the officers, many of whom had worried about leaving their appointments for a week, now wished the experience could last just a little bit longer. "I am extremely excited!" Evans said later. "In my 32 years as an officer, this is the first time there has been a men officers' conference and I have been overwhelmed [to see it]."[265]

At another officers' summit designed for both men and women, an outpouring of love and support became evident toward the Gaithers, still serving in South Africa. They had arrived in that country at a time of great political and economic uncertainty. The problems were massive. There was high unemployment among blacks, and white business owners and managers, who feared retaliation from blacks, were abandoning their homes and businesses and fleeing to Europe, Canada, the United States, and other African nations. At the same time, black immigrants from poor neighboring countries were arriving in large numbers, seeking jobs, which exacerbated the unemployment problem. There was a high crime rate in urban areas, where the middle class, which could have acted as a buffer between the exceptionally rich and the destitute, was virtually nonexistent. And the world seemed to expect from the country's new leadership a fast reversal of the effects of 40 years of apartheid.

Although the Gaithers had served through the 60s revolution in the United States, they could not have imagined the degree of poverty experienced by millions of blacks living in pathetic townships located just outside South Africa's opulent cities. "It was not so much a surprise as a shock!" said Colonel Eva Gaither. "And we both agree that the initial response to seeing wealth and poverty in such close proximity saddened and, frankly, even angered us." Colonel Israel Gaither said, "We have never seen people—officers included—living in such desperately poor conditions. But from such communities of the poor, we could drive for less than an hour and be in the world of the middle class or the well–to–do. It's taught us something about stewarding material resources."

At the Officers' Summit back home in the USA Eastern Territory, Major Carl Schoch, Development Department director and a friend of the Gaithers, went to the platform and made a passionate appeal to the officers to support needy families in the Southern Africa Territory; he requested a donation of $3,000. To his surprise, the officers contributed $14,000 on the spot. When the Gaithers received notice of the gift, they were standing in an office, alone, and tears welled up in their eyes. They were overwhelmed to think that all of these officers, so far away in the USA Eastern Territory, would care so much about the ministry in that part of the world, where officers have so little disposable income. The Gaithers offered a prayer of thanksgiving and asked God to bless the officers for their generosity and faith.

As the Gaithers continued their ministry in Southern Africa, they effectively built a bridge of hope that reached all the way back to the United States. Many USA officers and volunteers, both black and white, crossed that bridge. They offered their time, expertise, labor, and love of Christ. And those who could not make the journey offered financial support. Divisional commanders in the USA

Eastern Territory funded a mission team through a small annual donation. Funds also helped expand the Feet First Initiative, a youth–based outreach program launched during the 1999 All–Africa Games. As many as 1,700 young converts for Christ came forward through the ministry of Salvationist young people. Funds from the United States were used to purchase new Army flags and drums to replace old, worn ones. At a congress, the wind lifted 38 new flags to the warm African sun. The sight inspired the 700 Salvationist witnesses, Gaither later said in an open letter to Salvationists in the United States.[266]

In May of that year, another development concerning the Gaithers occurred. As a territorial leader, Israel Gaither became the first African–American officer to sit on the High Council, the international group of Army leaders who choose the next General. At that High Council, Gaither also became the first African American and youngest officer ever to be nominated for General. This development sent ripples throughout the Army world. Colonel Eva Gaither, still in South Africa, was flown to London to engage in the Council proceedings; at that time, wives of territorial leaders did not automatically attend, but the Council interviewed nominees' wives. Commissioner Helen Clifton, wife of Commissioner Shaw Clifton, another nominee, was also flown in to London from Pakistan to join her husband.

Despite the High Council's strong backing, Gaither withdrew his name from nomination that year, and the Council elected Commissioner John Larsson as General. The Gaithers returned to Southern Africa to complete their appointments as territorial leaders.

The goal–oriented Gaithers had set their sights on rebuilding the Army in that part of the world. Their "Mission 2005" initiative, which addressed the topics of leadership, evangelism, discipleship, stewardship, and expansion, would become the foundation upon which the rebuilding would take place. They hoped to double the number of corps in the territory to 300 and train and prepare 250 corps planters. The Gaithers pressed forward, using their skills as fund–raisers and program initiators. Colonel Israel Gaither also preached the Gospel at many corps and divisional meetings throughout the territory. Eva spread her influence by supporting the HIV/AIDS babies of Ethembeni, a home for abandoned children. She loved the African worship meetings and joined in and spread the love of Christ through dance, word, and song. Eva also started many family health programs that helped build her reputation as a sensitive, warm, caring, and inspirational leader.[267]

Ministry Milestones (1998–2001)

In 1998 Commissioner David Edwards releases Majors Victor and Rose–Marie Leslie to serve in territorial appointments in the Caribbean Territory.[268]

Majors Clifford and Edna Yearwood retire that same year. At a ceremony at Harlem Temple, Commissioners David and Doreen Edwards, Western Territory leaders, present retirement certificates to the Yearwoods and recognize them for a combined total of 77 years of service "to God and The Salvation Army." During the ceremony, Commissioner David Edwards echoes the sentiments of people who had traveled from all over the United States, Central America, the Caribbean, and England to attend the retirement ceremony for these Caribbean–born officers; Clifford from Panama, Edna from Jamaica. Although the Yearwoods had spent most of their careers in the Caribbean and Central America as corps and divisional leaders, they had also served for a time in the United States as corps officers at Boston (Roxbury) and Harlem Temple. During the weekend celebration, a wide variety of guests offer words of apprecia-

Clifford and Edna Yearwood (left)–

tion and musical selections, some of which were composed by Clifford Yearwood himself.

In the USA Eastern Territory, the Army's Haitian–American ministry continues to grow under Captains Luxene and Islande Claricius. Captain Luxene commences study toward a bachelor's degree in organizational management at Nyack College and Dr. Michel Christel, who had been involved in pioneering the Long Island work, goes to Spring Valley, N.Y. to launch another Haitian ministry there.

Commissioner Joe Noland, territorial commander, promotes the Johnsons to the rank of lt. colonel.

In 1999, Commissioner Joe Noland, the new USA Eastern territorial commander, promotes the Majors Abraham and Louise Johnson to lieutenant colonel. The announcement comes as a surprise to them during an annual Christmas program in New York City's Centennial Memorial Temple. Noland recognizes them for a combined total of 81 years of service as Salvation Army officers. Lt. Colonel Abraham Johnson, who later describes receiving the promotion as "exciting," reflects on the faithfulness of God by quoting 1 Thessalonians 5:24, "The one who calls you is faithful and He will do it."[269]

Majors Allan and Marjorie Wiltshire retire in a ceremony held at the USA Eastern Territory Headquarter's chapel, Railton Hall, which is crowded with friends and family. Retired Commissioner James Osborne, former national commander, conducts the ceremony and recognizes the Wiltshires for their faithfulness under fire during the U.S. invasion of Panama, where they had served as divisional leaders, and for their steadfastness while serving far from the limelight. "Your ministry may have been little–known, and your faces may not have graced the cover of *The War Cry,*" he says, "but you have proven to be [true] Salvation Army officers."

The Wiltshires acknowledge many officers for their help through the years. Major Allan Wiltshire particularly thanks "the dynamic duo," Commissioners James and Ruth Osborne, for being "genuine and caring leaders." The Wiltshire's son, Allan Jr., and daughters, Avonnie Wiltshire and Lieutenant Margaret Davis, lead the audience in "A Musical Salute to a Faithful God." Lt. Colonel Thomas Jones of National Headquarters and Major Clifford Yearwood deliver remarks representing the Wiltshires' officer colleagues. Among many other things, Yearwood jokingly recalls friendly rivalries between his and Allan's musical bands in their home country of Panama. In a more serious vein, Jones adds, "Thanks for keeping the faith ... the promises ... the flag ... and [your] family." Lieutenant Margaret Davis, paying tribute to her parents on behalf of the family, says, "Thank you for being loving parents and for staying on the high road." A special tribute by the Wiltshires' grandchildren, "Seek ye first the kingdom of God," completes the family's tribute.[270]

The Wiltshires retire. Major Maurice 'Eddie' Smith (left) holds the American flag.

Black officers in the Eastern Territory hold an African–American leadership conference, in Suffern, N.Y. Commissioner Joe Noland, territorial commander and keynote speaker, sounds a clear note of welcome during his address and acknowledges African–American Salvation Army history, dating back to the 1880s. Noland quotes Commissioner Railton who, back in the Army's early days in the United States, had articulated the Army's commitment to people of color. Among the 135 delegates attending the conference were Adult Rehabilitation Center beneficiaries, who are impressed to see so many officers of African descent committed to the Army as their church. Lt. Colonel Gilbert Reynders, program secretary, is moved by what he hears and sees at the worship service. "I didn't understand why [African Americans] needed to have this separate gathering. I now understand why," he says. One delegate who formerly resided at an Army veterans' residence in New York City announces his intention to become an officer. "I've finished my paperwork to become a soldier, [and] I want to go to officer school next year," he says.[271]

Commissioner Joe Noland speaks at the African–American leadership conference

The Gaithers meet Nelson Mandela, former president of South Africa and the man who changed the course of politics in that region. "Madiba" (the clan name that family and friends often used) welcomes the Salvation Army delegation in his office in Houghton, a Johannesburg suburb, where he receives visiting dignitaries. Security personnel and Mandela's private secretary escort Commissioners Gaither; Dr. Ivan May, national advisory board member; Captain Len Millar, territorial public relations secretary; and Major Jenny Harms, South African *War Cry* editor, into the beautifully appointed office.

Tall, gray–haired, and wearing one of his signature African print shirts, Mandela dominates the room as he rises from behind his desk. He shakes Commissioner Israel Gaither's hand firmly and immediately puts the party at ease with his graciousness. Gaither, reflecting on having seen on television Mandela's dramatic release from Robben Island in 1990 after spending 27 years as a political prisoner, says, "Watching that dramatic event unfold on the television screen, I never dreamed that God would give me the privilege of personally meeting you." Mandela's humility quickly surfaces as he makes it clear that his respect for The Salvation Army had made this meeting possible. "South Africa needs The Salvation Army," he says. For the next 30 minutes, the delegation discusses key aspects of the Army's work in South Africa and then agrees to continue contact and follow–up, particularly discussion about the Army's ongoing ministry in flood–ravaged Mozambique.[272]

Chapter 18

Recapturing the vision; restoring the passion

IN 2001, A FLOOD OF A DIFFERENT SORT THREATENED TO OVERWHELM the Army's ministry in California. Commissioners Edwards, territorial leaders, were called on to take extraordinary steps to keep the organization anchored firmly in its Christian principles and core values. The Domestic Partner debate had the potential to divide Salvationists, dominate their attention, and distract them from their primary ministry focus. The debate centered on laws demanding that social service agencies that receive government funds, such as the Army, extend benefits to domestic partners, including same–sex couples. There was no simple answer to the problem when it first arose in 1997 upon the Edwardses' arrival in the West, nor was there one now in 2001.

On the one hand, refusal to comply with the law would result in the Army's losing several million dollars in domestic program funding and attract intense criticism from gay–rights advocates, who had become a powerful force in California politics and popular culture. On the other hand, to accept the ruling and provide benefits to domestic partners would invite equally intense criticism from other Salvation Army territories and the larger evangelical

Commissioner David Edwards shares thoughts on the visioning process in Western Territory

Christian community. Edwards wrote, "It is an issue that The Salvation Army in the USA will have to resolve at some time .... This is a very divisive issue both within and without The Salvation Army. It would appear that, whichever way the Army goes on this issue, it would alienate a significant segment of our society."

As the debate unfolded, Edwards focused on the Army's mission and called for unity within the ranks. "There has been a great deal of internal debate over this issue, especially here in the Western Territory, where we have tried to make everyone aware of [its] complexity ...," wrote Edwards. "This issue has proven to be quite divisive. There are as many who hold positions on either side—and we should be quite free to do so. We can differ in our opinions about what the decision should be on this issue or any issue. But I would plead with all who read this column that we do not allow this decision to divide us in our ministry nor hinder us in the pursuit of our mission. This is God's Army. He brought it into existence for that purpose. Let us pray for Him to continue to give us the needed guidance to accomplish His holy will."

However, the Army struggled to hear the still, small voice of God over a tumultuous storm of controversy that spiraled out of control when the Western Territory, on its own, decided to "extend access to employee benefits to one legally domiciled adult." Like a category five hurricane, the debate over that decision threatened to tear the Army from its traditional roots and fling it into uncharted ethical and political territory. Phone calls and e–mail messages from high–profile individuals, as well as evangelical and pro–family organizations, flooded the Army's national and four territorial offices, urging it to reverse the decision. And, in a matter of days, the Army did. "We deeply regret the perception that the Commissioners' Conference surrendered any biblical principles in making the original decision," read an official Commissioners' Conference

Statement. "This review has resulted in the rescinding of the policy statement…."[273]

When the political storm finally spent itself, Edwards took the territory through a "visioning process," one that had never been tried before. The initiative placed responsibility on officers, soldiers, and volunteers at every level to come up with a vision for the work of the Army—"just where they are," he said. The process required a change in mindset. The command and controls that existed between Territorial Headquarters and the field gave way to an approach that was more intent on partnership. Growth took place as a result, not so much in numbers but in the maturity of the people involved, Edwards said.

Focusing on multicultural issues, Edwards, who was also known as a prayer warrior, placed emphasis throughout the territory on communicating with God and giving wide latitude to officers such as Lt. Colonels Mervyn and Shirley Morelock, territorial prayer warriors, to do the same. Edwards wrote, "Whether they be black or white, people need to be treated with respect; they need to be given opportunity; and should not be judged by the color of their skins or racial origins." On ministering to a multicultural community, he said, "[the ministry] should identify closely with people whom we serve. If the community happens to be multicultural, then its leadership and membership should reflect that multicultural disposition. While I am not one who supports a system of quotas, as I believe that we should find the best people to do the task, it does say something to people either about the organization or about the community if only one or two cultures in that multicultural environment seem to dominate in the organization rather than all of them."[274]

Ministry Milestones (2001–2002)

Major Victor Leslie returns to the U.S. from the Caribbean Territory to serve as the divisional secretary for business in the Southern California Division and is later appointed as the general secretary (second in command) in that division. The former financial secretary had earned a doctorate in Jurisprudence (law degree), an M.B.A. (management and business), an M.A. in religious studies, a B.S. in management, certificates in chemical dependency studies and planned giving, and a diploma in biblical and religious studies. Three years later, the Army appoints him as the territorial finance secretary for the USA Western Territory, making him the first person of African descent to hold that position in the United States. His wife, Rose–Marie, serves as divisional Women's Ministries secretary in the Southern California Division. Also highly educated, with a certificate in early childhood education, a B.S. in nursing (summa cum laude), a B.A. in social work, and a M.A. in human services administration, the Army later appoints her to the Western territorial headquarters as assistant Territorial Women's Ministries secretary.[275]

In 2002, General John Gowans presents retirement certificates to Commissioners David and Doreen Edwards. He commends their excellent ministry of nearly 90 years of combined service as Salvation Army officers. He praises Doreen, commending her for loving people and displaying a steadfast commitment to ministry. He acknowledges David's steady hand and courage. On a special video presentation highlighting their officer careers, the narrator says, "There is no uncertain sound in the power of their message nor in the performance of their lives. They go about their duties with great courage and dignity, without fanfare, humble in every respect. They taught us to see a vision for our Army and challenged us to actualize that vision." Major Linda Markiewicz, representing Territorial Headquarters officers, had worked with the couple both in the West and at International Headquarters. In commenting on David's strength of purpose and persistence, she refers to him as "the Darth Vader of the Western Territory."[276] Indeed he was tall, dark, and spoke with a resonance that resembled that of the infamous "Star Wars" movie villain as voiced by James Earl Jones.

Edwards, known for his humor and passion for souls, was a devoted leader and friend to many, both inside and outside The Salvation Army. He overcame the Vader stereotype by defining himself rather than allowing others to define him. He had admired both South African President Nelson Mandela and Colin Powell, retired U.S. Army General, chairman of the Joint Chiefs of Staff, and Secretary of State, for displaying this ability. "I would like to think that people looking at us, my wife and me, and our lives in years to come, will arrive at the same conclusions," Edwards wrote, "that we were people who were as proud of our origins as anyone else was of theirs; that we loved all of God's people and wanted for all of them the same things that we wanted for ourselves. We are all God's children."

Edwards once wrote that he would like to believe the Army had based all his appointments on merit, his commitment to the cause of Christ, and his successful track record—not just because of race. "While no one should be allowed to make us less the persons than God intended us to be because of our color or racial origin, neither should we allow anyone to use that as an excuse or crutch for not achieving all that we have the potential to be by God's grace." At the conclusion of their retirement service, the Edwardses thank people they had worked with through the years and say that their greatest joy came from always leaving people better for having met them.[277]

That same year, the USA Eastern Territory holds an African Heritage Leadership Cultivation Seminar at Star Lake Camp in New Jersey. "Do you know why you are here this weekend? Do you really know? Do you understand that WE WANT YOU? If you've ever needed to be wanted before, you are wanted now!" says Colonel James M. Knaggs, territorial secretary for personnel. He delivers those powerful words to prospective Army officers and employees of African descent during the seminar's opening meeting. As a white man who had helped teach music to black children in Cleveland during the Civil Rights Movement, Knaggs passionately explains that there is a need to reach others who don't know the Lord. "And the only way we are going to get there," he says, "is with your help!"

Lt. Colonels Abraham and Louise Johnson, Daniel Diakanwa, Captains James LaBossiere and Charles Roberts, Colonels Franklyn and Joan Thompson, and Captain Lydia Pearson lead the meetings with informative workshops and stimulating, thought–provoking panel discussions. On Sunday morning, Cadets James and Melinda Jones of the 2002–2003 Crossbearers session share their testimonies. The couple had attended the seminar in 2000. Cadet Melinda says, "Two years ago, I sat where you are sitting, wondering about The Salvation Army. Today, I am about to be commissioned as a Salvation Army officer. God is truly amazing!"[278]

~

Lt. Colonels Johnson officially retire from active officership after serving a combined total of 85 years in ministry. Fifty–one years earlier, young Abe had knelt at the mercy seat in the Star Lake Camp tabernacle to accept God's call to become an officer. Now, he was once again at that mercy seat, surrounded by other officers, family members, and friends.

Commissioners David and Doreen Edwards, retired Western territorial leaders, conduct the ceremony on behalf of Commissioner Joe Noland, territorial commander. David says that the retirement of the Johnsons marks "the end of an era." He praises their leadership and reminds the audience that the Johnsons had entered The Salvation Army when black officers struggled for acceptance. He contrasts that time with 2002, saying that more African Americans are joining the ranks and serving in leadership. "Many are well educated and extremely gifted. They have the potential and the capacity to lead in any community, not just black communities." Edwards thanks the Johnsons for contributing to this change in circumstances. When Edwards says that the Johnsons believed in serving all people—regardless of race or nationality, there is sustained applause. "Abe and Louise Johnson are certainly among those few who can be counted as legends in their own lifetimes," he says.

Johnsons' retirement

Lt. Colonel Judy LaMarr, speaking for herself and her husband, Lt. Colonel William LaMarr, Greater New York divisional commander, says, "Abe and Louise Johnson have always been our peers. The one thing that I respect the most about them is that they have a true love for souls," LaMarr says. Another representative speaker compares Abe Johnson to legendary Jackie Robinson, who broke the color line in baseball. Diakanwa describes the Johnsons as his "spiritual parents in the faith." Pastor John Hagler, Louise's youngest brother, describes his sister as a "lovely, strict, sincere, dedicated, diligent, and committed" Christian. In response, the Johnsons thank God and encourage everyone to "stay on our course through Salvation Army ministry. Trust God through the Holy Spirit."[279]

On June 9, 2002, Delilah "Dee" Collier is admitted to the Order of the Founder. Before a capacity crowd gathered for Commissioning Weekend in the New Jersey Performing Arts Center in Newark, the Salvation Army senior soldier of the Hartford Citadel Corps in Connecticut sees a video presentation that describes her legacy. It reveals a life of dedication and "surrender to the will of God." Collier, who, like nearly 3,000 other people, had come to see the Crossbearers session become officers, was surprised when her own face appeared on the large screens.

Commissioner Joe Noland admits Delilah Collier to the Order of the Founder

The video chronicles 30 years of service by Collier, who held several local officer positions and served on the faculty of the Soldiers National Seminar on Evangelism and of Code BLUE, a local officer–training program. She also had served on the Multicultural Commission and the Current Issues Commission and shared her testimony at the Army's International Millennial Congress in 2000 before more than 14,000 soldiers. Her work on these committees became legendary in the Eastern Territory. She sent money and encouragement cards to cadets from her corps who went to training to become Salvation Army officers. "I just wanted the young people to know that we cared, and were praying for them. That kind of support means so much," she said. Collier served God with every fiber of her being. She managed a household of 12, worked part time for the local school district in Hartford, and graduated from college with a teaching certificate. She also became an outstanding representative for The Salvation Army in Charter Oak Terrace, one of the largest housing projects in the city.

Commissioner Joe Noland, territorial commander, had taken notice of how Collier had expressed her concern about the issues facing members of Hartford Citadel. He nominated Collier for the Order of the Founder award, he said, because her compassion for others touched his heart. Collier, who holds a master's degree in early childhood education, had taught 5th graders for 28 years and had helped develop curriculum for her inner–city school district. At Rawson Elementary School, Collier was instrumental in organizing a morning prayer session among faculty. And she managed, discreetly, to share her faith with students. Many who knew the mother of seven and grandmother of 17 also knew of her love for Christ and others. One daughter, Patricia Wood, who was an envoy (corps officer) herself said: "Growing up, I remember my mother always putting people first ... always making sacrifices for people. We never knew how poor we actually were because she would always find a way to give to somebody, even if she had to take from herself. Yet, somehow, on Christmas and holidays, we always had what we needed. My mother just has a servant's heart."[280]

In November of that year, in Washington, D.C., Brigadier Victor Wilson is promoted to Glory. Among those who pay tribute to him are the Wiltshire family, who present themselves in word and song. The National Capital and Virginia Band play "Ten Thousand Angels." It is a fitting tribute to a man who had served God through The Salvation Army in the United States, the Caribbean, and Central America. Says one speaker, "He made an enormous impact on the lives of many individuals, groups, organizations, and societies, near and far."[281]

That same year, in the Eastern Territory, Major George Evans is also "promoted to Glory." At his funeral, representative speakers reflect on his life and ministry at the following corps: Jeanette, Pa.; Pittsburgh Temple/Arlington, Pa.; Newark Central, N.J.; Door of Hope in Jersey City, N.J.; Brownsville, N.Y.; Bushwick, N.Y.; Cleveland Hough; Pittsburgh West Side, Atlantic City, N.J.; and Philadelphia Temple. Evans had also served as divisional youth secretary in Greater New York.[282]

In the Western Territory, Major Rose Marie Leslie is appointed a delegate to the International College of Officers (ICO).

Chapter 19
Mission *Still* Matters Most!

"'...being confident of this, that he who began a good work in you will carry it on to completion, until the day of Christ Jesus,"

—Paul (Phil. 1:6).

First African–American TC, Chief of the Staff, and NC

Israel L. and Eva D. Gaither returned from South Africa in 2002 to become territorial leaders, making Commissioner Israel Gaither the first African American to serve as a territorial commander in the United States. (Commissioner David Edwards, who had served as territorial commander in the West, was of Caribbean origins.) "Mission Matters Most!" became Gaither's battle cry and motto, and he articulated it with great passion during his installation service at the annual Old Orchard Beach camp meetings in Maine.

"During the whirlwind time of transition," Gaither said of himself and his wife, Commissioner Eva Gaither, "both of us placed ourselves before God for the receiving of His vision for the territory. I'm being led to focus on the centrality of the mission—understanding what it means for the future, fixing it in our actions, dreams, and undertakings." Gaither believed that a focus on Salvation Army mission would seal the successes of the past while opening doors of opportunity to the future.

When he explained his and Eva's reaction to the news that they would be returning to the United States, Gaither said, "When we arrived at our quarters [that day in South Africa] the first thing we did on closing the kitchen door behind us was something we have always done throughout the years of our service each time we have received word of a forthcoming change of appointment, we have prayed together—in the kitchen."[283]

General John Larsson

The Gaithers soon found themselves again praying in the kitchen. Installed as territorial leaders on Aug. 3, they received a call just a few weeks later from General–Elect John Larsson, who asked Commissioner Israel Gaither if he would serve as his Chief of the Staff, second in command of The Salvation Army worldwide. Commissioner Eva would serve as World Secretary for Women's Ministries and World President of Salvation Army Scouts, Guides, and Guards. The Gaithers, who had just been warmly welcomed home after their sojourn in Southern Africa, had looked forward to spending time with family and friends and were still exhilarated by their Old Orchard Beach experience and the anticipation of leading the USA Eastern Territory.

They received the news as a shock of "seismic proportions," Commissioner Israel Gaither said. "We had no idea whatsoever that we were being considered for these significant responsibilities." Gaither broke the news to the USA East Territorial Executive Council in private session, following which he and Commissioner Eva traveled to Territorial Headquarters to announce the change to officers and employees, just minutes before the news was shared with the Army world.

Starting with the words of the Apostle Paul, Commissioner Israel Gaither addressed his audience by saying, "I will miss you. I thank my God every single time I remember you. I always pray with joy because of your partnership in the Gospel, in this special way—for 103 days. Be confident of this, that He who began a good work in you, will continue; will carry it on to completion, until the day of Jesus Christ."

Gaither pointed out that during his short tenure as

commander of the USA Eastern Territory, he had enjoyed several "first and last" experiences. "We conducted one series of Old Orchard Beach meetings, one Spiritual Sunday at the School for Officer Training, dedicated one new building, conducted one officer retirement service, one divisional camp meeting weekend, [attended] one Commissioners' Conference, one National Advisory Board meeting, one Territorial Headquarters Officers' Retreat, and one funeral of a precious and very special retired officer. So, I guess our photos can legitimately hang on the walls with the other former territorial leaders, although we've only served you for a very short time."

Commissioners Israel L. and Eva D. Gaither

The unexpected announcement was received with a mixture of sorrow for a departure that would come so soon and joy that the Gaithers had received such an honor. When Gaither was asked to be Chief of the Staff, he said he and Commissioner Eva shared several days of "spiritual exercises" together before their international appointments were formally announced. "God made it very clear to me that I had simply been a vessel of His message, a servant of the USA Eastern Territory for a short period of time. I do not own the vision 'Mission Matters Most!' nor is the territory my personal property. I am a steward."

Reflecting on the lessons they had learned about submission to the will of God, Gaither said, "We are continually astounded at the way God mysteriously works in our lives. This was one of those occasions when He disrupted what we thought was best. But His Spirit has reminded me that when my wife and I signed our officer covenants in 1964, we placed ourselves fully at His disposal. He has a right to do what He pleases. And all we want is to be certain that we are doing His will, in His place, and at His time. If we don't model what faithfulness to the mission means during circumstances like this, then you might lose some belief in what officers are supposed to be. And we don't want that guilt on our heart. If we believe that God's sovereign will is in place and is certain for us and for the Eastern Territory, all will be well." Commissioner Eva Gaither said, "What a journey! I am amazed at the privileges that God has given us as Salvation Army officers. So many people have made this journey a great joy."

During a special sendoff in November at Centennial Memorial Temple in New York City, Gaither paid tribute to her children: Mark of Pittsburgh, Pa.; Michele Gaither–Sparks of Wilmore, Ky.; their spouses; and their grandson, Isaiah Highland Sparks. Quoting the Apostle Paul, she said, "'...being confident of this, that he who began a good work in you will carry it on to completion, until the day of Christ Jesus' (Phil. 1:6). I love the Lord, this man [her husband], and this mission, and believe that we are in the complete will of God."

Harlem Temple's New Sounds for Christ choir and the New York Staff Band filled the hall with Gospel music and the strains of "Hail to the Chief." The Territorial Arts Ministry team presented a humorous sketch, and the Media Ministries Bureau offered several video presentations, including one from General–Elect John Larsson himself.

Larsson spoke from the very office in London where Commissioner Israel would soon assume his new post. "If you are wondering why I selected the Gaithers to take up these international roles," Larsson said, "the reason you are sorry to see them coming out is the very reason why they are needed on the international scene. You know of their warmth and their sensitivity—their passion for the Lord, their passion for mission. And it is these qualities that will make such a difference for the Army on the international

Commissioners Lawrence R. and Nancy A. Moretz

scene." As Larsson held up the Chief of the Staff's flag, he reminded the audience that Gaither would be needed to help plan strategy for the Army's ministries in 109 countries worldwide. "I know you will be proud of them," he said. "I know you will be praying for them, that they will go in the strength of the Lord."

Commissioners Lawrence R. and Nancy A. Moretz, the USA Central Territory leaders, were appointed to succeed the Gaithers in the East. The moment the Moretzes learned of the new appointments, they said, they dropped to their knees. "Nancy and I went to prayer, kneeling in my office, making the desk a mercy seat," Commissioner Lawrence said. The Moretzes, like the Gaithers, were members of the 1964 Heroes of the Faith session in the Eastern Territory, and they had developed a strong and vital friendship with the Gaithers that had dissolved the color line; they had experienced mutual love and affection for some 40 years. "We've participated in each other's weddings. Our children are friends. Our families have grown together, shared joys and sorrows," he said. The Moretzes adopted the Gaithers' slogan, with a slight modification—"Mission *Still* Matters Most!" During the Gaithers' send–off, Moretz took his message from the words God delivered to Moses in Deuteronomy 4:1–9: "Only be careful, and watch yourselves closely so that you do not forget the things your eyes have seen or let them slip from your heart as long as you live. Teach them to your children and to their children after them." Gaither, the only African American who had ever been a divisional commander, personnel secretary, chief secretary, or territorial commander, said he felt like Moses, who knew a better day would come.[284]

During the next four years, Commissioner Israel Gaither served as the Salvation Army's Chief of the Staff, the first African American to hold the position since the founding of the organization in 1865. As the Army's chief executive officer, Gaither served as second–in–command of the worldwide organization. Commissioner Eva Gaither served as the World Secretary for Women's Ministries, an executive responsibility for the advancement of women in developed and developing sectors of the world. During their service at The Salvation Army's International Headquarters in London, the Gaithers traveled to more than 30 countries and made as many as 50 visits to Salvation Army territories in order to provide support, guidance, and pastoral care to the leaders in those regions.

Israel's reputation for being an efficient administrator and gifted speaker continued to grow as he addressed thousands of Salvationists and Christians worldwide. He received a number of honors for his global leadership and ministry, including an honorary Doctor of Humane Letters degree from Asbury College in May 2005 in Wilmore, Ky.

On January 20, 2006, at the Sunbury Court Conference Centre in London, the High Council convened to elect the 18th General of The Salvation Army. Army leaders from around the world would decide who would be the successor to General John Larsson, scheduled to retire at midnight on April 1 of that year. Commissioner Israel Gaither, as Chief of the Staff, summoned all active commissioners and territorial commanders to this historic council. It was the largest one to date, with 102 members, including 86 commissioners and 16 colonels.

Once again the Council nominated Gaither for the office of General along with four others: Commissioners Shaw Clifton, Hasse Kjellgren, Carl Lydholm, and Christine MacMillan. Two other members, Commissioners Phillip Needham and Linda Bond, were nominated but declined to stand for election.

The Council took up Day 8 of the process with the questioning of candidates and spouses. Then, on Saturday, Jan. 28, the candidates gave their speeches, sharing their vision for The Salvation Army. Colonel Michael Marvell, territorial commander in Denmark, served as media and liaison officer and kept a diary of the High Council. He recorded what happened next.

> ...Attention then turned to the table in the center of the hall as the Council, in hushed silence, moved into the voting procedure. The table was covered with a dark–red velvet cloth bordered with a golden fringe. On the tablecloth, embroidered in gold letters, which faced each member of the Council as he or she approached to place their ballot paper in one of the two ballot boxes, were the words 'Holiness unto the Lord.' The voting began at 11:35 a.m. and was completed at 3:55 p.m., with a shortened break for lunch.
>
> Commissioner Shaw Clifton accepted the Council's choice, kneeling, together with Commissioner Helen Clifton, at the table, which now... had become a Holiness Table (altar). On rising, he thanked the Council for the love and the trust it had given him, and in quiet but emphatic voice, he stressed how totally dependent he was and would always be on God and the prayers of Salvationists everywhere. The General–elect then paid warm tribute to the other candidates, and this was greeted with loud and prolonged applause. He also thanked God for Commissioner Helen Clifton. 'She is my support, my counselor—and she keeps me on the right track,' he said.
>
> With the result declared and the other formalities completed, the President (Commissioner Is-

> rael Gaither) emphasized the sacredness of what had taken place. To underline this, he quoted from the Orders of Procedure: 'The voting figures and number of ballots shall not be published within a period of 10 years after the dissolution of the Council.' Everyone understood what he meant. This had not been a race or a competition, not an obstacle course or a talent competition. It had been the selection of a new leader from among a group of Jesus' disciples, all equally committed and dedicated to His service. The choice—and God's blessing upon it—eclipsed all procedures and figures.

Although Gaither did not become General of The Salvation Army, God had another appointment in store. On May 12, 2006, at Centennial Memorial Temple in New York, during a solemn and historic ceremony, General Shaw Clifton installed Commissioner Israel L. Gaither as the first African–American U.S. national commander and Commissioner Eva D. Gaither as national secretary for Women's Ministries.

For the Gaither family, the meeting represented a long–awaited homecoming.

"It's good to be home," Israel said, looking out into the 1,400–seat auditorium, nearly filled to capacity. Leaders from every USA territory, officers, soldiers, adherents, and members of the National Advisory Board were on hand for this historic event. The Army's 26th national commander continued, "We've been away a long time, but it has been worth it."

General Clifton said, "Although we've known the Gaithers for only 11 years, they have become part and parcel of our lives. It is a privilege to stand with your new national leaders of The Salvation Army in the United States. They are held in highest regard in circles at International Head-

General Shaw Clifton

quarters. They have distinguished themselves in recent years as world leaders of The Salvation Army. They are here for pure, authentic, and godly reasons."

Clifton expressed his belief that God wants the Gaithers to lead a Christ–centered, Calvary–conscious Army that is coherent in doctrine and cognizant of its place on the "ecclesiological spectrum." And that this be accomplished "by the power of a risen Savior, not our own skills or mightily impressive professionalism." Turning to the Gaithers, the General said, "These are the right people at the right time."

Facing transition and challenge

"We've experienced The Salvation Army in ways that have not left us the same; but America is not the same either," said Gaither. "We are facing challenges like we have never known. It is a disturbing time in America; we are on the crossroads of spiritual and moral transition."

Gaither also made it clear that the Army was poised and ready to respond to these challenges and had wide support.

> We have been profoundly moved by the power of the presence of this uniform. We've been humbled by the respect the Army has received from church, civic, and business leaders. They have said to me, 'We need The Salvation Army. Will you speak with us? Will you walk with us? Will you help us?'

Gaither said that former South African President Nelson Mandela had told him in a private meeting that South Africa needed The Salvation Army. "But so do South Los Angeles, South Florida, the South Side of Chicago, South Jersey, and every place where this Salvation banner flies—America needs The Salvation Army!" Gaither said passionately.

> America is in a culture war. There is a battle for the hearts and minds of those on the margins. There is a deliberate attempt to mute the voice of the Church and sideline the influence of the believer. Someone must say 'no' to wrong and 'yes' to right. Somebody's got to do it; why not us?
>
> This is our time; the time for a sanctified army of men and women to make good on our promises. It is time for Salvationists in America to become soldiers!"
>
> I plead to you tonight to get ready to engage spiritual warfare like never before. This is not the time for the Army to slip behind the sanctuary of the citadel. This is the largest Army in the world; with the greatest power the world will ever know—this is the Army of the Lord—a mighty army![285]

Chapter 20

The future of people of African descent in The Salvation Army in the United States

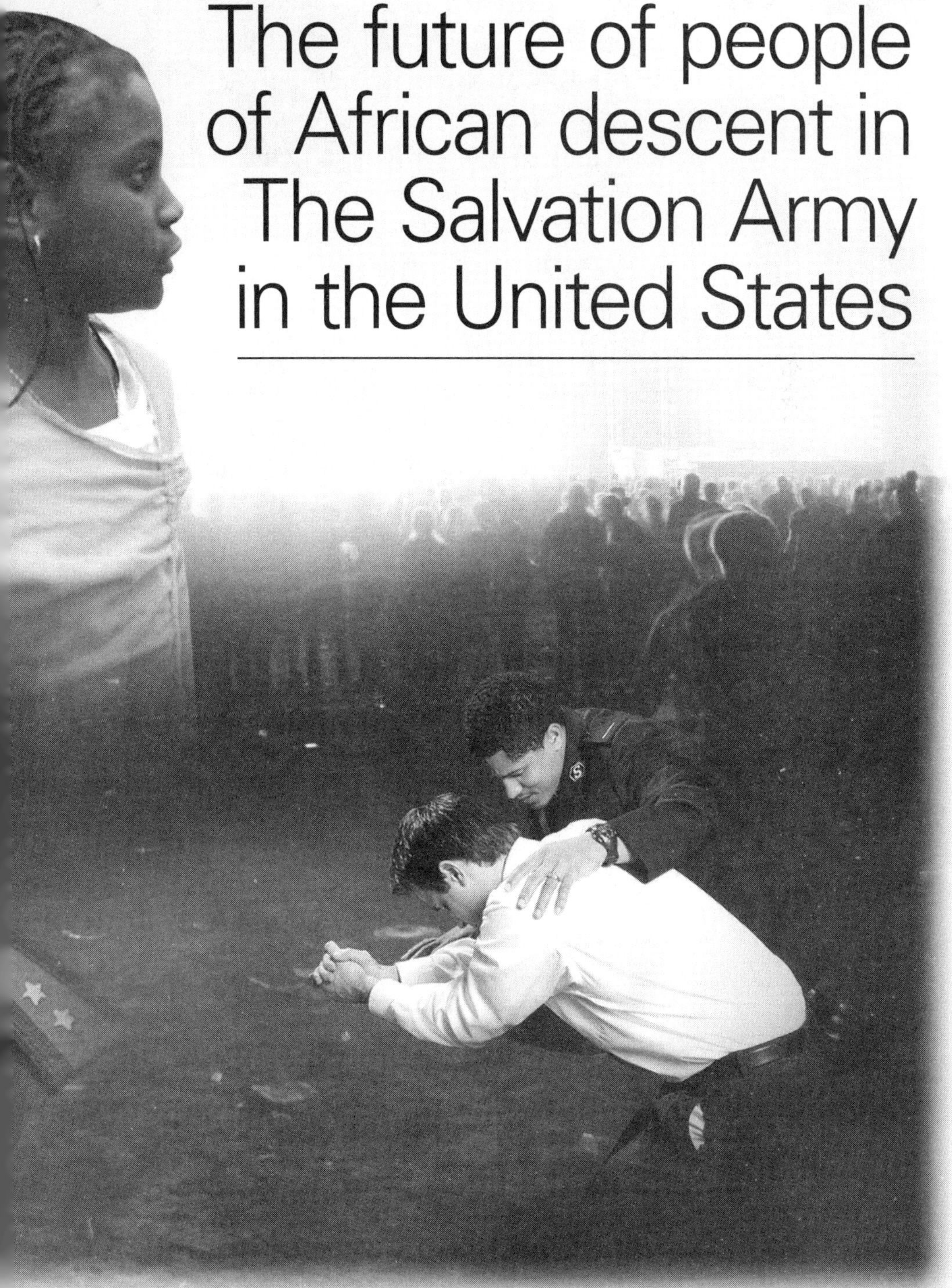

"The Negro personality is yet an unknown quantity. His moral character, intellectual ability, and spiritual capacity are as yet comparatively undiscovered. We only see him in a savage state or at most just emerging from slavery; and even now where in individual cases he has had equal opportunities, he will favorably compare with the white man. It is quite possible for us to argue, therefore, that of civilization, education, and Christian influence, he will equal if he does not actually surpass the white man in those things, which now make the latter so much the superior."

—Founder William Booth, speaking to his troops in South Africa, 1890, as published in "*Field to Field,*" an article published in *All the World*

TODAY, THE PERSONALITY, MORAL CHARACTER, INTELLECTUAL ABILITY, and spiritual capacity of people of African descent is no longer an "unknown quantity" in The Salvation Army. The Founder would be pleased to know of the efforts by both white and black Salvationists through the years to create a favorable climate for the inclusion of blacks within its ranks. At the Army's inception in the United States, Commissioner Railton declared "If [blacks] will not join themselves with other races, we will go farther still, and there will be found officers ready to leave off association with their own race in order to rescue those of another." Commissioner Frank Smith, one of many white officers who worked diligently to realize Railton's dream of racial diversity, launched the "Great Colored Campaign and combined attack on the South." He said, "We are determined, by the help of God, to be among the first white

Christian communities of America who would faithfully and wholly break down this wall of partition separating the white from the colored, whom the Lord has brought from a common captivity and bondage."

Recognizing the Army's commitment to diversity

Those efforts, which began in those early days and continued in modern times, have not gone unnoticed by Salvationists of color. "We are deeply indebted to God and The Salvation Army for the tremendous opportunities we have been provided over the years of our officership to become the persons we are today," says Commissioner David Edwards. "And while the Army has not always been the organization that we would have liked it to be (which organization ever is?), [Commissioner Doreen Edwards and I] can truly say that at no time have we ever found that our color was a problem for Army administration. I have no doubt that our color and place of origin might have been considered a distinct advantage in determining certain appointments for us, but I would like to believe that these were not significant factors that were taken into account in making the final decision."[286]

Major Marjorie Wiltshire notes that, whenever possible, many white officers decidedly took the high road when it came to race relations. "My husband and I were involved in ministry in the USA Southern Territory for about 20 years," she said. "We are grateful for the opportunity afforded us to serve God and humanity. We were blessed to have had some wonderful leaders like the then Brigadier and Mrs. Ernest Holz, Colonel and Mrs. W.R.H. Goodier, Colonel and Mrs. John Needham, and the then Brigadier and Mrs. James Osborne, who were open and helpful."[287]

Captain (Dr.) K. Kendall Mathews says he is grateful to God for calling black officers to the ranks of The Salvation

Army. "It is not by chance that we [people of color] are a part of The Salvation Army, but by God's choice so that people may see Jesus in us as we serve others," he said. "Our struggles belong to us and they have contributed to build a unique character within us, making us who we are today in preparation for our future.... Our message of love and peace, no doubt, has been the bond that has held us together as a people who have a brighter future ahead in The Salvation Army."[288]

When an interviewer asked then–Chief of the Staff Commissioner Israel L. Gaither if he regretted entering training as such a young cadet (age 17), he said he thanked God for calling him before he was tempted to walk down another road in life. "There is no question in my mind that God called and prepared me for His right time—but I have wondered about the 'what if.' And I do believe that, had I pursued further formal studies, it would have taken me on another path and I would not be wearing this uniform. I would not be married to my wonderful wife, nor would I be blessed with great kids and awesome grandsons! I followed as I was led—'what if' has never been a problem." Gaither said that he was called by God to leave the church of his heritage to be not only a Salvationist but also an officer. "It was not just a call to the ministry," he wrote, "it was a definite call to officership and I can never deny it."[289]

More intentional effort needed

Having answered the call to service, Salvationists of color have faced racial and cultural challenges. "We were all trapped in a cultural time warp," said Major Marjorie Wiltshire regarding her service in the South. "And Army policy was dictated by the cultural mores. African heritage officers were victims of the status quo.... Many black officers have been lost from the Army because there was a lack of intentional caring on the part of the administration as well as our own fellow black officers. There is a need for pastoral care coupled with brotherly love and compassion from fellow officers." She continued, "Forty or more years ago in the Caribbean, we had a few well–qualified black leaders in administration but there were no others being prepared to take their places. Consequently, a huge gap was created that took many years to fill."

A survey of officers conducted in the Eastern Territory in 1999 by Major Raphael C. Jackson revealed that less than a third of the black officers surveyed believed that the gap has actually been filled. Only 25 percent agreed that the internal environment of The Salvation Army was "racially inclusive," while 61 percent disagreed with that statement. Those officers who disagreed did not see the problem as an organizational malady but one having to do with relationships between individuals. "Individual racism is very much alive," commented one respondent.[290]

Commissioner Edwards said that some black officers had been inconsistent when asserting their racial credentials, using them as tools of preference rather than principle. "I notice that there seems to be a kind of contradiction in the way some of us regard this issue of color and the way it is used in determining what jobs we are given," he said. "We want it to be a significant factor in those instances that we favor and cry foul when it is factored in to those situations that we do not favor. I do not think that we can have it both ways."

Edwards believes that one's calling should transcend the politics of color and that it should not be used as the reason behind one's appointment or *dis*appointment. "These officers did not become divisional or territorial leaders because they were black or of African descent, or in spite of being thus, but that they were territorial and divisional leaders who, by the way, were black and of African descent. While no one should be allowed to make us less the persons that God intended us to be because of our color or racial origin, neither should we allow anyone to use that as an excuse or crutch for not achieving all that we have the potential to be by God's grace."

Does racism still exist in the Army? Although Commissioner Gaither points out that he is still the only African American to have entered "key" leadership roles, he doesn't immediately attribute that fact to racism. "We still have some way to go, but we have traveled a great distance from where the Army once was. I don't suggest it is because of racism, but I am not proud that in the USA, I am still the only African American who has ever been a divisional commander, personnel secretary, chief secretary, or territorial commander. This is the 21st century, and for the Army still not to have officers of color in these leadership roles clearly signals the urgent need to give intentional attention to the early identification and development of not just officer–leaders—but also non–white leaders. And it must not be mere 'window dressing.' That has not ever been, nor is it now, acceptable to any segment of our community."

Daniel Diakanwa, African heritage consultant, says that, in addition to racial issues, cultural and theological differences also hamper the recruitment of African Americans. During his service as Cross–Cultural Ministries Bureau director, he discovered that the Army's worship style, culture, and decision to abstain from observing the sacraments were problematic for African Americans. "The fact that The Salvation Army does not administer water baptism and communion makes it difficult for blacks to consider the Army as a church," he said. "African Americans view The Salvation Army as a white Christian organization. Its ranking system, uniform, and symbols do not attract them. Furthermore, while blacks have benefited tremendously from the Army's social services, its lack of involvement in the Civil Rights Movement has alienated many blacks, especially their leaders, from The Salvation Army."[291]

Faced with such challenges, how can the Army hope to ensure a future for people of African descent, particularly

African Americans, in its ranks? Diakanwa does not see these issues as insurmountable but as open invitations for more deliberate, intentional action in recruiting African Americans. He believes that today's Army needs to follow the model established years ago in the South by Commissioner Frank Smith. "The future of Salvationists of African descent lies [in] their willingness to aggressively recruit more black officers in The Salvation Army," he said. "While there may be a considerable number of *soldiers* of African descent within the U.S. Salvation Army, the number of black *officers* remains insignificant. We need an aggressive campaign that includes financial and material resources, qualified Salvationists of African descent at territorial levels to plan recruitment seminars, visits to Christian colleges and seminaries, and other means of recruitment."

Jackson's survey of officers in the Eastern Territory, which included officers of African descent, indicated that there is wide support for diversity programs and all respondents, including those of African descent, thought such programs should be mandatory. In his remarks, Jackson also noted that, "This is an encouraging figure that shows that both groups see the need for better understanding."[292]

Imitating the success of other groups

However, Diakanwa also believes blacks should follow the example of other ethnic and affinity groups in the Army who have increased their own numbers. He says the onus to lead the campaign should not be on the Army entirely; black Salvationists must also shoulder this responsibility. "Unlike other ethnic officers who have encouraged their young people to join the ranks, officers of African descent have not generally prepared their qualified young people for officership. The future of blacks in The Salvation Army will not necessarily depend upon [the efforts of] Army leadership, but mostly upon the concentrated efforts of officers of African descent to recruit their young people and show them a positive image of our international and inclusive Army of God."

Captain Mathews concurs. "It is our responsibility as African Americans, who serve in this international movement, to encourage and enlist the membership of others who make up the heritage and culture, which promotes African–American mobilization in the Army. Our African–American officers must view ourselves as servants who are making a positive contribution to the cause of Christ while simultaneously dispensing service as a joyful example for new recruits to follow."

'Every correct motivation'

Gaither explains how black officers can achieve this goal. "We do it by being the best God–glorifying Salvationists possible," he says. "Salvationists of color are able to stand as solid models of what it means to be a Salvationist—especially in urban America. We need to be people of holy character and intention, knowledgeable of our heritage, fully committed to God and this mission, and convinced of its effectiveness.... We need Salvationists of color to be soldiers, not just 'members'![293]

However, words of caution also come from Diakanwa and Gaither. Says Diakanwa, "Blacks should not be recruited for the sake of adding numbers to the ranks, but for the sake of meeting the immeasurable spiritual and social needs of our African–American communities," Gaither adds another qualifier: "The first essential is *not* about 'promotion.' Every officer is a leader. The focus of the question is obviously on 'key' leadership roles and functions. But this attraction must not be for the sake of place, position, or power. The attraction is to serve the Kingdom with every correct motivation—then the organizational issues of strategy and deployment can be correctly addressed."

Edwards points out that although black Salvationists

are distinctive in The Salvation Army, they are not a "special needs" group. He said that, in many ways, they have the same needs as everyone else. "[Commissioner Doreen and I] do not think that our needs are any different as people of color [from] any other people. People need to be treated with respect, they need to be given opportunity, and should not be judged by the color of their skins or their racial origins." According to Jackson's, Eastern Territory–wide survey, unlike most white officers, many African–American officers still feel that, because of their race, they are not given the opportunity to grow to their full potential.[294]

Reflecting the 'community's multicultural disposition'

However, Edwards is quick to point out that the Army's ranks should adequately reflect the communities it serves. "At the same time, we would suggest that wherever The Salvation Army exists, it should identify closely with people whom it serves. If the community happens to be multicultural, then [the Army's] leadership and membership should reflect the multicultural disposition. While I am not one who supports a system of quotas, as I believe that we should find the best people to do the task, it does say something to people either about the organization or about the community if only one or two cultures in that multicultural environment seems to dominate in the organization rather than all of them."

Major Marjorie Wiltshire says that the Army should cross territorial boundaries if necessary, in order to reflect a community's multicultural disposition through "inter–territorial appointments" and follow the example set by affinity groups such as Hispanic Salvationists. "Copy what's being done with Hispanics—make non–commissioned battlefield commissions (sergeants, envoys, and auxiliary captains) and place them in charge of ministries. Ethnic ministers who have come from other countries could be pressed into use in ministries among their own people [here in the Army]. And second–career individuals could be pressed into use." According to Jackson's survey, the Army has a severe shortage of African–American officers with 16–24 years of experience. He wrote:

> The fact that almost all the African–American officers with 25 or more years experience are in or near their sixties and, as such, nearing their retirement. Since, in general, this is the area that key leadership is found, the prospect for immediate African–descent leadership is not as hopeful as the future may be. Even the future may not be so bright if we cannot slow down the attrition of African–American officers leaving the ministry.[295]

What does the future hold?

Recent appointments of African–American officers to positions overseas (Commissioner Gaither as territorial leader in South Africa and Chief of the Staff at IHQ; Majors Robert and Hester Dixon as territorial leaders in Liberia, Africa; and Major E. Lewanne Dudley as financial secretary in Nigeria) are milestones in Army history. Heretofore, only officers of European or Caribbean descent have held such appointments. For Gaither, this is a sign of a bright future for African–American officers. "The future is absolutely wide open to African–American Salvationists who would be available for God's use as officers," he said. "But 'we' must be willing to make ourselves available. African–American officers will be stretched and informed by offering themselves for overseas service." He acknowledged that redeployment of African–American officers overseas would create a "severe problem" at home, "but such sacrifices for the greater good of the mission must often be undertaken. It's about willing availability. The future is bright with opportunity!"

Mathews shares Gaither's vision for a bright and promising future. "God has not brought us this far in The Salvation Army to leave us.... Even during our time of trouble, [He] is still our very present help.... Today, our soldiers and officers have the power from God to serve in unity with no regard to rank or skin color. Our serviceableness to the needy and with the like–mindedness of Christ will be the spiritual glue that will hold us together.... From soldier, to General, and every rank in between, let's unite as one and march into [Satan's] camp and take back what he has stolen from us. It's not by chance that we are a part of The Salvation Army, but by God's choice, so that people may see Jesus in us as we serve others."

Jackson adds the following caveat:

> The Army can take the lead in diversity more effectively than any other organization, if they make it a core value. They have the potential of making the corporate atmosphere fertile for the cultivation of minority officers.[296]

Chapter Notes

Chapter 1

1 Charles Mayzleck, Division of Markets, Ohio Dept. of Agriculture, Reynoldsburg, Ohio, 2005. In 1872, farmers raised approximately 8 million sheep in Ohio and sold them at $2.30 per head. A leg would have sold for around 50 cents, retail.
2 James Jermy's address as listed on page 323 in the "J" section of the local Cleveland, Ohio, phone book, 1874–75.
3 F. De L. Booth–Tucker, *The Life of Catherine Booth, the Mother of The Salvation Army* (Fleming H. Revell Company, New York, 1870), p. 37. This was his mailing address on correspondence to William Booth.
4 Description of James Jermy based on photos provided by the Salvation Army's Archives and Research Center, Alexandria, Va.
5 James Jermy's address as listed on page 270 in the "J" section of the local Cleveland, Ohio, phone book, 1872–73.
6 Robert Sandall, *The History of The Salvation Army, Volume 1, 1865–1878* (Thomas Nelson and Sons, Ltd, New York, 1950) p. 244.
7 Norma T. Roberts, *The Black Salvationist: People of African descent in The Salvation Army, USA* (New York, The Salvation Army USA Eastern Territory, 1995), p. 14.
8 Sandall, p. 248.
9 Ibid, p. 244.
10 Ibid, p. 244.
11 Ibid., p. 36. The quote is from a letter Jermy wrote to William Booth, Sept. 2, 1872.
12 Ibid.
13 Ibid.
14 Hudla Friederichs, *Romance of The Salvation Army*, (Cassell and Company, Limited, London, 1907) pp. 180–182. Friedrichs, a contemporary of William Booth (he wrote the preface to the book), believed that James Fackler had contacted Booth long before Jermy arrived in Cleveland. According to Friederichs, Fackler sought assistance in his ministry and, enamored by what he had heard about Booth's work in England, wrote to encourage him to begin a work in Cleveland. Regarding the first meeting between Fackler and Jermy, Friederichs wrote, "…the two men met, and lo and behold! The minister was the writer of the letter urging Mr. Booth to come over and help Cleveland, Ohio." David Malcolm Bennett, author of *The General: William Booth* (Xulon Press, Longwood, Fl., 2003) questions the validity of Friederichs' claim, despite Booth's endorsement of her book. She also wrote *The Life of General Booth* (Thomas Nelson and Sons, Ltd., New York, actual publication date not known; printed after *Romance of The Salvation Army*).
15 Booth–Tucker, p. 37. The quote is from a letter Jermy wrote to William Booth, Sept. 2, 1872.

16 St. John Ervine, *God's Soldier: William Booth, Volume 1* (New York: The MacMillan Company, 1953), p. 480.
17 Booth–Tucker, p. 38. The quote is from a letter William Booth wrote to James Fackler, Sept. 20, 1872.
18 Ibid.; Gariepy, "A Profile of Salvation Army History in Cleveland, Ohio: Cleveland hosts first Salvation Army Work in U.S.," a paper prepared for WZAR and selective distribution in connection with the Super Sesqui Observance in Cleveland, July 1, 1971, pp. 1–2.
19 Ibid., p. 40. William Booth was laid aside for six months, unable to take part in any meetings.
20 Ibid., p. 38. The quote is from a letter William Booth wrote to James Fackler, Sept. 20, 1872.
21 *Cleveland Plain Dealer*, March 8, 1873, page number unknown.
22 *Rowell's American Newspaper Directory, Cleveland City Directory*, 1955; Herbert A. Wisbey, Jr., "A Salvation Army Prelude," *The Ohio Historical Quarterly*, Vol. 64, p. 80.
23 Commissioner Edward Carey, "Mission Flag Hoisted in Cleveland," *The War Cry* (The Salvation Army, USA National Headquarters), Feb. 9, 1980, p.10.
24 *The Christian Mission Magazine*, May 1873, p. 144.
25 *The Christian Mission Magazine*, October 1873, p. 168
26 Carey, "Mission Flag Hoisted in Cleveland."
27 Ibid, p.11.
28 Ibid.
29 *Rowell's American Newspaper Directory, Cleveland City Directory*, 1955; Wisbey, Jr., "A Salvation Army Prelude: The Christian Mission in Cleveland, Ohio," *The Ohio Historical Quaterly* no. 64, 1955, pp. 77–81.

Chapter 2

30 Lillian Taiz, *Hallelujah Lads & Lasses: Remaking the Salvation Army in America, 1880–1930*, (The University of North Carolina Press: Chapel Hill, 2001), p. 22.
31 Edward H. McKinley, *Marching to Glory: The History of The Salvation Army in the United States, 1880–1992*, Second Edition, (William B. Eerdmans Publishing Company: Grand Rapids, Michigan,1995), p. 10.
32 Ibid, p. 11.
33 St. John Ervine, *God's Soldier: William Booth, Vol. 1,* (Macmillan Company: New York, 1953), p. 485. McKinley, *Marching to Glory*, p. 10. Taiz, p. 25.
34 Ibid.
35 Leslie M. Harris, *In the Shadow of Slavery: African Americans in New York City, 1626–1863* (University of Chicago Press: Chicago, 2003), pp. 279–288. On Monday, July 11, 1863, five days of mayhem and bloodshed broke out in the streets of New York City to protest the Civil War draft. Approximately 100 people were killed. Irish New Yorkers feared that the Emancipation Proclamation enacted in January would flood the labor market with freed slaves and fresh competition. The Irish workers sharply criticized the federal government for intruding on their local affairs on behalf of the "nigger war." The rioters had initially targeted military and governmental targets. But by the afternoon of the first day, they began to attack black people and things symbolic of black political, economic, and social power. This included a black fruit vendor, a 9–year–old boy, and the Colored Orphan Asylum on Fifth Avenue, which was burned to the ground. Rioters also murdered

several black dockworkers in an attempt to run the black male working class out of town. This riot followed a pattern similar to the anti–abolition riot of 1834 in that city.

36 McKinley, p. 65. *The War Cry*, July 18, 1885, p. 1.

37 Diane Winston, *Red–Hot and Righteous: The Urban Religion of The Salvation Army* (Harvard University Press: Cambridge, Mass., 1999), p. 26. *New York Times*, March 16, 1880, p. 8. Sallie Chesham, *Born to Battle: The Salvation Army in America* (Chicago: Rand McNally & Co., 1965), p. 62.

38 Taiz, p. 27.

39 Herbert A. Wisbey, Jr., *Soldiers Without Swords: A History of The Salvation Army in the United States* (The Macmillan Company: New York, 1955), p. 6

40 McKinley, p. 19. Before The Salvation Army issued its first official songbooks based on European–styled music, it often used African–American spirituals during worship meetings, which inspired whites and greatly encouraged the attendance and participation of blacks.

Chapter 3

41 Susan Altman, *The Encyclopedia of African–American Heritage* (Facts on File, Inc.: New York, 1997), p. 90. African slaves brought the banjo to the United States in the 17th century. The banjo gained national attention when white musicians in 19th–century minstrel show troupes adopted it.

42 Anonymous, "Self Related Experience of a Former Minstrel." *Albany Times*, Aug. 18, 1884, p. 2.

43 *The Cleveland Gazette*, June 14, 1884, p. 1.

44 Commissioner Frank Smith, "A Night with One of the Coloured Corps," *All the World* (Salvation Army International Headquarters: London), April 1886, pp. 82–84.

45 Ibid.

46 Museum of the City of New York, Fifth Avenue; *New York Times Magazine*, part II, May 18, 1986, p. 36; *New York Post*, June 17, 1986, p. 12; French Embassy at the United Nations. Rebecca M. Joseph, Ph.D., "The Black Statue of Liberty Rumor" An Inquiry into the History and Meaning of Bartholdi's *Liberté éclairant le Monde,* Final Report," Northeast Ethnography Program, Boston Support Office, National Park Service, Sept. 2000. Dr. Joseph contends that, although the statue was dark copper in color, originally based on the image of an Egyptian woman in chains, and presented by one anti–slavery society to another at the end of the Civil War, there was no intent by the statue's designers to portray the plight of black American slaves, nor to memorialize them for their contribution to ending slavery in the United States, and that any appearance of these ideas in the statue's evolution was purely "coincidental." Howard Dodson, Christopher Moore, and Roberta Yancy, *The Black New Yorkers: The Schomburg Illustrated Chronology*, 2000, p. 85; shows a full–page image of one of Auguste Bartholdi's mid–nineteenth–century drawings considered by some to be an early model for the Statue of Liberty. The image shows a long–haired, dark–skinned woman holding an American flag in her right hand, the scales of justice in her left, and broken shackles at her feet. Directly below the shackles is written "Presented by August Au, Esq., LIBERTY."

47 *The War Cry*, Jan. 24, 1885, p. 2

48 McKinley, p. 45. Samuel Logan Brengle's personal letter written in St. Petersburg, Fla., to Adjutant David Farrar in Danbury, Conn., on Feb. 12, 1936; Brengle's personal letter written in St. Petersburg, Fla., to Uldine Utley in New York City on March 11, 1936.

49 "The Beck Family: The Colored Jubilee Singers," *The War Cry*, Nov. 18, 1893, p. 8; "Captain Alexander Beck," *The War Cry*, Nov. 23, 1894, p. 5
50 Captain B. A. Ironside, "A Year's War on the Pacific Coast," *The Conqueror* (The Salvation Army: Los Angeles:1896) pp. 546–548.
51 Winston, p. 100.
52 Edward Abeles and Nathan D. Mann, "I'se Gwine to Save Yo' Soul: Salvation Song," M. Witmark and Sons, Inc., 1897.
53 St. John Ervine, pp. 480–81; (referred to earlier? Need first names) Douglas and Duff, *Commissioner Railton*, p. 74; *The War Cry*, July 18, 1885, p. 1.
54 James E. Beane, "Early Black Salvationists in America," a paper prepared for presentation at the Territorial Historical Commission Conference, Territorial Headquarters, Sept. 14–15, 1974, pp. 2, 6. *The War Cry*, July 18, 1885, article on the 1898 edition of the *Orders and Regulations for Social Officers*, the Army indicated that people would not be barred from its social programs based on skin color.
55 *The War Cry*, July 11, 1885, NP; James E. Beane, "Early Black Salvationists in America"; Allan Satterlee, *Sweeping Through the Land: A History of The Salvation Army in the Southern United States* (The Salvation Army Supplies: Atlanta, Ga.,: 1989), p. 35.
56 McKinley, p. 65; Beane, "Early Black Salvationists in America."; Satterlee, p. 35. Braithwaite may have been caught up in the schism that essentially split the organization into two salvation armies. Thomas E. Moore, whom William Booth had chosen to lead the U.S. branch, "defected" when he incorporated the organization against Booth's will. Booth eventually replaced Moore with Frank Smith, but it is believed that Moore convinced Braithwaite to join forces with him.
57 McKinley, p. 65.
58 Commissioner Frank Smith, *The Salvation War in America*, Chapter VI, "Here, There, and Everywhere," pp. 136–37.
59 McKinley, p. 65.
60 *The War Cry*, July 18, 1885, p. 1
61 Smith, pp. 136–37.
62 Winston, p. 26; *The New York Times*, March 16, 1880, p. 8; Sallie Chesham, *Born to Battle: The Salvation Army in America* (Chicago: Rand McNally & Co., 1965), p. 62.
63 *The War Cry*, Dec. 26, 1885, p. 7.
64 Smith, p. 139.
65 David Barton, "Setting the Record Straight: American History in Black & White," digital video disc (DVD) presentation published by WallBuilders, 2005. Between 1882 and 1964, 4,743 lynchings took place in the United States. Of that number, 3,446 victims were black, 1,297 white. Langston Hughes, Milton Meltzer, and C. Eric Lincoln, *A Pictorial History of Black Americans* (Crown Publishers: New York, 1983), pp. 97, 232–34, 266–67. Ronald L. F. Davis, Ph. D., "Creating Jim Crow: In–depth Essay," The History of Jim Crow, California State University, Northridge, sponsored by New York Life, Inc., (website) www.jimcrowhistory.org/resources/resources.htm, 2005. Railroad companies sold tickets to attend lynchings, whites hawked body parts of dead victims as souvenirs and brought their children to watch the torture and death of blacks, newspapers carried advance notices, and participants proudly posed for pictures of themselves with the burned corpses of lynched men and women and allowed the images to be reproduced on picture postcards.
66 McKinley, p. 67. *The War Cry*, July 14, 1894, pp. 8, 21; July 21, 1894, p. 8; December 28, 1895, cover and p. 2; May 1899, p. 8.

67 Taiz, p. 37, footnote; actual number of corps openings is not clear. As many as 300 may have opened by 1886, but Smith himself admits many of those opened and closed quickly. Commissioner Frank Smith, *The Salvation War in America: Under the Generalship of Rev. William Booth* (The Salvation Army Headquarters and Trade Department: New York, 1886), p. 74.

68 "A Kind Letter from Principal Washington," *The Conqueror*, Oct. 1896, p. 475.

Chapter 4

69 *Lifting the veil; or acts of Salvationists*, author unknown. *The War Cry*, July 28, 1894, reported on the "Colored Contingent" in a meeting in Leicester and published stories about African–American men who gave testimony during the International Congress of 1894, namely "George," "Uncle Solomon," and "Comrade Bailey," who "was once deep–dyed in drunkenness and sin."

70 Philip Durham, Everett L. Jones, *The Negro Cowboys* (University of Nebraska Press: Place of Publication, Sept. 1, 1983) pp. 3–4.

71 Nat Love, *The Life and Adventures of Nat Love, Better Known in the Cattle Country as "Deadwood Dick," by Himself: a True History of Slavery Days, Life on the Great Cattle Ranges and on the Plains of the "Wild and Woolly" West, Based on Facts, and Personal Experiences of the Author* Los Angeles, Calif., 1907 (University of North Carolina at Chapel Hill website, http://docsouth.unc.edu/neh/natlove/).

72 Julie Wittington, Archives and Research Center, USA Eastern Territorial Headquarters, West Nyack, N.Y., 1998.

73 *The War Cry*, Aug. 1, 1914.

74 Sabrina L. Miller, "Untold story of the *Titanic*: a museum exhibit reveals what many don't know—a black family was on board," *The Chicago Tribune*, Feb. 20, 2000, p. 1.

75 Captain Lambert Bailey, from a letter to Commander Evangeline Booth about the opening of the "Coloured People Work" in the U.S., July 25, 1913.

76 Norma T. Roberts, *The Black Salvationist: People of African descent in The Salvation Army, USA*, p. 69.

77 Colonel Samuel Logan Brengle, "Impression of the I.C.C.," *The War Cry,* Aug. 15, 1914, p. 9.

78 (Website) "Telescoping the times: the age of Imperialism, 1850–1914." Indians, resenting the fact that the British were treating them unfairly, formed two groups, the Indian National Congress and the Muslim League. Both began to push for change. In the early 1900s, they called for self–government. (McDougal–Little:Houghton Mifflin Company, (cited Nov. 29. 2007) http://mclane:fresno.k12.ca.us/wilson98/Assignments/ImpCH11.html.

79 Jennifer V. Jackson, Mary E. Cothran, *Journal of Black Studies*, Vol. 33, No. 5, "Black versus black: the relationships among African, African American, and African Caribbean persons" (University of Maryland: College Park, May 2003), p. 20. Although the groups have similar interracial struggles that create some semblance of common bonds, they fail to appreciate their common heritage.

80 Caille Millner, *Jinn Magazine*, "The Caribbean/African–American gap can be bridged with understanding" (Pacific News Service: San Francisco, 1999), www.pacificnews.org/jinn/stories/5.02/990126–pan–african.html.

81 Belinda Carberry, "Teaching African Literature in English" (Yale–New Haven Teachers Institute: New Haven, Conn., 2005); Raffael Scheck, "They Are Just Savages: "German

Massacres of Black Soldiers from the French Army in 1940," *The Journal of Modern History*, (University of Chicago Press), p. 325. Lerone Bennett Jr., "The 10 biggest myths about black history," *Ebony*, Feb. 1984, p. 25.

82 William Loren Katz, *Black Indians: a hidden heritage* (Aladdin Paperbacks edition, an imprint of Simon & Schuster: New York, 1997), p. 10. *Jan Nederveen Pieterse, White on Black: Images of Africa and Blacks in Western Popular Culture* (Yale University Press: New Haven, 1992) pp. 9, 108–11, 202. Pieterse writes, "It has often been observed that race is not a reality but a social construct. That is the point of departure of this book.... The legacy of several hundred years of western expansion and hegemony, manifested in racism and exoticism, continues to be recycled in western culture in the form of stereotypical images of non–western cultures."

83 Doris Bailey–Burton, "My Life Experience Portfolio: Helping Others," New York City (unpublished manuscript), p. 4.

84 Ibid., p. 5.

85 Roberts, p. 65.

86 Alan Brinkley, *American History, A Survey, Volume II: Since 1865* (USA McGraw–Hill, Inc.: Place of Publication, 1995), p. 645.

87 Ibid., pp. 432–433. Colonel Richard Ernest Holz, "The Salvation Army and the Negroes of the Southern States of North America," *The Officer* (Salvation Army International Headquarters: London), July 1914, p. 478.

88 Holz, pp. 477–478.

89 Brinkley, pp. 432–433.

90 Holz, pp. 478–479.

91 Brinkley, p. 423. Reconstruction governments established a large network of schools for former slaves: 4,000 schools by 1870, staffed by 9,000 teachers (half of them black) teaching 200,000 students (approximately 12 percent were freedmen). In the 1870s, there was a comprehensive educational system in the South. By 1876, more than half of all white children and about 40 percent of all black children were attending schools in the South.

92 *The War Cry*, Nov. 12, 1932, p. 1.

93 Brinkley, pp. 644–645.

94 Ibid., p. 682.

95 Lt. Colonel Jacob A. Hohn, from a letter to Major Allan Wiltshire at USA Eastern Territorial Headquarters regarding "Chappy," July 13, 1999.

96 Bailey–Burton, p. 12.

97 Roberts, p. 72.

98 Whitworth Bosch, Allan, *The Salvation Army in Chicago, 1885–1914,* (University of Chicago, 1965), p. 60.

99 Karen Young, "A 'Gideon' of the Chicago Slums," *Priority!* (Salvation Army USA Eastern Territory, West Nyack, N.Y.), Winter 2006, p. 56.

100 Colonel John W. Paton, from a letter to Colonel Willard S. Evans in New York regarding Mabel V. Broome, Jan. 23, 1984. Colonel Willard S. Evans, from a letter in response to Colonel Paton in Chicago, Ill., Feb. 9, 1984. Officer's Service History and Corps History records, Central Territory.

101 Commissioner Edward Carey, "Mission Flag Hoisted In Cleveland," *The War Cry*, Feb. 9, 1980, p.11.

102 Roberts, p. 69 (unpublished biographical sketch).

103 Ibid., p. 68 (unpublished biographical sketch).

104 Ibid., p. 70 (unpublished biographical sketch).

105 L. Masco Young, "Little Rock's Angel of Mercy: pretty Salvation Army officer unselfishly toils to help Arkansas' needy Negroes," *Our World* newspaper (Little Rock, Ark., 1952), pp. 56–59.
106 Roberts, p. 65 ,unpublished biographical sketch.
107 "Salvation Army Marks Founding: Tablet set at site of 1889," *The Cleveland Plain Dealer*, Nov. 4, 1944, NP.
108 Mrs. S/Major M. Smith promoted to Glory," *The War Cry*, "May 25, 1957, p. 15; Major Maurice E. Smith, unpublished biographical sketch, Nov. 21, 2005.
109 Smith, unpublished biographical sketch.
110 "United in Marriage," *The War Cry*, Aug. 26, 1944, p. 11.

Chapter 5

111 "Christianity Beautiful," *Arkansas State Press, City Edition*, April 15, 1949, p. 1; L. Masco Young, *Our World,* p. 59.
112 Lt. Colonel Florence Turkington, letter to Colonel Holland French at USA Eastern Territorial Headquarters regarding then–Second Lieutenant Norma T. Roberts, July 21, 1948.
113 Young, *Our World,* pp. 56–59.
114 Jerry Neil, *Arkansas Gazette*, July 7, 1949, NP.
115 Young, *Our World,* pp. 56–59. Neil, *Arkansas Gazette*.

Chapter 6

116 Brigadier Edward Carey, letter written to Colonel Samuel Hepburn at USA Eastern Territorial Headquarters regarding the Cleveland East 33rd Street Corps, March 2, 1949; Purviance, letter written to Carey at Northeastern Ohio Divisional Headquarters, regarding the Cleveland East 33rd Street Corps, March 24, 1949; "The Salvation Army Central Area Corps," dedication ceremony program, Sunday May 22, 1949.
117 McKinley, *Somebody's Brother: A History of The Salvation Army Men's Social Service Department 1891–1985* (The Edwin Mellen Press: Lewiston/Queenston, England, 1986), p. 185.
118 Ibid., pp. 185–186.
119 Brown vs. Board of Education decision declares separate but equal schools unconstitutional—"Supreme Court of the United States, Brown v. Board of Education, 347 U.S. 483 (1954) (USSC+) 347 U.S. 483 Argued Dec. 9, 1952; Reargued Dec. 8, 1953; Decided May 17, 1954. Appeal from the United States District Court for the District of Kansas.
120 McKinley, *Somebody's Brother*, p. 186.
121 Answers.com, "Marian Anderson: biography" http://www.answers.com/topic/marian–anderson.
122 Promotion to Glory and Funeral Service program (obituary) Maryland, for Brigadier Victor S. Wilson, Nov. 2, 2002. Also Roberts, pp. 63–64. Unpublished biographical sketch.
123 "Mrs. S/Major M. Smith, Promoted to Glory," *The War Cry*, May 25, 1957, p. 15; Major Maurice E. Smith, unpublished biographical sketch.
124 Harmon Tate interview at the Mystic Valley Corps, Massachusetts Division, "Oral History" series, USA Eastern Territory Museum Archives.
125 Commissioner Ernest I. Pugmire, "Some effects of Prejudice and Discrimination on the Personality of Children," *Testament to Youth: The Salvation Army's Report to the Mid–Century*

White House Conference On Children and Youth, (The Salvation Army National Headquarters: New York City, 1950), p. 37.

Chapter 7

126 Major Abraham Johnson, "Reflections on Past, Present, and Future," a paper presented at the African Heritage Symposium Leadership Development Conference, Hillside Inn and Conference Center, East Stroudsburg, Pa., Oct. 21, 1998. Warren L. Maye, unpublished notes from the Johnsons' retirement program at Star Lake Tabernacle, July 20, 2002; Maye, "Lt. Colonels Johnson retire: mark the 'end of an era,' " *Good News!* (Salvation Army USA Eastern Territory, West Nyack, N.Y.), Sept. 2002, p. 11

127 A. Johnson, "Reflections on Past, Present, and Future."

128 Lt. Colonel Dorothy Purser, unpublished interview with Maye, Williams Memorial Residence, New York City, 2004; Maye, "She Fears Not," *Priority*!, Fall 2004, pp. 37–43; unpublished biographical sketch.

129 Major Vivian Taylor–Childs interview with Maye, Dec. 2004; unpublished testimony.

130 Ibid.

131 Ibid.

132 Roberts, p. 70 (unpublished biographical sketch).

133 Lieutenant Hester Dixon, "Sharing from the heart: I serve an army that battles the toughest enemy of all—poverty," *Ladies Home Journal*, Dec. 1985, p. 20.

134 "Mrs. S/Major M. Smith, Promoted to Glory," *The War Cry*, May 25, 1957, p. 15; Unpublished biographical sketch.

135 Maye, unpublished notes from the Johnsons' retirement program at Star Lake Tabernacle, July 20, 2002; Maye, "Lt. Colonels Johnson retire: marks an 'end to an era,' *Good News!*, Sept. 2002, p. 11.

136 "Worker's $500 Aids SA's Drive," *Cleveland Plain Dealer*, April 20, 1958, NP.

137 McKinley, *Somebody's Brother*, p. 186.

Chapter 8

138 Brigadier W. R. H. Goodier, divisional commander, National Capital Division, "The Poor People's Campaign and The Salvation Army," position statement, no date, pp. 1–2.

139 Shumel Ross, www.infoplease.com/spot/marchonwashington.html, Aug. 14, 2006.

140 Ernest R. Holz, , "Where do we stand on Civil Rights?", *New Soldiers*,1965, NP, USA Eastern Territory Heritage Museum.

141 A. Johnson, "Reflections on Past, Present, and Future."

142 "1963: Kennedy shot dead in Dallas," On this Day website, Nov. 22, 1963, bbc.co.uk, http://news.bbc.co.uk/onthisday/hi/dates/stories/november/22/newsid_2451000/2451143.stm.

143 Maye, unpublished notes from the Johnsons' retirement program.

144 Purser, unpublished interview with Maye, Williams Memorial Residence, New York City, 2004; Gariepy, *Challenge Response: A Documentary on Christianity in Action in the Inner City* (The Salvation Army Northeastern Ohio Division: Cleveland, 1994), pp. 111–116.

145 Majors Allan and Marjorie Wiltshire, retirement ceremony, March 10, 2000, USA Eastern Territorial Headquarters; Retirement ceremony program biography.

146 Roberts, p. 69 (unpublished biographical sketch).

Chapter 9

147 McKinley, *Marching to Glory*, p. 260.
148 Susan Flack, M.A., "Jim Crow Legislation Overview" (California State University: Northridge, Date). Article written for "The History of Jim Crow" series (website) http://www.jimcrowhistory.org/resources/lessonplans/hs_es_jim_crow_laws.htm.
149 Maye, conversations with the Gaithers in Johannesburg, South Africa, Mozambique, and Swaziland in the Southern Africa Territory, Dec. 2000.
150 Captain Dean Pallant, " 'God called me and prepared me,' says Army leader," *Salvationist* (Salvation Army International Headquarters (IHQ): London). Taken from IHQ website, 2005, a two–part interview with Chief of the Staff Commissioner Israel L. Gaither.
151 Paul Lombardo, "Eugenic Laws Against Race Mixing," Social Origins of Eugenics, Image Archive on the American Eugenics Movement (Doland DNA Learning Center, Cold Spring, STATE, Harbor Laboratory website http://www.eugenicsarchive.org/html/eugenics/essay7text.html).
152 McKinley, *Marching to Glory*, pp. 260–261.
153 "1965: Black nationalist leader shot dead," On this Day (website) http://news.bbc.co.uk/onthisday/hi/dates/stories/february/21/newsid_2752000/2752637.stm (cited Dec. 10, 2007).
154 Maye, telephone interviews conducted with Harper, Dec. 31, 2004.
155 McKinley, *Marching to Glory*, pp. 260–261; Promotion to Glory service for Major George H. Evans (program obituary), Jan. 29, 2000, The Salvation Army Philadelphia Roxborough Corps, Philadelphia, Pa.
156 Roberts, p. 69; Unpublished biographical sketch; "Soldiers of Uncommon Valor: A tribute to Salvationists of African Heritage" video, Office of Media Ministries, USA Eastern Territory, as told by Major A. Margaret (Yarde) Samuel; Gariepy, *Challenge Response,* p. 13.
157 Promotion to Glory service for. Evans; Brownsville Corps annual dinner program, "Marching into the 21st Century," biography of Evans, May 15, 1993.
158 Majors Cleo and Carmen Damon, "Retirement Dinner and Service," Feb. 18–20, 2005, Naples, Fla.; Majors Allan and Marjorie Wiltshire, letter written to the Damons in Ocala, Fla., March 3, 2005.
159 "LeHigh Recreation Center Dedication Service" program, Philadelphia, Pa., Dec. 1, 1946; "Philadelphia Canteens Serve at City's 'Biggest Fire,' " *The War Cry*, Feb. 9, 1963, NP.
160 Dixon, p. 20.
161 Jack Chamberlain, "Youth follows in dad's footsteps to train for Salvation Army post," *Roanoke Times* (Roanoke, Va., 1967), NP.

Chapter 10

162 McIntyre, "Facing Ghetto Problems—As I see it," unpublished paper, New York City, Sept. 1968.
163 Ibid.
164 Attending the meeting were: Brigadier and Mrs. B. Barton McIntyre, Brigadier Lebert Bernard, Major and Mrs. Hugh Norris, Major Dorothy A. Purser, R.N., Major Lilian Yarde, Captain and Mrs. Abraham Johnson, Captain Israel L. Gaither, Captain Ronald Lowery, Captain Francine Freeman, Lieutenant George Evans, Lieutenant Noel V. Christian, Lt. Carmilla Gaither (Israel Gaither's sister, who was eventually promoted to Glory), and Lt.

Vhonda Ridley. Also invited were Auxiliary Captain and Mrs. Alfred Jones and Captain Elizabeth Reed, but they could not attend.

165 McIntyre, "Black Officers' Meeting," a letter written to Colonel J. Clyde Cox at Territorial Headquarters, May 26, 1969; Lt. Colonel John D. Waldron, "Black Commissioned Officers' Meeting," a letter written to McIntyre at Territorial Headquarters, June 2, 1969; Colonel J. Clyde Cox, "Black Commissioned Officers' Meeting," a letter written to Waldron, June 10, 1969; Waldron, "Black Officers' Meeting," letters written to Captain Israel L. Gaither at the Homewood Corps, June 23 and August 28, 1969; Major Dorothy A. Purser, "Report on the meeting of active black officers serving in the Eastern Territory" (held at the Eastern Territorial Congress, June 1969).

166 Rise B. Axelrod, Charles R. Cooper, *Reading Critically, Writing Well: A reader and guide,* (St. Martin's Press: New York, D), pp. 10, 21.

167 Holz, *New Soldiers.*

168 Purser, "Report on the meeting of active black officers serving in the Eastern Territory" (held at the Eastern Territorial Congress, June 1969).

169 A. Johnson, "Reflections on Past, Present, and Future."

170 Maye, "'Discovering our roots': Seminar delegates explore their heritage," *Good News!,* June 2002, p.5

171 Gariepy, *Challenge Response,* pp. 49–56.

172 Maye, interview with Majors Timothy and Grace Thomas, Harlem Temple Corps, 2002; "A Celebration of Life," Promotion to Glory program for Major Timothy Thomas, Gaston, N.C., July 16, 2004; Major Patricia Mack, "Major Timothy Thomas promoted to Glory," *Good News!* Sept. 2004, p. 14.

173 Gariepy, *Challenge Response,* pp. 63–71.

174 Alvin H. Darden Jr., M.D., letter to Gerald White, editor of the *Cincinnati Enquirer*, Sept. 30, 1968; Captain Karl E. Nelson, letter written to Lt. Colonel Evelyn Skinner, William Booth Memorial Hospital administrator; Maye, "She Fears Not," *Priority!,* Fall, 2004, pp. 37–41; Norman H. Murdoch, *A Centennial History: The Salvation Army in Cincinnati 1885–1985* (The Salvation Army: Place of Publication, 1985), p. 61.

Chapter 11

175 "Hough Salvation Army Officers Transferred," *Call and Post* (Place of Publication), June 24, 1972, NP.

176 Milt Servias, "Salvation Army Approach to Minority and Inner City Needs: Black Leadership Conference, How? When? Where?" Nashville, Tenn., meeting notes, 1972.

177 Promotion to Glory service for Major George H. Evans.

Chapter 12

178 Dr. Ronald W. Holz, "Major Events in Salvation Army Music: Milestones during the life of William Booth," Asbury College, Wilmore, Ky.

179 Wyatt T. Walker, *Somebody's Calling My Name: Black Sacred Music and Social Change* (Judson Press: Valley Forge, Pa., 1979), pp. 127–180.

180 Ibid., pp. 62, 78, 84, 98, 180.

181 "The Colored Work," *The War Cry*, June 16, 1894, NP.

182 Linda D. Johnson, "Heritage Museum inspired by Holy Spirit," *Good News!,* July 17, 1998, pp. 1, 5; Julie Chesham Whittington, Salvation Army Heritage Museum Center, USA

Eastern Territorial Headquarters, West Nyack, NY.; Warren L. Maye, "Do what you must do: Rev. Bernice King delivers evangelistic message," *Good News!* May 29, 2001, pp. 1, 3.

183 Bailey–Burton, p. 17.

184 Bailey–Burton, p. 32.

185 Ibid.

186 Gariepy, "7,000 Celebrate Christ! At USA Eastern Congress: Kenneth Burton, 'Man of the Year,' " *The War Cry*, Aug. 1, 1992, p. 19; Robert Mitchell, "Moved by the Music," *Priority!* Summer 2001, pp. 12–15; Craig Evans, "Ken Burton, Bandmaster to Bank On," *The War Cry*, March 7, 1998, pp. 10–11.

187 "Profiles of Salvationism: An Open–Door Policy," *The War Cry*, Sept. 10, 1994, pp. 6–8.

188 Allan Wiltshire, Jr., biographical sketch prepared for the Regional African Heritage Convocation "Stand and Withstand," Oct. 21–22, 1995, New York; program brochure, p. 16; "Onward! Christian Soldiers," *The Young Salvationist* (The Salvation Army USA National Headquarters, Alexandria, Va.), Oct. 1992, p. 11.

189 "The Salvation Army Heritage Hill Band 110th Anniversary (1884–1994)," Grand Rapids, Michigan, program brochure, pp. 1–2.

190 Captain Frank Duracher, "An Interview with Margaret Wiltshire–Davis," *The War Cry*, Jan. 21, 1989, pp. 10–11.

191 "Under Two Flags," *The War Cry*, Sept. 12, 1992, pp. 1, 16–17.

192 Maye, "Perfect Pitch," *Priority!*, Summer 2002, pp. 15–18.

193 Kenneth Burton, notes on blacks in Salvation Army music in the USA Eastern Territory, Nov. 15, 2005.

194 L. Johnson, "Welcome of Nolands, cadets crackles with excitement," *Good News!*, Oct. 9, 1998, pp. 1, 4–5.

195 Maye, "Northern Ireland 'Harmony Tour' shows unity is possible," *Good News!* Vol. 15, No. 8 (put date instead), p. 8.

196 Steven C. Hohn, "Shout!" *Good News!*, March 28, 2001, p. 7.

Chapter 13

197 Major Gwendolyn Jones, unpublished biography, October 25, 2005.

198 Ibid.

199 Maye, "She Fears Not," *Priority!*, pp. 37–41.

200 "Colonel McIntyre and wife conduct evangelistic campaign," *Call and Post,* Nov. 16, 1974, NP; June 7, 1975 (is this another article?).

201 Janice F. Munson, "Women in the pulpit? For some, it's old hat," *The Plain Dealer*, Dec. 13, 1975, Section B, p. 1.

202 Daniel N. Diakanwa, "Focus on Cross–Cultural Ministries," *Good News!,* Oct. 1994, p. 9

203 Maye, "Martin Luther King, Sr., was a friend of the Army," *The War Cry*, Jan. 12, 1985, p. 4; Maye, " 'Daddy' King's message of hope," *Good News!,* Jan. 1995, p. 11.

204 Major Grace Cumberbatch, unpublished autobiographical sketch, Oct. 19, 2005.

205 Roberts, pp. 6–7; Captain Israel L. Gaither, letter to Major Dorothy Breen, territorial literary secretary, regarding *The Black Salvationist*, May 25, 1979.

Chapter 14

206 David Wilson, "Constructing a 'Black–on–Black' Violence: The Conservative Discourse," University of Illinois, Place? Department of Geography (website) http://www.acme–journal.org/vol1/wilson.pdf.

207 "Homicide Trends in the U.S.: Age Trends," U.S. Department of Justice, Office of Justice Programs, Bureau of Justice Statistics, www.ojp.usdoj.gov/bjs/homicide/teens.htm; C.A. Bell; "Female Homicides in United States Workplaces, 1980–1985," National Institute of Occupational Safety and Health, Morgantown, WV, 26505, 1991, http://www.ajph.org/cgi/content/abstract/81/6/729, referenced Aug. 17, 2006.

208 M. Wiltshire, "My perspective," an unpublished autobiographical sketch, Oct. 21, 2005.

209 Captain Allan Wiltshire, Sr., "Cultural Awareness & Minority Ministries (Black Culture)," a paper presented at The Salvation Army National Social Services Conference, Kansas City, Missouri, March 27, 1984.

210 Maye, " 'Sarge': The Man With a Holy Smile," *Priority!*, Summer 2000, pp. 45–48; Merle Howe, oral history interview with Edward Gooding; "A Fisher of Men: He dares to go where most would fear to tread…," *The War Cry*, Aug. 28, 1993, pp. 18, 19.

211 Major Victor Leslie, unpublished autobiographical sketch, March 2005; Warren L. Maye, personal interview with Major Victor Leslie, March 12, 2005.

212 Joanie Perkins Potter, "Tom Skinner: The Man, The Prophet, The Legacy," *Urban Family: The Magazine of Hope & Progress*, (Publisher: Place of Publication), Fall 1994, pp. 6–11; Tom Skinner Associates 15th Anniversary journal.

213 Maye, "Judged 'Faithful,' " *Priority!* Fall 1999, p.11.

214 Rev. Tom Skinner, sermon given at a Friday Evening at the Temple meeting in New York City, Nov. 2, 1979.

215 Dixon, *Ladies Home Journal,* pp. 20, 23.

216 Roberts, p. 69; Unpublished biographical sketch; "Soldiers of Uncommon Valor: A tribute to Salvationists of African Heritage" video, Office of Media Ministries, USA East, as told by Major A. Margaret (Yarde) Samuel; Gariepy, *Challenge Response*, p. 13.

217 McKinley, *Marching to Glory*, pp. 324–325.

218 Cynthia Brown Austin, "Fully Surrendered," *Priority!*, Fall 2002, pp. 27–30; Maye, "Army's highest honor awarded," *Good News!,* July 2002, p. 2.

219 Maye, telephone interviews conducted with Major Stephen Harper, Dec. 31, 2004.

220 Wiltshire, unpublished biography of Majors Lonneal and Patty Richardson, Jan. 6, 2005.

Chapter 15

221 McKinley, *Marching to Glory* p. 329.

222 Dixon, *Ladies Home Journal,* pp. 20–23.

223 Maye, "Celebrating God's faithfulness: Majors Wiltshire retire;" "Under fire in Panama, Wiltshires stayed true to their own 'Operation Just Cause' " *Good News!,* Easter 2000, p. 5.

224 "YPSM Clara Paige: Order of the Founder," *The War Cry,* July 22, 1989, p. 11.

225 Major Lydia Pearson, "Major Lydia Pearson, Cleveland (Miles Park), Ohio," an unpublished autobiography, Dec. 11, 2005.

226 "Hall of Service Honors Black Officers; Provides Youth with Role Models," *Good News!,* Feb. 1988, p. 9. By 2005, Hispanics of all races had become the fastest growing segment of Salvation Army soldiers in the USA Eastern territory.

227 Diakanwa, "Focus on Cross–Cultural Ministries," *Good News!,* Oct. 1994, p. 9; McKinley, *Marching to Glory,* p. 325.
228 Diakanwa, "History of the first Haitian corps in the Southern Territory and the USA," via e–mail, Oct., 26, 2005.
229 Captain Robert Dixon, "Black Salvationism: Past, Present & Future," *Good News!,* February 1988, pp. 1, 4–9; Captain George Evans, "The Black Salvationist" (work in progress regarding the Cleveland (Central Area) Corps, Ohio. ADHOC Committee, Dec. 1, 1978.
230 Diakanwa, "Brief History of Haitian Ministry in the Eastern Territory," a paper written Oct. 20, 2005.
231 Maye, telephone interviews with Major Stephen Harper, Dec. 31, 2004.
232 Diakanwa, "Focus on Cross–Cultural Ministries"; McKinley, *Marching to Glory*, p. 325.

Chapter 16

233 Diakanwa, presentation at a symposium on African–American recruitment and preparation in Ashford, Conn., 1993. Maye, telephone interview Sept. 24, 2005.
234 Diakanwa, "Focus on Cross–Cultural Ministries."
235 Maye, interview with Daniel N. Diakanwa, 1990.
236 Pearson, "Major Lydia Pearson, Cleveland (Miles Park) Ohio," unpublished autobiographical sketch.
237 Cuesta Benberry, *Always There: The African American Presence in American Quilts* (Kentucky Quilt Project: Place of Publication, 1992), p. 62.
238 Dr. Wyatt Tee Walker, "The Story of Gospel Music: The Power in the Voice," a video documentary, British Broadcasting Corporation (BBC), 1996.
239 Captain Janet Love, "A Quilt of God's Love," *Cross–Cultural Vision*, Issue no. XXII, p. 13.
240 Lieutenant K. Kendall Matthews, LSW/BSW, "Urban Corps & Institutional Social Services: How are we perceived, bridging the gap from client to soldier," a paper written for The Salvation Army African American Council of War in the USA Central Territory, 1994.
241 Matthews, LSW/BSW, "Urban Corps & Institutional Social Services," 1994.
242 Jennie Keast, "Doing a New Thing," *Priority!*, Spring 1999, p. 11; Warren L. Maye, "Planting for the harvest," *Good News!,* Oct. 1994, p. 4.
243 Diakanwa, "History of the first Haitian corps in the Southern Territory and the USA,"
244 Unpublished biographical sketches of Colonels Franklyn and Joan Thompson.
245 Maye, "100 Years in Harlem Marching to the Glory of God," *The War Cry*, June 5, 1993, pp. 10, 11; Warren L. Maye, "A cherished past, a challenging future: Harlem Temple Corps celebrates centennial," *Good News!,* Dec. 1992, p. 8. In 1892, New York's black community lived in Seneca Village (know today as Central Park) before moving to Harlem. Prior to 1825, blacks lived primarily in lower Manhattan (Wall Street area).
246 Wiltshire, unpublished biography of Majors Lonneal and Patty Richardson.
247 Major Grace Cumberbatch, unpublished autobiographical sketch, Oct. 19, 2005.
248 Diakanwa, "Brief History of Haitian Ministry in the Eastern Territory"; Kenneth Speranza, "Greater New York opens ministry to Haitians on Long Island," *Good News!*, Feb. 1995, p. 9.
249 Unpublished biographical sketches of Colonels Franklyn and Joan Thompson.
250 "Movin' On Up," *Emerge,* May 1997, p. 16.
251 Edwards, "The Road Ahead in a Multi–Cultural World," a paper delivered at the International Conference of Leaders, Melbourne, Australia, April 1998; Edwards, "Edwards

Pays Tribute to Aunt Who Led Him to Christ," *New Frontier* (The Salvation Army USA Western Territory: Place), Date. pp. 1, 10.

252 "Trophies of Grace: A collision course to hell," *The War Cry,* Nov. 25, 1995, pp. 6–7; "Army Captain Named 'Woman of Achievement,' " *Priority!,* Summer 1999, p. 12.

253 Lt. Colonel William D. MacLean, "Appointed to serve the world," *Good News!,* July 1996, p. 7.

254 Leslie, unpublished biography, October 24, 2005.

255 Major Maurice Edward Smith, unpublished biography.

256 L. Johnson, "Reconciliation is watchword in the 'new South Africa,' " *Good News!* pp. 1, 7.

257 Captain E. Lewanne Dudley, "Blessing Overcomes Insult," *The War Cry*, Jan. 25, 1997, p. 2.

258 Dudley, " 'Friends forever': One officer's experience at the International College for Officers," *Good News!,* Jan. 16, 1998, p. 5.

Chapter 17

259 Maye, "African Heritage Symposium explores 'rainbow' of possibilities," *Good News!,* Nov. 20, 1998, pp. 1, 4; Major Abraham Johnson, "Reflections on Past, Present, and Future."

260 Major George H. Evans, personal testimony presented at the USA Eastern Territory's Men Officers' Summit, Hershey, Pa., 1999; Promotion to Glory service for Major George H. Evans.

261 L. Johnson, "Gaithers appointed to lead Southern African Territory," *Good News!* Oct. 23, 1998, pp. 1, 7.

262 L. Johnson, " 'Journey in Hope' brings spirit of repentance, reconciliation," *Good News!,* July 3, 1998, pp. 1, 4–5.

263 Maye, " 'Soldiers of uncommon valor' chronicled in new video," *Good News!,* Nov. 6, 1998, pp. 1, 3.

264 Edwards, "The Road Ahead in a Multi–Cultural World," April 1998.

265 Evans, personal testimony, 1999; Maye, " 'Blazing with Holiness': Men Officers' Conference fans spiritual flame," *Good News!,* June 13, 1999, pp. 1, 12.

266 Maye, " 'Mission matters most': Commissioners Gaither return," *Good News!,* June 2002, pp. 1–2.

267 Maye, personal interviews with the Commissioners Gaither in Mozambique, Swaziland, and Johannesburg, South Africa, Dec. 2000.

268 Leslie, unpublished autobiographical sketch, Oct. 24, 2005.

269 Maye, " 'Shepherds and servants' promoted to lieutenant colonels," *Good News!,* p. 4; Maye, "New appointments." *Good News!,* p. 2.

270 Majors Allan and Marjorie Wiltshire, retirement ceremony remarks, March 10, 2000, USA Eastern Territorial Headquarters.

271 Maye, " 'Red–hot' conference attracts African Americans to Army," *Good News!,* May 12, 2000, pp. 1, 5.

272 Major Jenny Harms, "Gaithers meet Mandela," *Good News!,* Oct. 25, 2000, p. 5.

Chaper 18

273 Edwards, "Mission and ministry … that is what it is all about," *New Frontier*, Oct, 27, 2001, pp. 3–4; Allie Martin and Jody Brown, "Salvation Army Nixes Divisive Policy Change," AgapePress: Christian News Service, Nov. 12, 2001, http://headlines.agapepress.

org/archive/11/122001a.asp; Commissioners Conference Statement, Nov. 12, 2001. Maye, interview with Commissioner David Edwards via e–mail, May 30, 2002.

274 Maye, interview with Commissioner David Edwards, May 30, 2002.

275 Leslie, unpublished biography, March 2005; Oct. 24, 2005.

276 "Commissioners Edwards enter retirement," *New Frontier*, June 30, 2002, p. 1.

277 Maye, interview with Commissioner David Edwards, May 30, 2002.

278 Maye, " 'Discovering our roots,' " *Good News!,* June 2002, p. 5.

279 Maye, unpublished notes from the Lt. Colonels Johnson retirement program at Star Lake Tabernacle, Saturday, July 20, 2002; Maye, "Lt. Colonels Johnson retire: mark the 'end of an era,' " *Good News!,* Sept. 2002, p. 11.

280 Maye, "Army's highest honor awarded," *Good News!,* July 2002, p. 2; Austin, "Fully Surrendered," *Priority!,* Fall 2002, pp. 27–30.

281 Promotion to Glory and Funeral Service program (obituary), Maryland, for Brigadier Victor S. Wilson, Nov. 2, 2002.

282 Promotion to Glory service for Major George H. Evans.

Chaper 19

283 Maye, "'Mission matters most:' Commissioners Gaither return," *Good News!,* June 2002, pp. 1–2.

284 Commissioner Israel L. and Eva D. Gaither, farewell addresses to officers and employees at Territorial Headquarters, Nov. 2002; Maye, "Gaithers hailed as leaders, friends in 'very personal' sendoff," *Good News!* pp. 1, 6; Captain Dean Pallant, " 'God called me and prepared me,' says Army leader," *Salvationist*, International Headquarters website, 2005, two–part interview with Chief of the Staff Commissioner Israel L. Gaither.

285 Maye, "USA welcomes the Cliftons to install the Gaithers as national leaders," *Good News!*, June 2006, pp. 1, 4.

Chaper 20

286 Maye, interview with Commissioner David Edwards, May 31, 2002.

287 Major Marjorie Wiltshire, "My perspective," an unpublished autobiographical sketch, Oct. 21, 2005.

288 Captain K. Kendall Matthews, "My View of The African–American Salvationist," unpublished writing, Oct. 22, 2005.

289 Pallant, *Salvationist,* "'God called me and prepared me,' says Army leader," International Headquarters website, 2005, a two–part interview with Chief of the Staff Commissioner Israel L. Gaither.

290 Major Raphael C. Jackson, "Recruitment and Cultivation of African–American Candidates for The Salvation Army:" A Project Report Presented to the Faculty of the Degree Completion Program, Nyack College, Nyack, N.Y., Sept. 1999, pp. 40–41.

291 Daniel Diakanwa, "What officers of African descent think about the future of blacks in The Salvation Army," unpublished writing, Oct. 18, 2005.

292 Jackson, p. 41

293 Maye, interview with Commissioner Israel L. Gaither via e–mail, Nov. 1, 2005.

294 Jackson, p. 38

295 Ibid., p. 53

296 Ibid., p. 67

Biographies

Warren L. Maye, B.F.A., M.A., is editor and contributing writer of *Good News!*, the Salvation Army's USA Eastern Territory monthly news magazine, as well as contributing editor and writer to *Priority!*, a quarterly magazine about people touched by the Army's ministry nationwide. Mr. Maye has chronicled the Salvation Army's work for 27 years, serving as an editor, writer, and art director at National, USA Eastern territorial, and Greater New York divisional headquarters. He has worked in publishing for more than 30 years, and has designed history textbooks for Harper & Row Publishers (now HarperCollins), as well as other publishing companies. He and his wife, Dr. Marilyn Maye, co authored *Orita: Rites of Passage for youth of African Descent in America* (2000).

Daniel N. Diakanwa, B.A., M.P.S., M.P.A., is research coordinator for *Soldiers of Uncommon Valor: the history of Salvationists of African descent in the United States*. He has worked for 22 years in various positions in The Salvation Army, including director of the USA Eastern Territory's Multicultural Ministry Bureau (1991–1994) and as its African heritage consultant (1994–2001). Mr. Diakanwa has also served as pastor of the former Brooklyn Citadel Corps in New York City. He has published three books including *Key to Intercultural Ministries* (2000), *Global Ministry in a Global Society* (2007), *and Understanding, Assisting and Counseling, Immigrants* (2007).

Selected Bibliographies

Books

Altman, Susan. *The Encyclopedia of African–American Heritage*. New York: Facts on File, Inc., 1997.

Barnes, Cyril. *With Booth in London: A London Guide*. London: The Salvation Army International Headquarters, 1986.

Barton, David. *Setting the Record Straight: American History in Black and White*. Aledo, TX: WallBuilders Press, Inc., 2004.

Booth, William. *In Darkest England and the Way Out*. 6th ed. London: Charles Knight & Co. LTD, 1970.

Booth–Tucker, F. de L. *The Life of Catherine Booth:The Mother of The Salvation Army*. New York: Fleming H. Revell Company, 1870.

Brengle, Samuel Logan. *Helps to Holiness*. 2nd ed. London: Salvationist Publishing and Supplies, LTD., 1965.

———. *The Soul–Winner's Secret*. 2nd ed. London: Salvationist Publishing and Supplies, LTD., 1969.

Brinkley, Alan. *American History, a Survey, Volume II: Since 1865*. New York: McGraw–Hill, Inc, 1995.

Brown, Kent L., ed. *Medicine in Cleveland and Cuyahoga County: 1810–1976*. Cleveland, OH: The Academy of Medicine of Cleveland, 1977.

Chesham, Sallie. *Born to Battle: The Salvation Army in America*. Chicago: Rand McNally & Co., 1965.

Davis, Russell H. *Black Americans in Cleveland from George Peake to Carl B. Stokes 1796–1969*. Washington, DC: The Association for the Study of Negro Life and History, 1985.

Diakanwa, Daniel N. *Key to Intercultural Ministries: A Biblical Perspective on Human Reconciliation*. Bronx. N.Y.: New Covenant Publications,

2000.

Dorsey, Allison. *To Build Our Lives Together: Community Formation in Black Atlanta, 1875–1906*. Athens: University of Georgia Press, 2004.

Eason, Andrew Mark. *Women in God's Army: Gender and Equality in the Early Salvation Army*. Edited by Eleanor J. Stebner. Vol. 7, *Studies in Women and Religion*. Waterloo, Ontario: Wilfrid Laurier University Press, Canada, 2003.

Ervine, St. John. *God's Soldier: General William Booth*. Vol. 1. New York: The Macmillan Company, 1953.

Friederichs, Hulda. *Romance of The Salvation Army*. London: Cassell and Company, Limited, 1907.

Gariepy, Henry. *Christianity in Action: The Salvation Army in the USA Today*. Wheaton: Victor Books, 1990.

———. *General of God's Army: The Authorized Biography of General Eva Burrows*. Wheaton, Ill.: Victor Books, 1993.

———. *Challenge Response: A Documentary on Christianity in Action in the Inner City in Response to Riots, Racism, Poverty, Crime, and Spiritual Need*: The Salvation Army Northeast Ohio Division and the Hough Multi–Purpose Center, 1994.

Gerber, David A. *Black Ohio and the Color Line 1860–1915*. Edited by August Meier. 10 vols. Vol. 10, *Blacks in the New World*. Urbana: University of Illinois Press, 1976.

Green, Roger J. *War on Two Fronts: The Redemptive Theology of William Booth*. Atlanta: The Salvation Army Supplies, 1989.

Harris, Leslie M. *In the Shadow of Slavery: African Americans in New York City, 1626–1863*. Chicago: University of Chicago Press, 2003.

Herbert A. Wisbey, Jr. *Soldiers with Swords: A History of The Salvation Army in the United States*. New York: The Macmillan Company, 1955.

Holz, Ronald W. *Heralds of Victory: A History Celebrating the 100th Anniversary of the New York Staff Band and Male Chorus 1887–1987*. New York: The Salvation Army, 1986.

Jan Nederveen Pieterse. *White on Black: Images of Africa and Blacks in Western Popular Culture*. New Haven: Yale University Press, 1992.

Jennifer V. Jackson, Mary E. Cothhran. "Black Verses Black: The

Relationships among African, African–American, and African–Caribbean Persons." *Journal of Black Studies* Vol. 33, no. 5 (2003).

Katz, William Loren. *Black Indians: A Hidden Heritage*. New York: Simon & Schuster, 1997.

Langston Hughes, Milton Meltzer, Charles Eric Lincoln. *A Pictorial History of Black Americans*. New York: Crown Publishers, 1983.

Linton, Calvin D., ed. *American Headlines Year by Year*. Nashville: Thomas Nelson Publishers, 1985.

Love, Nat. *The Life and Adventures of Nat Love, Better Known in the Cattle Country as "Deadwood Dick" by Himself: A True History of Slavery Days, Life on the Great Cattle Ranges and on the Plains of the "Wild and Wooly" West, Based on Facts, and Personal Experiences of the Author*. 2nd ed. Baltimore: Black Classics Press, 1988.

McKinley, Edward H. *Somebody's Brother: A History of the Salvation Army Men's Social Service Department, 1891–1985*. New York: The Salvation Army, 1986.

———. *Marching to Glory: The History of The Salvation Army in the United States, 1880–1992*. Grand Rapids, Michigan: William B. Eerdmans Publishing Company, 1995.

———. "The Foundation Principles of the Religion of Jehovah—The Salvation Army and Multiculturalism in Perspective." Atlanta, Georgia, 1998.

Millner, Caille. *The Caribbean/African–American Gap Can Be Bridged with Understanding* [Internet]. Pacific News Service, 1999 [cited Nov. 29, 2007]. Available from www.pacificnews.org/jinn/stories/5.02/990126–pan–african.html.

Morrison–Reed, Mark D. *Black Pioneers in a White Denomination*. Boston: Beacon Press, 1984.

Parks, Rosa. *Rosa Parks: My Story*. New York: Penguin Putnam Books for Young Readers, 1992.

Philip Durham, Everett L. Jones. *The Negro Cowboys*. Lincoln: University of Nebraska Press, 1983.

Richards, Miriam. *Army Beliefs and Characteristics*. 3 vols. Vol. 2. London: The Salvation Army International Headquarters, 1969.

Robert A. Watson, Ben Brown. *The Most Effective Organization in the U.S.: Leadership Secrets of The Salvation Army*. New York: Crown

Publishing Group, 2001.
Roberts, Norma T. *The Black Salvationist*. West Nyack, NY: The Salvation Army Eastern Territory, U.S.A., 1997.
Sandall, Robert. *The History of The Salvation Army: Volume I 1865–1878*. New York: Thomas Nelson and Sons Ltd, 1950.
Satterlee, Allen. *Sweeping through the Land: A History of The Salvation Army in the Southern United States*. Atlanta, GA: The Salvation Army Supplies, 1989.
Smale, Philippa, ed. *The Salvation Army 2005 Yearbook*. Edited by Charles King, *The Salvation Army Yearbook*. London: The Salvation Army International Headquarters, 2005.
Smith, Frank. *The Salvation War in America for 1885: Under the Generalship of Rev. William Booth*: The Salvation Army Headquarters and Trade Department, 1886.
Storey, William Kelleher. *Writing History: A Guide for Students*. Oxford, New York: Oxford University Press, 1999.
Taiz, Lillian. *Hallelujah Lads & Lasses: Remaking The Salvation Army in America, 1880–1930*. Chapel Hill and London: The University of North Carolina Press, 2001.
Van Tassel, David D., and John J. Grabowski, eds. *The Encyclopedia of Cleveland History*. Bloomington, Indiana: Indiana University Press, 1996.
Walker, Wyatt T. *Somebody's Calling My Name: Black Sacred Music and Social Change*. Forge, Pa.: Judson Press, 1979.
Winston, Diane. *Red–Hot and Righteous: The Urban Religion of The Salvation Army*. Cambridge, Mass.: Harvard University Press, 1999.

Selected Articles

"A Resource for the Army World." *The War Cry*, April 13, 1991, 9.
The New York Times, March 16, 1880, 8.
"The Salvation Army: Self–Related Experience of a Former Negro Minstrel." *Albany Times*, August 18, 1884.
"The Beck Family: The Colored Jubilee Singers." *The War Cry*, November 18, 1893, 8.

"The Colored Work." *American War Cry*, June 16, 1894.
"Lifting the Veil; or Acts of Salvationists." *The War Cry* 1894.
"The Colored Work." *The War Cry*, June 16, 1894, 3.
"Captain Alexander Beck." *The War Cry*, November 23, 1894, 5.
"The Commander at Epworth Heights." *The War Cry*, September 21, 1895, 2–4.
"1914 International Congress: Tea at the Astor Estate." *The War Cry*, August 1, 1914, 1.
"9 Injured as Blast Rips Maternity Hospital of Salvation Army Here." *Cleveland Press*, March 12, 1940.
"Booth Hospital to Mark 50th Year." *Cleveland Plain Dealer*, September 29, 1942.
"Salvation Army Marks Founding." *Cleveland Plain Dealer*, November 4, 1944.
"United in Marriage." *Southern War Cry*, August 26, 1944.
"Evangeline Booth to Help Salvation Army Drive Here." *Cleveland Plain Dealer*, June 1, 1947.
"Salvation Army's Cellar Golf Links Is Tricky Course." *Cleveland Plain Dealer*, August 10, 1947.
"Salvation Army on Budget of $900,000." *Cleveland Plain Dealer*, March 21, 1950.
"Salvation Corps to Hail 84 Years." *Cleveland Plain Dealer*, March 5, 1955.
"2 Social Agencies Study Move to Hough Area." *Cleveland Press*, October 4, 1957.
"Mrs. S/Major M. Smith Promoted to Glory." *Southern War Cry*, May 25, 1957, 15.
"Worker's $500 Aids Sa's Drive." *Cleveland Plain Dealer*, April 25, 1958, 52.
"Hough Center Pushed, 2 Other Drives Delayed." *Cleveland Press*, October 7, 1966.
"Two Strategic Locations." *Cleveland Press*, August 31, 1966.
"Salvation Army Plans Hough Center." *The Plain Dealer*, March 4, 1966.
"Mayor Rings Salvation Army Christmas Bell." *Cleveland Press*, November 24, 1967.

"Salvation Army's Hough Multi–Purpose Center Is Dedicated." *Cleveland Press* 1969.

"She Runs for the Glory of God." *The War Cry*, September 5, 1970, 12–13.

"Salvation Army Plans to Move, Expand Facilities for Alcoholics." *Cleveland Press*, June 9, 1971.

"Salvation Army to Open Center." *The Plain Dealer*, December 17, 1971.

"News Briefs." *The War Cry*, August 21, 1971, 20.

"Salvation Army Plans a Salute." *Cleveland Press*, August 21, 1971.

"Center Marks Anniversary." *Cleveland Press*, September 8, 1971.

"Alcoholics Center: The Salvation Army Dedicated Its Harbor Light Center Yesterday." *Cleveland Press*, June 21, 1971.

"Busy Scouts." *Press*, November 3, 1971.

"Hough Salvation Army Officers Transferred." *Cleveland Call and Post*, June 24, 1972.

"New Chiefs at Booth Memorial." *Cleveland Press*, May 2, 1972.

"Brig. Purser to Administer Philly Clinic." *The Cleveland Press*, September 19, 1972.

"Colonel Mcintyre and Wife Conduct Evangelistic Campaign." *Call and Post*, November 16, 1974.

"Colonel Dorothy A. Purser." *Cleveland Press*, February 20, 1974.

"Salvation Army Honors Major Yarde." *Call and Post*, September 6, 1975.

"A Testimonial Banquest in Honor of Lt. Colonel and Mrs. B. Barton Mcintyre." *Call and Post*, June 7, 1975.

Orders and Regulations for Corps Officers of the Salvation Army. London: The Salvation Army International Headquarters, 1976.

"Captain Maurice Smith and Two Junior Solders from the Compton Corps." *The Young Soldier*, January, 1976.

"The Halls Will Be Alive with Sound of Music, Thanks to $30,770 Grant." *The Plain Dealer*, August 25, 1977.

"Retirements from Active Service: Major and Mrs. Vivian Scale." *The War Cry*, December 9, 1978, 8.

"Salvation Army Offers Music Lessons." *The Cleveland Press*, July 12, 1978.

"Recommendations of the National Planning and Development Commission Ministry to Minorities Committee." Atlanta, Georgia, 1983.

"Anith B. Fitts Salvation Army Pioneer Extraordinary." Pittsburgh, PA: Homewood–Brushton Corps, 1983.

"The Salvation Army Bedford Temple Corps 60th Anniversary Celebration." In *Advisory Council Civic Luncheon: Reflections and Projections – Six Decades*. Brooklyn, NY, 1984.

Proclaiming Christ: Friday Evening at the Temple. New York, NY, 1984. flyer – brochure.

"Martin Luther King, Sr., Was a Friend of the Army." *The War Cry*, January 12, 1985, 4–5.

"Australia for Christ: The Salvation Army National Bicentennial Congress, Sydney, May 24–30, 1988." 1988.

"Army Leadership Takes Stand against Racism." *Good News!*, February, 1988, 5.

"African Officer Shares Vision of Evangelism." *Good News!*, February, 1988, 5.

"Let Every Salvationist Break This Modern Curse." *Good News!*, February, 1988, 8.

"Forum Addresses Issues Specific to Black Salvationists." *Good News!*, February, 1988, 1–7.

"'Extraordinary Soldier' Merits Order of the Founder Award for Compassionate Ministry: Ypsm Clara Paige Honored Posthumously." *The Southern Spirit*, August 21, 1989.

"The Order of the Sounder Honoring Ypsm Clara Paige Being Presented, Posthumously." *The Southern Spirit*, July 10, 1989.

"1884–1994: 110th Anniversary the Salvation Army Heritage Hill Band, Grand Rapids, Michigan." Grand Rapids, MI, 1994.

"Malden Man Honored by Salvation Army at Recent Volunteer Recognition Luncheon." *Medford Daily Mercury* 1995, 3.

Abeles, Ed., and Nat D. Mann. "I'se Gwine to Save Yo' Soul: Salvation Song." M. Witmark and Sons, 1897.

Agnew, Major Fletcher. "Commissioner Estill Commissions Western Cadets." *The War Cry*, July 6, 1914, 9.

Banks, Kenneth E. "Salvation Army to Aid Both Mother and Child." *The*

Plain Dealer, April 19, 1972, 12.

Berkow, Ira. "No. Robinson Wasn't First." *The New York Times*, April 6, 1997, 3.

Bernstein, Richard. *New York Times Magazine*, May 18, 1986, 36.

Bryant, James H. "The Salvation Army Boys' Club Richmond Virginia." Richmond, VA: The Salvation Army, 1968.

Campbell, Capt. W.B. "The Charioteers." *The War Cry*, June 23, 1894, 6.

Carey, Edward. "Mission Flag Hoisted in Cleveland." *The War Cry*, Feb. 9, 1980, 11.

Carney, Glandion. "Stepping into the Future: Diversity and the Army." *Good News!*, April 24 1998, 3.

Chamberlain, Jack. "Youth Follows in Dad's Footsteps to Train for Salvation Army Post." *Roanoke Times* 1967.

Dalziel, Colonel William R. "The Chief of the Staff and Mrs. Mapp Lead Canada's Golden Jubilee Congress to a Victorious Conclusion Commissioner and Mrs. Hay Support." *The War Cry*, November 12, 1932.

Davis, Ronald L. F. *Creating Jim Crow: In–Depth Essay* California State University, 2003 [cited November 28, 2007]. Available from www. jimcrowhistoryorg/creating2.htm.

"Focus on Black History Month." *Good News*, August 28, 1993, 12.

Dixon, Hester. "Sharing from the Heart." *Ladies' Home Journal*, December, 1985, 20–23.

Docter, Robert. "Legally Domiciled Adults Will Be Able to Access Benefits." *New Frontier*, October 27 2001, 1, special section.

Duracher, Frank. "An Interview with Margaret Wiltshire–Davis." *The War Cry*, January 21, 1989, 10–11.

Edwards, David. "Get out Your Trumpet—Get Ready to Blow." *New Frontier*, July 30 1997, 2,4.

———. "Mission and Ministry...That Is What It Is All About." *New Frontier*, October 27 2001, 3, 4.

Erving, Julius. "I Was Blessed before I Was Born." *The War Cry*, May 14, 1983, 4–5.

Evans, George H. "'The Black Salvationist' Regarding the Cleveland Ohio Central Area Corps." Cleveland, OH, 1978.

Pearson, Lydia. "Confronting Racism." *Good News!*, June 9 2001, 3.

Scott, Spencer. "$2 Million Hough Center Keeps Evans Active." *Good News*, February, 1988, 4.

Sparks, Gordon. "Black Salvationists Speak Candidly." *Good News*, February, 1988, 7.

Smith, Harry C. "The Salvation Army." *The Cleveland Gazette*, June 14, 1884, 2.

Young, L. Masco. "Little Rock's Angel of Mercy." *Our World*, November, 1952, 56–59.

Gaither, Israel L. "The Future Responsibilities of Blacks." *Good News!*, February, 1988, 6–9.

Hohn, Steven. "'Shout!' Gospel Concert Filled with the Spirit." *Good News!*, March 28 2001, 7.

Holz, Richard Ernest. "The Salvation Army and the Negroes of the Southern States of North America." *The Officer*, July 1914, 477–480.

Ironside, B. A. "A Year's War on the Pacific Coast." *Conqueror* 1896, 546–48.

Johnson, Abraham. "Building Unity in the Army." *Good News*, February 1988, 7–9.

———. "Reflections on Past, Present and Future." 1998.

Johnson, Linda. "'Journey in Hope' Brings Spirit of Repentance, Reconciliation." *Good News!*, July 3 1998, 1, 4–5.

———. "Gaithers Answer Call to 'Come and See'." *Good News!*, December 1998, 1, 5–6.

Lyle, Robin. "Facing Racial Reconciliation." *Good News!*, September 5 1997, 2.

Marshall, T. C. "Our Apostle to the Colored People." *The Conqueror*, October 1896, 473–75.

Maye, Warren L. "General Burrows (R) Brings Message of Hope to Harlem Temple, N.Y." *The War Cry*, December 4, 1993, 14–15.

———. "Lt. Colonels Johnson Retire: Mark the 'End of an Era'." *Good News!*, September 2002, 11.

Miller, Susan. "Christ or Color: The Salvation Army's Black Heritage." *The War Cry*, February, 1984, 1,8.

Miller, Sabrina l. "A Museum Exhibit Reveals What Many Don't Know—a Black Family Was on Board." *The Chicago Tribune*, February 20,

2000.

Munson, Janice F. "Women in the Pulpit? For Some, It's Old Hat." *The Plain Dealer*, December 13, 1975.

Needham, Phil. "The Domestic Partner Issue, Extending Benefits and The Salvation Army: Personal Reflections and Conclusions." *New Frontier*, October 27 2001, 1.

Neil, Jerry. "Christianity Beautiful." *Arkansas Gazette*, April 15, 1949.

Oller, John. "Youths 'Locked' Behind Open Door: Center Gives Offenders a Taste of Responsibility." *Plain Dealer*, August 7, 1978.

Ragan, Jennifer. "Forum Focuses on Issues, Education." *New Frontier*, October 30, 1998, 5.

Rutledge, Archibald. "Prohibition and the Negro." *The Outlook and Independent*, May 28, 1932.

Smith, Frank. "A Night with One of the Coloured Corps." *All the World*, April 1886, 82–84.

Wisbey, Herbert A. Jr. "A Salvation Army Prelude: The Christian Mission in Cleveland, Ohio." *The Ohio Historical Quarterly* 64, no. 1 (1955): 77–81.

Internet Sources

Telescoping the Times: The Age of Imperialism, 1850–1914 [Internet]. McDougal–Little, Houghton Mifflin Company, 1999 [cited Nov. 29 2007]. Available from http://mclane:fresno.k12.ca.us/wilson98/Assignments/ImpCH11.html.

Learn to Live Together The Salvation Army UK Territory, February 2000 [cited 2003]. Available from http://www.salvationarmy.org.uk/en/Library/publications/salvationist/2000/02–05/2000.02.05salvationist_05–02–2000_p2.xml.htm.

Ellis Island & Statue of Liberty [Internet]. American Park Network, 2007 [cited November 28, 2007]. Available from www.americanparknetwork.com/parkinfo/content.asp?catid=85contenttypeid=35.

Acknowledgements

I am thankful to the officers who attended the "Candidates Recruitment Among Minorities Conference" held in April 1972. Together they created the vision for the first chronological history about people of African descent in The Salvation Army. Their efforts led to the work of Major Norma T. Roberts, who, thirty years ago, wrote *The Black Salvationist: People of African Descent in The Salvation Army USA,* which laid the groundwork for and served as the inspiration for *Soldiers of Uncommon Valor: the History of Salvationists of African Descent in the United States.* I am deeply indebted to Major Roberts for her courage as a writer and as a history–making Salvationist in her own right.

I am also grateful to all the territorial commanders in the USA Eastern Territory who supported this project from inception through completion, including Commissioner Ronald G. Irwin; Commissioner Joe Noland, Commissioner Israel L. Gaither, now national commander; and Commissioner Lawrence R. Moretz, the current territorial commander. The USA Eastern Territory's Territorial Committee for Salvationists of African Descent and the Territorial Publications Council, which reviewed and approved the manuscript, also served in a strongly supportive role.

During the early stages of this project, Major Allan Wiltshire and Daniel N. Diakanwa worked diligently to coordinate nationwide Salvation Army research teams that collected Army documents, articles, and photos upon which most of the narrative is based.

I appreciate the work of officers and Army employees who led the research teams in three other U.S. territories, including Major Janet Love, cross–cultural ministries coordinator in the Central Territory; Francis Dingman, former museum coordinator, Geir Engoy, former cross–cultural ministries secretary, and Captain Robert Rudd in the Western Territory; and Major Maurice "Eddie" Smith in the Southern Territory.

Special thanks to Colonel Henry Gariepy, O. F.*, for his contributions as writing coach, instructor, and mentor during this process, as well as for being an inspiration and role model to me and others down through the years.

I truly appreciate the "eagle eye" and "editorial scalpel" of Linda D. Johnson, literary secretary for the USA Eastern Territory, who helped bring clarity to the text. And thanks also to Louise Capuano, Dr. Marilyn Maye, Kenneth Burton, O.F.*, Major E. Lewanne Dudley, and Lt. Colonel Abraham Johnson for taking the time to carefully proofread the manuscript.

Many thanks to the librarians at many urban library systems whose tireless efforts unearthed many documents and articles about The Salvation Army that had been printed in daily newspapers, magazines, and books. I particularly thank the New York Public Library's Schomburg Center for Research in Black Culture; the Cleveland Public Library; the Free Library of Philadelphia; University Libraries, University at Albany, State University of New York; the Albany Main Library; the New York State Library; and the Central Arkansas Library System.

Much thanks to Major Frank Klemanski, Trade secretary, for his indomitable spirit and infectious enthusiasm for this project.

I also thank graphic designers Damian Windley, Lily Chen, Karena Lin, and Keri Johnson, art director, for integrating photos, drawings, and text to create a book that is a pleasure to read. And I would be remiss if I did not offer a special "thank you" to senior designer Peter Hanke. Although he suffered from terminal illness, he nevertheless spent numerous hours designing many of the chapter openings—sometimes during weekends—until the very end of his life on Dec. 28, 2007.

To every individual who has helped make this book possible—please accept my sincere and heartfelt thanks.

Warren L. Maye

**O.F. stands for Order of the Founder, the highest honor that can be conferred on a Salvationist.*

Credits

Chapter opening captions (clockwise)

Chapter 1

Pages 12–13: Salvation Army Founder William Booth and wife Catherine; James Jermy and James Fackler meet for the first time; African Americans hold and open–air meeting; George Scott Railton and "Seven Lassies" arrive in New York City; and Jermy and Fackler pray for converts in Cleveland's African–American community.

Chapter 2

Pages 24–25: A *Harper's Weekly* drawing shows black women participating in a Railton meeting in New York City; an early African–American corps enrolls many junior soldiers; a *War Cry* illustration in 1894 shows a black woman "Charioteer" participating in an open–air meeting; and actors in Philadelphia reenact the inauguration of The Salvation Army in the United States.

Chapter 3

Pages 32–33: Slaves pick cotton in the Deep South; Evangelist Alexander Beck and family minister in California; Booker T. Washington congratulates the Army on its social service initiatives; Auntie Mae Norton of California testifies to the power of God; and a slave woman reflects on her life of pain and struggle.

Chapter 4

Pages 50–51: Early Salvationists attend the 1914 International Congress and Salvationists in stars–in–stripes uniforms in share African–American music and Civil War stories during the1894 International Congress.

Chapter 5

Pages 70–71: Norma T. Roberts in Little Rock, Arkansas in 1952: helping a small child, kneeling in prayer at the Salvation Army Center, and visiting a local family.

Chapter 6

Pages 78–79: Singer Marian Anderson; Harmon Tate; Victor Wilson; Cleveland Central Area Corps, center of the "colored corps" designation controversy; African–American soldiers march into WW2; Harmon Tate as a session mate; and a corps leader teaches music to children.

Chapter 7

Pages 88–89: Abraham Johnson, Vivian Taylor–Childs, and Dorothy Purser share their stories of trial and victory.

Chapter 8

Pages 98–99: Ku Klux Klansman; the Salvation Army crest; *TIME* magazine's cover story on Senator Robert Kennedy; the Statue of Liberty stands as a beacon of hope to immigrants as well as African–Americans struggling to live free; African–Americans ride in the front of the bus for the first time; and black leaders, Dr. Martin Luther King Jr., Rev. Ralph David Abernathy, and Malcolm X discuss the challenges black people face in gaining social and economic equality in America.

Chapter 9

Pages 106–107: Stephen Harper, Israel L. Gaither speaks with Salvation Army supporters; Robert and Hester Dixon teach small children in Brooklyn, N.Y.; a black man drinks from a Jim Crow water fountain in the South; black Salvationists conduct an open–air meeting on a busy city street; Dr. Martin Luther King Jr., leads a civil rights march; and George and Carmen Evans enter training school as cadets.

Chapter 10

Pages 118–119: African Americans participate in a Salvation Army open–air meeting; B. Barton and Mildred McIntyre; Abraham Johnson and corps members minister to neighborhood children; officers and soldiers of the Miles Park Corps in Cleveland marches through the community; Timothy Thomas as a lieutenant.

Chapter 11

Pages 132–133: A man in Cleveland receives social services from the Salvation Army; George Evans encourages a health–care worker; seniors gather for a special dinner at a corps; children enjoy an afternoon in the pool; and Salvationists hold an open–air meeting in Harlem.

Chapter 12

Pages 142–143: Patrick Morris conducts a band rehearsal, soldiers play their instruments at Harlem Temple; the Heritage Hill Band ministers in Michigan; Eric Dina plays cornet; the New Sounds for Christ perform in concert; Bill Rollins leads the Eastern Territorial Songsters; Margaret Davis poses for a CD jacket; the School for Officer Training's Gospel Choir sings for a delegation of Christian writers; Allan Wiltshire Jr., plays piano.

Chapter 13

Pages 176–177: Dr. Martin Luther King Sr., speaks at a rally (© Owen Franken/CORBIS); the book *The Black Salvationist: people of African descent in The Salvation Army, USA* is released; President Jimmy Carter prays for the nation; Lt. Colonel Dorothy Purser at home in Manhattan; Brian and Gwendolyn Jones; men of all races gather for outdoor fellowship; and Brigadier Gladys Goddard and George and Carmen Evans pose during an award ceremony.

Chapter 14

Pages 188–189: Edward Gooding receives the Order of the Founder; Lonneal Richardson; Stephen and Diane Harper; Allan Wiltshire Sr., spends time with young boys in a local community; Delilah Collier; Victor and Rose–Marie Leslie; and Judge Clarence Barry–Austin.

Chapter 15

Pages 202–203: American troops gather around Allan Wiltshire in the aftermath of the U.S. invasion of Panama; Robert and Hester Dixon serve as territorial evangelists; Wilfred H. Samuel preaches the Word of God; people kneel, asking God to answer their prayers; Israel L. Gaither leads singing during a African heritage symposium with Abraham Johnson and Daniel Diakanwa (left); Commissioner David Edwards and members of the Commissioner's Conference; the Johnsons receive an award from General Eva Burrows and Commissioner Andrew S. Miller; and Commissioner David Edwards hugs a child during a African heritage symposium.

Chapter 16

Pages 214–215: African–American officers and soldiers gather in New York for a heritage symposium; Lt. Colonel Angeline Hofman listens as John Stewart share his testimony during an ARC rally in New York City; K. Kendall and Katrina D. Mathews with members of their corps in the Central Territory; members of the Eastern Territory's first Cross–Cultural Ministries Department; seventy commissioned officers, cadets, and local officers of the Eastern Territory meet in New England for an historic symposium on African–American recruitment and preparation; Robert Watson Jr., serves as Cross–Cultural Ministries Department secretary; and K. Kendall Mathews shakes hands with Martin Luther King III.

Chapter 17

Pages 234–235: Eva D. Gaither cradles an HIV/AIDS baby in South Africa; Dennis Young talks about African–American recruitment during a heritage symposium in the Eastern Territory; an officer in Mozambique, Africa, newly commissioned by Commissioner Israel L. Gaither, territorial commander, raises his fist in recognition of the power of God; men pray together during a men's retreat in Pennsylvania; Major Lydia Pearson leads a discussion during a symposium on racial attitudes in The Salvation Army; Major Yvon Alkintor and Envoys Islande and Luxene Claircius celebrate the opening of the first Haitian Corps in the Eastern Territory; (below) Commissioners Gaither and Commissioners Joe and Doris Noland pray in Mozambique, Africa with a woman and her children who have moved into a new home provided by The Salvation Army; Lt. Colonel Abraham Johnson and Major Richard Munn pray together during a men's retreat in Pennsylvania; Commissioner Joe Noland preaches in South Africa; and Commissioners Gaither meet with South African President Nelson Mandela.

Chapter 18

Pages 252–253: In the Western Territory: Hawaiian Salvationists celebrate their heritage; officers, soldiers, and family members huddle in prayer; an Asian Salvationist celebrates her heritage; an African–American cadet witnesses to people on the streets of Los Angeles, Calif.; a homeless man searches for answers; the Army seeks to serve people of all ages and to lead them into a saving knowledge of Jesus Christ; and the Golden Gate Bridge serves as a metaphor for the Salvation Army's ministry, providing a path to eternal Salvation by way of the Cross.

Chapter 19

Pages 262–263: Timbrelist performs with tambourine; Salvationists march through the streets; a young Salvationist wears a WW1 Doughnut Girl uniform during a parade in New York City; General Paul A. Rader appeals to Salvationists to reconcile their racial differences; Major Norma T. Roberts continues her advocacy for the poor and disenfranchised masses; young Salvationists march with flags and gifts in hand during a commissioning of cadets in the East; and officers pay tribute to Tom Ferguson, poet and composer during the unveiling ceremony of the Eastern Territory's Heritage Museum.

Chapter 20

Pages 274–275: Young girls pledge allegiance to God and The Salvation Army; a woman soldier kneels in prayer; the Salvation Army captain's uniform awaits an owner; and a young Salvationist leads a man to Christ as a multitude other people stand, waiting to hear the Gospel message (© Peter Boel Nielsen/Getty Images).

Index

Italic indicates illustrations.

D

E

F

G

H

I

J

K

L

M

N

Q

R

S

T

Y

Glossary

Adherent: A person who regards The Salvation Army, as his/her spiritual home, but has not made a commitment to soldiership.

Adult Rehabilitation Center (ARC): Serves men and women with social, emotional, and spiritual needs who have lost the ability to cope with their problems and provide for themselves. The centers provide adequate housing with work, group and individual therapy in clean wholesome surroundings. Physical and spiritual care prepares beneficiaries to re–enter society and return to employment. Work therapy includes the collection and repair of discarded materials and the operation of thrift stores in which the restored materials are sold at moderate prices. Proceeds from these stores assist in supporting the program of the centers. Frequently people who are rehabilitated reunite with their families and resume normal lifestyles. Sometimes they become Salvationists or officers.

Advisory Board: A group of influential citizens who, believing in the Army's program of spiritual, moral, and physical rehabilitation and amelioration, assist in promoting and supporting Army projects.

Articles of War (Soldier's Covenant): The statement of beliefs and promises, which every intending soldier is required to sign before enrollment.

Auxiliary Captain: A mature Salvationist who is beyond the age limit for full officer training, who holds a warrant of appointment as distinct from commissioned rank, and who may undertake corps or social work similar to that of a commissioned officer.

Blacks: People of African descent who are typically characterized by skin color or by racial classification. Political, sociological, geographical, or cultural circumstances may also define who is "black."

'Blood and Fire': The Army's motto;

refers to the blood of Jesus Christ and the fire of the Holy Spirit.

Boys Adventure Corps (SABAC): is a recreation and camping venture originally designed for boys, but now includes girls. In addition to games, children are encouraged to earn merit badges by achieving specific and varied objectives that measure skill and Christian character.

Cadet: A Salvationist in training for officership

Candidate: A soldier who has been accepted for officer training

Certificate in Recognition of Exceptional Service: The certificate is awarded to Salvationists (officers and soldiers) and friends who work in or for The Salvation Army, whose work, although not being considered for recommendation to the Order of the Founder, or the Order of Distinguished Auxiliary Service, has been of such outstanding value that it should be placed on permanent record. The service being recognized is outstanding in length or quality, work of an unusual nature for the benefit of the Army not being overlooked. General Arnold Brown adopted the award internationally in May 1980, having been in use in Canada since before 1971.

Chief of the Staff: The officer second in command of the worldwide Salvation Army

Circle Corps: A number of societies grouped together so as to form one corps, under the charge of the same officers

Citadel: A hall used for worship.

Colors: The tricolor flag of the Army; Its colors symbolize: the blood of Jesus Christ (red), the fire of the Holy Spirit (yellow) and the purity of God (blue).

Command: A smaller type of territory (division), directed by commanding officer, or divisional commander

Commission: A document conferring authority upon an officer, or upon an unpaid local officer, such as a secretary, treasurer, or bandmaster.

Congress: Central gatherings often held annually and attended by most officers and many soldiers of a territory, region or division. Salvationists would attend an international congress from nations around the world.

Corps: A Salvation Army unit established for the preaching of the Gospel and service in the community

Corps Cadet: A young Salvationist who undertakes a course of study and practical training in his or her corps, with a view to becoming efficient in Salvation Army service.

Corps Planter: A commissioned Salvation Army officer, envoy, or Lieutenant who has repeatedly demonstrated an ability to successfully launch new corps (churches).

Corps Sergeant–Major: The chief local officer for public work who assists the corps officer with meetings and usually takes command in their absence (comparable to a head deacon).

Dedication Service: The public presentation of infants to the Lord; this differs from christening or infant baptism in that the main emphasis is upon specific vows made by the parents concerning the child's upbringing.

Division: A number of corps grouped together, under the direction of a divisional commander.

Envoy: A local officer whose duty is to visit corps, societies, and outposts, for the purpose of conducting meetings; An envoy may be appointed in charge of any such unit.

General: The officer elected to the supreme command of the Army throughout the world. All appointments are made, and all regulations issued, under the General's authority (see under High Council).

Halfway House: A center for the rehabilitation of alcoholics, drug addicts, or parolees

Harbor–Light Center: A reclamation center, usually located in inner–city areas.

High Council: Composed of the Chief of the Staff, all active commissioners, including the spouse of the General, and all territorial commanders and their spouses. The High Council elects the General in accordance with the Salvation Army Act 1980.

Holiness Movement: A direct outgrowth from Methodism and the ideas of John Wesley. William Booth, founder of The Salvation Army, had a strong Holiness background and included important Holiness doctrines in his own organization. Other Holiness denominations in the United States are the Pilgrim Holiness Church; Church of the Nazarene; and Church of God, Anderson, Indiana.

Home–going service: A funeral ceremony characterized by an enthusiastic celebration of the life and ministry of a Christian who has died.

Home League: The Salvation Army's international women's organization, which was founded in 1907 by Mrs. Bramwell Booth (see also: Events/ Home League).

International Headquarters (IHQ): The offices based in London, England, in which the business of the world-wide Salvation Army is conducted.

International Secretary: An officer appointed by the General to supervise and represent, at International Head-quarters, Army work mainly overseas.

Junior Soldier: A boy or girl who, having professed conversion and having signed the junior soldier's promise, becomes a Salvationist.

League of Mercy: Salvationists who visit prisons, hospitals, and needy homes, in their own time, bringing the Gospel and rendering practical aid.

Local Officer: A soldier appointed to a position of responsibility and authority in the corps; carries out the duties of the appointment without being separated from regular employment or receiving remuneration from the Army.

Mercy Seat or Penitent Form: A bench provided as a place where people can kneel to pray, seeking salvation or sanctification, or making a special consecration to God's will and service. The mercy seat is usually situated between the platform and main area of Army halls as a focal point to remind all of God's reconciling and redeeming presence.

Ministry: The act of using one's skills, talents, and gifts to share the Gospel message with others. Ministry is often characterized, among other things, to mean; preaching, teaching Sunday school, music and singing, public speaking, facilitating community outreach programs, and visiting the sick.

Officer: A Salvationist who has left secular concerns at God's call and has been trained, commissioned, and ordained to service and leadership. An officer is a recognized minister of religion.

Order of Distinguished Auxiliary Service: On Feb., 24, 1941, General George Carpenter instituted this order to mark the Army's appreciation of distinguished service rendered by non–Salvationists who have helped to further its work in a variety of ways.

Order of the Founder: Instituted on Aug., 20, 1917 by General Bramwell Booth, this Salvation Army order of merit marks distinguished or memorable service such as would, in spirit or achievement, specially commended itself to the Founder, William Booth.

Outpost: A locality in which Army work is carried on and where it is hoped a society or corps will develop.

Promotion to Glory: The Army's description of the death of Salvationists; The phrase seems to have originated towards the end of 1882, when The War Cry (Dec., 14, 1882, p. 2), included reports with headlines such as "Promotion of Sister Muxlow from Earth to Heaven," and "Private Rudd goes to Glory from the Open–air." Another report, headed "Promotion from Cheltenham to Glory," appeared in The War Cry, (Dec., 16, 1882 p. 2).

Ranks of officers: Cadet lieutenant, lieutenant, captain, major, lt. colonel, colonel, commissioner, general.

Red Shield: A symbol identifying a wide range of Army social and emergency services.

Red Shield Appeal: An annual financial appeal to the general public.

Red Shield Center: A club for military personnel.

Salvation: The work of grace which God accomplishes in a repentant person whose trust is in Christ as Savior, forgiving sin, giving meaning and new direction to life, and strength to live as God desires. The deeper experience of this grace, known as holiness or sanctification, is the outcome of wholehearted commitment to God and enables the living of a Christ–like life.

Satan: In Christianity, the enemy of God, the lord of evil, and the tempter of human beings. He is sometimes identified as Lucifer, the leader of the fallen angels.

Saved: See Salvation

Self–Denial Appeal: An annual effort to raise funds for the Army's worldwide operations; also known as the annual appeal in some countries.

Sergeant: A local officer appointed for specific duty, usually in a corps.

Session: A class of officers who are either in training or have graduated from a Salvation Army college or school of officer training. In addition to the year of graduation, the Army distinguishes each session with a name (i.e., "Greathearts" session). The name is adopted worldwide by all sessions graduating in the same year.

Sessionmate: Officers who are members of the same graduating class (session) of a specific Salvation Army school or college for officer training.

Soldier: A converted person at least 14 years of age who has, with the approval of the census board, been enrolled as a member of The Salvation Army after signing the articles of war.

Songsters: A Salvation Army choir whose mission is to communicate the Gospel primarily through music. Songster "Brigades" are typically composed of selected soldiers from various corps who give their time voluntarily.

Swearing–In: Public enrollment of Salvation Army soldiers

Territory: A country, part of a country or several countries combined, in which Salvation Army work is organized under a territorial commander

Territorial Headquarters (THQ): The main administrative and primary command office for a territory from which the business of The Salvation Army is conducted.

Timbrels: Salvation Army worship leaders who typically use the tambourine as their primary musical instrument. A "Timbrel Brigade" performs choreographed movements that may involve juggling tambourines or colorful ribbons between one another.

Young People's Sergeant–Major (YPSM): A local officer responsible for the young people's work, under the commanding officer.

Zonal secretary: An officer appointment covering a geographical zone, which may include a designated combination of territories, commands, and/or regions.

GLOSSARY